Rights Enabled

Drawing on extensive firsthand fieldwork and analysis of original sources, Katharina Heyer offers a deeply comparative study of the transformation toward a global model of disability law and politics. Using three case studies—Germany, Japan, and the United Nations—she traces the uniquely American origins of this disability rights model and explores its influence on the law and politics of other countries.

Though Germany and Japan were already leaders in developing sophisticated (though segregated) disability welfare states, German and Japanese disability activists became "rights tourists" and apprenticed themselves to American activists, learning how disability rights work in the United States and then importing this model to their own countries. Consequently, a new combination of rights and welfare policy evolved in Germany and Japan to promote equality for the disabled. By following the progress of disability rights to a global platform—the UN—Heyer develops a framework for rights globalization. At the same time, she demonstrates that while notions of disability, equality, and rights become reinterpreted and contested as they move through various political contexts, ultimately the result may be a more robust and substantive understanding of equality.

Rights Enabled is a truly interdisciplinary work, combining sociolegal literature on rights and legal mobilization with a deep cultural and sociopolitical analysis of the disability category developed in disability studies. It raises important issues for comparative rights scholarship, the global reach of social movements, and the uses and limitations of rights-based activism.

Katharina Heyer is Associate Professor of Political Science at the University of Hawai'i.

Rights Enabled

THE DISABILITY REVOLUTION, FROM THE US, TO GERMANY AND JAPAN, TO THE UNITED NATIONS

Katharina Heyer

University of Michigan Press
Ann Arbor

Published in the United States of America by the
University of Michigan Press
Manufactured in the United States of America
♾ Printed on acid-free paper

2018   2017   2016   2015   4   3   2   1

A CIP catalog record for this book is available from the British Library.

Library of Congress Cataloging-in-Publication Data

Heyer, Katharina.
    Rights enabled: the disability revolution, from the US, to Germany and Japan,
    to the United Nations / Katharina Heyer.
        pages   cm
    Includes bibliographical references and index.
    ISBN 978-0-472-07247-7 (hardback) — ISBN 978-0-472-05247-9 (paper) —
    ISBN 978-0-472-12082-6 (ebook)
    1. People with disabilities—Civil rights.   2. People with disabilities—Political
activity.   3. Sociology of disability.   4. Equality.   5. Human rights.   I. Title.

HV1568.H49   2015
323.3—dc23

                                                            2014044072

Contents

Acknowledgments

I am grateful for the many hearts and minds that have contributed to this work. First and foremost are the Japanese and German disability activists who generously gave their time to help me understand their hopes, fears, and visions of a more just society. Special thanks go to Osamu Nagase, Yoshikazu Ikehara, Shoji Nakanishi, Keiko Higuchi, Theresia Degener, Bettina Theben, Hans-Günther Heiden, and the staff of the Institut Selbstbestimmt Leben Berlin.

Research support for this project came from the American Bar Foundation's Dissertation Fellowship, the German Institute for Japanese Studies in Tokyo, and from a teaching release at the Department of Political Science at University of Hawai'i at Manoa.

Because this book began as a dissertation I would like to acknowledge my dissertation chair, Kathy Ferguson, who cheerfully encouraged me to follow my instincts and change my research topic in midcourse to write about what truly inspired me. I had begun my scholarly career as a comparative constitutional scholar comparing women's equal rights legislation but soon became fascinated with the writings of feminist disability rights scholars. Making connections between women's rights and disability rights was both personally and professionally rewarding and renewed my commitment to interdisciplinary scholarship.

I will always be grateful to Jon Goldberg Hiller for introducing me to sociolegal scholarship and to the Law and Society Association, which has become my intellectual home for the last decade. I have received invaluable feedback on my work in its various stages during our annual meetings, especially from Michael McCann, Anna Maria Marshall, David Engel, Frank Munger, Scott Barkley, Marianne Constable, and Michael Waterstone, who have all modeled the kinds of scholarship I aspire to. I especially acknowledge Sagit Mor, with whom I have founded the Disability Legal Studies collaborative research network within the LSA.

The University of Hawai'i is a fabulous place to work and call home. I cheerfully acknowledge my colleagues in the Department of Political Science, the Center on Disability Studies, and the William S. Richardson School of Law. Avi Soifer, Hokulani Aikau, Steve Brown, and Jon Goldberg Hiller all read parts of this manuscript and sustained me with their support and friendship.

Previous versions of this work have been published in *Law & Social Inquiry* and the *Asia-Pacific Law & Policy Journal*. Parts of chapter 3 appeared as "The ADA on the Road: Disability Rights in Germany" (*Law & Social Inquiry* 2002), and parts of chapter 4 appeared as "From Special Needs to Equal Rights: Japanese Disability Law" (*APLPJ* 2000). I thank these publishers for their permission to use this material in this book. I also thank Melody Herr, Susan Cronin, and Kevin Rennells at the University of Michigan Press for their care and professionalism in handling this manuscript.

I am continuously nourished by my friendship with Sondra Cuban, Hediana Utarti, and Heike Pahl, as well as the connections I share with my siblings Inge, Peter, Andreas, and Désirée across continents and bloodlines. Finally, my deepest gratitude goes to David and our children, Lukas and Nikolas, who light my world with love and laughter.

Introduction: Rights Enabled

I have no legs,
But I still have feelings,
I cannot see,
But I think all the time,
Although I'm deaf,
I still want to communicate,
Why do people see me as useless, thoughtless, talkless,
When I am as capable as any,
For thoughts about our world.

(CORALIE SEVERS, 14, UNICEF)

"IT'S ABOUT ABILITY"

The United Nations Children's Fund opened its brochure explaining the UN Convention on the Rights of Persons with Disabilities with this poem and a reminder that "it's about ability." The poem speaks to the 650 million children and adults who live with disabilities: "their abilities are overlooked and their capacities are underestimated" (UNICEF 2008, 4). The poem invites children to contemplate the meaning of disability and human rights by reading about the experiences of children with disabilities around the world who, like the author of this poem, are frequently considered "lacking," "useless," and not capable of contributing meaningfully to their communities and to the world. Indeed, the assumption that disability signifies the opposite of ability remains deeply ingrained in our thinking about disability. The disruption of this idea, and the reclaiming of disability identity and pride, is a more recent phenomenon, borne out of larger movements calling for rights and equal citizenship status for marginalized communities. The evolution of disability from stigma and charity to rights and empowerment lies at the heart of this book. How did disability law and politics become a question of equal rights and full inclusion? How did it emerge as a human rights issue?

On August 25, 2006, the United Nations adopted the Convention on the Rights of Persons with Disabilities (CRPD), which recognized the rights of the world's largest minority. It was a historic date: "At no time in history has the confluence of domestic and international efforts challenged lawmakers, scholars, and activists to work together for the creation of binding international, regional, and domestic laws to protect the basic human right of people with disabilities to dignity and equality" (Kanter 2003, 242). As the first human rights treaty of the twenty-first century, the CRPD spells out a comprehensive approach to disability rights, recognizing both formal rights to equal opportunities and substantive rights to social and economic equality.

And yet the idea that disability is a human right, a legitimate addition to the global pantheon of rights, was unthinkable just twenty years earlier when most countries relied on charity, social welfare, segregated institutions, and sometimes employment quotas to incorporate people with disabilities or mitigate the suffering brought about by their exclusion. How did the disability rights model so rapidly transplant a century of thinking about disability as an issue of welfare? What has been won and lost by thinking of people with disability as rights holders entitled to full participation and equality?

Rights Enabled tells the story of this global shift to disability rights. It examines the "confluence of national and international efforts" that Arlene Kanter refers to above, which created an international movement to expand global thinking on disability as an issue of equal rights, inclusion, dignity, and, most crucially, human rights. This movement began with the growth of disability consciousness during the 1970s and 1980s that posited disability as a source of social oppression, rather than as a form of medical deviance. This movement revolutionized traditional thinking about disability away from a "medical model" and toward a "social model" that focused on disabling environments and attitudes—rather than individual impairments—as the true source of disability.

The first political expression of the social model was the 1990 Americans with Disabilities Act (ADA), the world's first comprehensive disability antidiscrimination law. The ADA defines disability discrimination as a civil rights issue and identifies people with disabilities as a protected minority. It explains the exclusion of people with disabilities from the public sphere not as a result of personal shortcomings or defects but as a direct result of inaccessible social environments.

Seeing the world in this way requires a radical shift in perspective. It forces us to question social arrangements that were previously seen as natural and inevitable for not fully responding to the diversity of needs represented in it. It invites us to pay less attention to a person's physical or mental impairments and to focus instead on the disabling environments and social structures surrounding that person. Accordingly, it has empowered people to make claims such as "I am not disabled by the fact that I can't walk, but by the fact that your building is not wheelchair accessible," or "I do not feel disabled being Deaf,[1] but the lack of sign language interpreters is limiting my ability to communicate with those who hear."

The ADA and the new paradigm of disability that it embodies have issued a profound challenge to American disability law and policy. How to create a society that is truly inclusive? How to provide people with disabilities with the same opportunities in employment, education, housing, health care, and public transportation provided to the nondisabled? How to talk about equal rights and special needs when it comes to providing equal access?

The ADA's unprecedented disability equality approach catapulted the United States into an unaccustomed position of leadership in the human rights community and played a central role in a global "paradigm shift" in thinking about disability as a rights issue. As the first international model of such a disability rights approach, the ADA has inspired disability activists across the globe to rethink disability as a civil rights issue and to organize political movements to begin the process of introducing similar legislation in their home countries.

This new approach to disability has found its way into regional and international human rights documents, culminating with the adoption of the 2006 UN Convention of the Rights of Persons with Disabilities that once again revolutionized how the international community was to think about disability rights. The CRPD offers a more comprehensive approach to disability equality and goes beyond the initial promise of the American-inspired rights model. It embraces both a formal approach to equality, which promises equal protection and nondiscrimination, and a more substantive approach to disability equality, by mandating the provision of "reasonable accommodation" and forms of positive action measures. More important, it posits that positive action—which it defines as "specific measures which are necessary to accelerate or achieve de facto equality" (Article 5.4)—fits squarely into a comprehensive understanding of equality. The UN Convention thus reflects an understanding of disability equality that incorporates an official respect for and recognition of disability difference. Moreover, it posits that the refusal to recognize disability difference (by refusing to provide reasonable accommodations, for example) should be considered a form of disability discrimination. Twenty-six years after the passage of the ADA the disability rights model has been expanded to include a substantive form of equality for people with disabilities—how did this happen?

Rights Enabled follows the journey of the disability rights model across national and ideological boundaries. It asks: How do rights travel? What medium do they travel by, and how are they transformed once they reach foreign shores? The book begins with the American origins of the rights model by analyzing how the U.S. disability rights movement waged a cultural struggle to analogize disability to race, gender, and other civil rights. This struggle culminated in passage of the ADA, which simultaneously became a tremendous inspiration to disability activists around the globe. The U.S.-inspired disability rights model offered personal empowerment and rights consciousness as an alternative to the dependency and segregation experienced under the medical model, enticing many disability activists across the globe to become "rights tourists." Apprenticeships with American activists allowed these travelers to learn what it means to live with disability rights and the social and political differences these rights created: the ability to navigate an accessible public sphere; to shop, play, live, learn, and work along with their nondisabled peers; and, ultimately, to actively demand equality and citizenship. Returning home, these activists were determined to graft the American rights model onto existing disability welfare policy; for as much as they were inspired by equal rights, they were also worried about relinquishing much more advanced degrees of social welfare and the recognition of disability difference that these welfare regimes offered to them.

Two of these countries inspired by the American example were Germany and Japan, and the experience of Japanese and German activists provides the main focus of this book. Both countries were considered leaders in Asia and Europe regarding their political commitment to maintaining an extensive but still segregated disability welfare state, symbolized most prominently by disability employment quotas and separate education systems. Both countries hold political traditions that embrace the state as a guarantor of rights and welfare and that eschew the use of law and rights as a tool for social change. Finally, both countries share historical and political ties to the

United States during the immediate postwar period, when the U.S.-led Allied Occupation of both countries instituted social and economic reforms that became the basis of their respective welfare states. As such, Germany and Japan provide ideal settings to trace the movement of the disability rights model into two countries that were committed to the disability welfare model and to think about the global forces and national pressures that create and reform legal ideas.

Rights Enabled locates two points of contact that transformed the rights model. The first is the Japanese and German initial contact with the rights model as activists in these countries looked toward the Americans with Disabilities Act as a model for reform. The second point of contact was provided by the CRPD and its comprehensive approach to disability rights. Once again German and Japanese disability activists and legal reformers looked toward the international arena as they prepared for a second wave of reforms to incorporate the demands of disability equality and full inclusion. The transplantation of American-style rights regimes into European and Asian contexts offers a unique case study for thinking about law and globalization, rights as a mediator of equality and difference, and legal ideas as a source of political inspiration.

THE ADA AS A GLOBAL MODEL

Theresia Degener and Gerald Quinn, two prominent European disability scholars, have claimed that the Americans with Disabilities Act "has had such an enormous impact on foreign legal development that one is tempted to say that the international impact of this law is larger than its domestic effect" (Degener and Quinn 2002). Indeed, as the first political expression of the disability rights model, the ADA has become a global model for other countries to rethink their political and legal approaches to disability difference. The passage of the ADA set off an immediate wave of reform in the 1990s (most prominently in Great Britain in 1995), and by the time the UN Convention was passed the rights model had spread to more than forty legal systems, including the European Union.

Rights Enabled analyzes the ways that the U.S.-inspired rights model traveled the globe and set foot in countries with radically different approaches to disability law and policy. It also examines the ways in which disability rights in a global model seek to reform the American civil rights model, providing a critical analytical lens for thinking about rights American-style. American disability activists paid a high price for equal treatment—trading welfare for rights—something that their German and Japanese followers were eager to avoid. This new generation of activists could build on the political promise of rights—to frame demands and to bestow autonomy and humanity—in order to create a new approach to disability that was equally rooted in a political commitment to social welfare and substantive notions of equality.

This book develops a framework for analyzing the disability rights model's impact on disability policy formation, implementation, and social movement generation. It studies the ways in which disability rights transplants might either support or contradict local legal culture, and how they might generate new approaches to legislating disability rights. Its extensive firsthand fieldwork and analysis of primary sources shows how German and Japanese activists use rights talk to commit to and contest culturally specific approaches to disability rights, equality, and legal reform. Following the journey of disability rights from the United States to Germany and Japan and eventually to the United Nations raises important issues not only for comparative rights scholarship or globalization studies but also for our understanding of the uses and limitations of rights-based activism in the United States.

DOING DISABILITY RESEARCH

This book develops a framework for analyzing the disability rights model's impact on disability policy formation, implementation, and social movement generation. It examines the ways disability rights transplants travel the globe and generate new approaches to legislating disability nondiscrimination and equality mandates. Extensive case studies show how German and Japanese activists use rights talk to commit to and contest culturally specific approaches to disability rights, equality, and legal reform.

In the course of researching this book I conducted fieldwork in Berlin, Bonn, Berkeley, and Tokyo, where I visited centers for independent living, sheltered workshops, group homes, and a host of government-sponsored disability community and resource centers. I attended numerous conferences that brought together disability activists and bureaucrats grappling with the implication of the rights model for German and Japanese disability law. I was allowed to sit in on strategy sessions and consciousness-raising workshops. I interviewed German and Japanese activists who traveled to the United States to learn about disability rights and formed a new, "second generation" of disability activism. I also interviewed some of their American counterparts who became the first mentors of these "rights tourists" and began traveling the world to continue the spread of the rights model. I consulted primary sources for Japanese and German legal reforms and policy papers, as well as essays and articles published in the growing field of German and Japanese disability studies.

A NOTE ON LANGUAGE

When thinking about disability, attention to language and terminology is important. Disability rights activists focus on terminology—what do we call ourselves? what do we ask others to call us?—as an important political tool to reclaim a sense of identity and personhood. They seek to counter traditional medicalized views of disability, in which the person essentially "becomes" their disability, that are reflected in common language terms: people with disabilities are called "autistic," "retarded," "deaf," "crippled," "wheelchair-bound," and so forth. Recognizing the power of language, disability activists have responded by formulating what in the United States is called a "people-first" ideology to remind the nondisabled (or "temporarily able-bodied") population to "see the person before you see the disability." People-first language promotes the idea that someone's disability label is just a label, and not the defining characteristic of the entire individual

The most widely used and accepted terminology emerging from people-first language is the term "people with disabilities" rather than "the disabled" or "the handicapped." This change was evident at the highest levels in U.S. policy, when the title of the federal special education law was changed from the Education of All Handicapped Children Act to the Individuals with Disabilities Education Act in 1990, as well as with the ADA's rejection of the term "handicapped" from its model, Section 504 of the 1973 Rehabilitation Act, and subsequent use of people-first language. As a result of the now commonly accepted use of people-first language, the "handicapped child" becomes a child with a disability, the "spastic" becomes a person with cerebral palsy, and the "retarded child" becomes a child with developmental disabilities. Not all disability groups embrace the move to such language: the Deaf community, for example, expressly rejects it because they consider their deafness as a central part of their identities, and as contributing toward a Deaf culture.

Other critiques of people-first language have emerged from disability scholars in Great Britain, who claim that this move depoliticizes the ways that disability continues to be a source of stigma and discrimination. Rather than placing the person before the disability, they suggest the reverse, to draw attention to the ways in which people still are, despite official declarations to the contrary, viewed as products of their disabilities. British disability theorist Michael Oliver (1990) argues that people-first language blurs the distinction between impairment and disability, making the disability the "property" of the person rather than of the society, which is the true source of the person's disability. This denies the political nature of living with a disability and draws attention away from the social responsibility to mitigate it. The British model promotes the term "disabled people" as this places the disability before the person as a political statement to show that a disability is something that is "done" to a person rather than something a person "has."

During my fieldwork I was careful to use terminology used by the activists and policy makers I interviewed, although in most cases the "people first" model was the one more prominently used in both countries. German activists have followed the model by using the term *Menschen mit Behinderungen,* whereas Japanese activists rely on the traditional term *shōgaisha.* When referring to Japanese activists I follow Japanese custom by using family names before given names.

OUTLINE OF THIS BOOK

The book's first two chapters provide the theoretical framework to the global shift to a rights model of disability. A key component here is the uniquely American origin of the rights model. Thus, the first chapter, "The Disability Revolution: From Welfare to Rights," begins by looking at theoretical distinctions between the two predominant models of thinking about disability: a medical model, which views disability as physiological limitation, and a social model, which views it as a form of social oppression. What are the implications of these differences for disability policy? Do communities respond to the universally high unemployment rates for workers with disabilities by mandating employment quotas or sheltered workshops, as proposed by the medical model, or do they hope for full integration into the labor market with reasonable accommodations, as mandated by a rights-based model? Are students with disabilities' educational needs best met in integrated or segregated classrooms? These theoretical distinctions became key to the shift in disability policy occurring in the United States in the 1970s that spelled out the origins of the disability rights model. The idealistic framers of Section 504 of the 1973 Rehabilitation Act incorporated the first modest antidiscrimination mandate, consciously basing it on their experiences with civil rights law, particularly Title VI of the 1964 Civil Rights Act. The 1990 Americans with Disabilities Act then expanded this model into broader protections for both public and private accommodations and reasonable accommodations in employment. In this chapter I argue that the American turn to the rights model mandated a deliberate turn away from welfare. Indeed, the ADA was passed by an overwhelming majority in Congress and triumphantly signed by a Republican president as a way to get people with disabilities off welfare and turn them from consumers of tax dollars into productive, taxpaying citizens. This turn *to* rights as a turn *away* from welfare has important implications for our understanding of the adoption of the rights models by other countries, including Japan and Germany.

The second chapter, "Disability Rights as Civil Rights: The ADA and the Limits of Analogy," tells the story of the cultural battle waged for disability rights in the United States. American disability activists deployed powerful analogies to the struggles of other rights-based movements when making the case for disability rights. The civil rights analogy has provided a well-paved terrain for disability activists to negotiate their demands and supply the legislative foundation for the ADA. It has furnished a vocabulary and a frame of reference through which people with disabilities can articulate the difficulties they face in achieving equal treatment and full participation in society. It has enabled them to cast arguments in the form of rights—rather than needs or mere policy preferences—that resonate with fundamental values regarding equality, fair treatment, and equal opportunities. The disability civil rights analogy is powerful not only in the ways it enabled a political and legal response to disability discrimination. It also shook the very foundations of the civil rights paradigm. It is disability—more so than race and gender—that troubles the legal distinction between equality and difference. The ADA therefore significantly departs from previous antidiscrimination legislation in its reasonable accommodations mandate to ensure meaningful access to equal employment opportunities.

The ADA also departs from other civil rights statutes in its requirement that individuals prove that they are members of a protected class. The question of who counts as disabled has proven a considerable hurdle for plaintiffs in bringing disability discrimination lawsuits, as is evidenced by the ADA's treatment in the courts. Moreover, the addition of disability to the civil rights paradigm has tended to place boundaries around the category of disability and to limit it to a bipolar approach: a person is either disabled or not. But disabilities exist along a continuum and are subject to change throughout a person's life course. The ADA thus departs from a traditional civil rights approach that defines equality as sameness and eschews positive rights. This departure features prominently in the German and Japanese engagement with the ADA model. To what degree will the civil rights analogy, so inherent in the political successes of the American disability rights movement, be translated into a German and Japanese setting?

Chapter 3, "'Dreamland USA': American Disability Rights Travel to Germany," tracks the German struggle for an antidiscrimination law, which was directly inspired by the ADA and the mobilization strategies of the American disability movement. It tells the story of a new generation of German disability activists traveling to the United States as rights tourists to learn about the empowering effects of disability rights. Arriving back home from what they called "Dreamland USA," these rights tourists launched an unprecedented and widely successful media campaign to generate disability rights awareness. The chapter is the first comprehensive analysis of this media campaign, which generated support for a constitutional antidiscrimination amendment and a German version of the ADA, an "Equalizing Law."

Despite strong ties to American colleagues and mentors, German disability activists remain critical of what they consider the limitations of American notions of equality. The German Disability Equalizing Law combines antidiscrimination mandates with affirmative equality rights and rests on German traditions that posit the state as a provider of basic social rights. Like their American counterparts, however, German activists use rights talk to define disability as a category of positive identity and pride, to shift the focus from special needs to equal rights, and to generate a political movement. The chapter shows how the ADA became a symbol of the ways law can transform people with disabilities from objects of charity and welfare into equal citizens, even where it does not provide a blueprint for legal change.

Chapter 4, "From Welfare to Rights: Disability Law and Activism in Japan," follows the journey of the disability rights model to Japan and asks: What are the promises and challenges of transplanting notions of rights, equality, and independence into a Japanese setting? To what degree can Japan incorporate U.S.-inspired ideas of independent living, autonomy, and disability rights consciousness into a country that values family interdependence and eschews using the law as a tool for social change? In charting Japan's journey from welfare to rights this chapter identifies two central waves of reform, both inspired and strengthened by international developments. The first is the UN's International Year of Disabled Persons (1981) and the International Decade of Disabled Persons (1983–92), followed by the passage of the 1990 Americans with Disabilities Act. These two developments inspired a new generation of Japanese disability activists to radically rethink and reframe the basis of their activism. They also culminated in Japan's enthusiastic participation in the 2006 UN CRPD, which has obligated Japan to pass an unprecedented disability antidiscrimination law.

This chapter argues that the ADA and the UN human rights instruments provided a powerful template for the Japanese disability movement's activism for political and legal reform. They inspired a new generation of Japanese activists to replace traditional organizing tools with rights talk, rights consciousness, and disability pride. The new emphasis on rights and discrimination allows Japanese disability activists to frame their political demands as a human rights issue, using Western terminology of self-determination, independent living, and advocacy that is foreign to the Japanese political and cultural context. This use of such imports is strategic: it frames disability rights as a progressive and Western project that Japan must embrace to be considered truly international (*kokusaika*). At the same time, transplanting a rights model that is deeply rooted in American civil rights approaches poses unique challenges to Japanese disability activists. The assertion of rights and independence is considered fundamentally incompatible with Japanese political, legal, and social norms. Legal remedies traditionally hold less power for Japanese social movements than they do for their American counterparts. Disability laws and policies reflect specific historical, legal, and cultural assumptions about the meaning of disability, equality, and the law as a tool for social change. The American-inspired disability rights model provides tremendous inspiration for Japanese activists but poses tremendous challenges when they seek to implement the model into law and policy.

The fifth chapter, "Disability Rights as Human Rights," considers the impact of the UN Convention on the Rights of Persons with Disabilities on disability rights in developing countries. How does the new thinking about disability rights as inclusive and comprehensive influence German and Japanese disability law? Previous chapters have traced the initial contact with the rights model in Germany and Japan as activists in these countries looked toward the Americans with Disabilities Act as a model for reform. This chapter considers the second wave of influence provided by the CRPD. The UN Convention offers a more comprehensive approach to disability rights that goes beyond the initial promise of the American-inspired rights model. German and Japanese disability activists and legal reformers are encouraged by this new promise as they prepare for a second wave of reforms inspired by international law.

In the German case, the chapter examines the Convention's promise of "inclusive education" (Article 24) and uses it as a case study to mark the development of the rights model. Germany remains deeply invested in segregated education, and thus Germany presents an ideal case to uncover the workings of international norms. The continued legitimacy of segregated education in Germany stands in contrast with the rest of the world's slow convergence toward inclusive education. In the Japanese case, chapter 5 examines the impact of the CRPD's right to reasonable accommodations in employment policies (Article 27). Japan provides a useful example here because it remains committed to the national employment quota and believes that it can combine what traditionally are considered contradictory policies: the guarantee of equal opportunities in the form of antidiscrimination law, and the promise of equality of result in the form of the disability employment quota. The CRPD represents the growth of a disability rights model from its American origins, which limited rights as antithetical to welfare, to a comprehensive equality guarantee in disability human rights law. Mobilizing around the CRPD also represented a new form of rights-based activism for German and Japanese disability activists who are adopting an increasingly global outlook toward their efforts for legal reforms as they pressure their respective governments to fulfill the promises of the CRPD.

The book's conclusion, "Tools for Going Global," suggests both political and scholarly implications for the globalization of disability rights. This final chapter outlines "tools for going global" that have emerged from the UN Convention: an unprecedented degree of transnational activism that is placing pressure on national governments by using shame, submitting shadow reports, and deploying the CRPD's awareness-raising mandate to contribute to global norm transformation. The final chapter argues that the global reach of the American disability rights model offers a new perspective on the limitations of equality discourse and the politics of rights, a subject with which American rights scholarship has long grappled, but without global and comparative models. *Rights Enabled* adds original research both in a comparative context to expand the American literature on the limitations of rights discourse and also offers disability as a unique site for investigating these limitations.

CHAPTER ONE

The Disability Revolution:
From Welfare to Rights

When I was fourteen, I got polio. When the doctor took my parents aside my mother asked, "Will he live?" The doctor looked at her and said, "You should probably hope he dies because if he lives he will be nothing more than a vegetable for the rest of his life." Well, I'm here today as an artichoke. You know, they're a little prickly on the outside with a big heart and I'd like to call on all the vegetables of the world to unite. (Roberts 1983)

UNITING ALL VEGETABLES

Ed Roberts, one of the most well-known leaders of the U.S. disability rights movement, addressed the 1983 Australian National Assembly of Disabled Peoples International (DPI) with this powerful call to unity. It was another six years until the U.S. Congress would pass the Americans with Disabilities Act (ADA), defining disability as a civil rights issue and revolutionizing disability policy around the globe. As the world's first comprehensive disability antidiscrimination law, the Americans with Disabilities Act became a model of rights-based disability policy, inspiring disability rights activists around the globe to rethink the way they organized and framed their demands. But, speaking in 1983, Ed Roberts captured an earlier, equally powerful moment in the history of international disability activism. By calling for unity for those considered "vegetables," denied their humanity and basic rights to social and political inclusion, Roberts captured the spirit of a growing movement toward self-determination and disability pride. This movement had reached a turning point three years earlier, at the 1980 Winnipeg Congress of Rehabilitation International (RI), then the largest disability organization with an international membership. Like most disability organizations at the time, both RI's membership and approach were dominated by rehabilitation profession-als, illustrating a deepening divide between organizations *for* disabled people, such as RI, and organizations *by* disabled peoples themselves. Members with disabilities had long been critical of this power relationship and demanded equal representation of disabled people in RI's decision-making bodies. When these demands were refused, DPI broke away from RI, forming an inde-pendent disability organization with the motto "nothing about us without us." This became the movement's powerful mantra for years to come, as it captured the importance of addressing the paternalism, segregation, and marginalization that people with disabilities experienced in their lives and saw reflected in disability policy at the time. *Nothing about us without us* be-came the motto for DPI's founding meeting in Singapore in 1981, which coin-cided with the UN's International Year of Disabled Peoples (Driedger 1989).

Roberts's call for international disability activism catapulted the United States into an unprecedented leadership position in the international human rights community. The United States is rarely considered a leader in the devel-opment of human rights instruments, but the passage of the ADA in 1990 made it the global leader of disability policy. U.S. disability activists had al-ready formed their first fragile cross-disability alliances during the 1970s when the disability community united to protest for the inclusion of disability dis-crimination under Section 504 of the 1973 Rehabilitation Act. Section 504 fa-mously forbade disability discrimination by programs receiving federal funds, which was the first articulation of disability discrimination in U.S. policy, and was modeled closely after Title VI of the 1964 Civil Rights Act (Scotch 2001). The idea that disability discrimination was to be seen as analogous to race dis-crimination and needed the same protection under the law was considered radical at the time and a clear departure from traditional thinking about dis-ability. The refusal of both the Nixon and Carter administrations to sign the 504 regulations prompted the first disability-wide protest by a movement that had never acted in unity before. This was a formative moment for U.S. disabil-ity activists, who were struggling to unite a movement that was historically divided by disability type and that spanned a wide and often contradictory set of movement goals (Barnartt and Scotch 2001). Yet activists emerged from the protests with a strong sense of collective identity, inspired by the idea that dis-ability was more than just a personal experience and a medical category. Rather than a personal shortcoming, disability was to be experienced in po-litical terms—as a form of discrimination like that experienced by women or by people of color. As Simi Linton explains, "We are bound together, not by a list of our personal shortcomings, but by the social and political circumstances that have forged us as a group" (Linton 1998, 4).

American disability law and activism commanded world attention during the 1980s. Activists around the globe paid close attention to the initial antidiscrimination articulated in Section 504, the protests needed to make it a reality, and to the broad expansion of this mandate into the world's first comprehensive disability antidiscrimination law, the 1990 Americans with Disabilities Act. Activists from around the globe traveled to the United States during this period—primarily to Berkeley as the center of U.S. activism—to apprentice with leaders such as Ed Roberts, Judy Heumann, and others to learn about movement strategies. In 1983, Roberts cemented the international focus of disability activism by cofounding the World Institute on Disability in Oakland, California. With the aid of a MacArthur Foundation genius award in 1984, Roberts turned the World Institute on Disability into an influential public policy center that connects local and global activism. That same year he served as keynote speaker for DPI's First National Assembly in Melbourne, Australia, from which the artichoke citation is taken, cementing the movement's self-determination principles with his speech entitled "When Others Speak for You, You Lose."

Robert's call for unity was part of an emerging trend in disability law and activism. First was the rejection of the idea that people with disabilities need to be thought of as "vegetables"—passive recipients of medical interventions and public charity who could never speak for themselves. Roberts's own life story, well known in activist circles, was living proof of that rejection. He contracted polio as a teenager, which left him with virtually no functional movement and dependent on a respirator for breathing. He recalls his first experience with self-determination while still in the hospital:

> I decided that I wanted to die. I was fourteen years old. Now, it's very hard to kill yourself in a hospital with everything set up to save your life. But the mind is a powerful thing. I stopped eating . . . and dropped to 54 pounds. My last special duty nurse left, and the next day I decided I wanted to live. You see, that was a big turning point. Up until then, these nurses were available and doing things for me around the clock—I didn't have to make any decisions for myself because they were always there. When they all finally left, that's when I realized that I could have a life, despite what everyone was saying. I could make choices, and that is freedom. I started to eat again.[1]

Roberts continued his education from home, with an innovative school-to-home telephone system and his mother Zona's endless advocacy. He enrolled in the University of California at Berkeley in 1962, which was nationally known as the center of radical politics and progressive social movements. Berkley's politics offered a fertile ground to think about disability as a form of oppression, inspiring Roberts to apply lessons learned by civil rights and women's rights activists to his own life. He founded the Rolling Quads, an organization of students with disabilities who first lived in the campus infirmary but soon moved into the community and provided the basis for the country's first Center for Independent Living in 1972. There are now around 400 independent living centers in the United States, which have become models for self-help and advocacy for and by people with disabilities.

In 1975, Governor Jerry Brown appointed Roberts as director of California's Department of Rehabilitation—the same agency that had refused to serve him fourteen years earlier when they deemed him too severely disabled to ever work. His eight-year tenure as Department of Rehabilitation director fundamentally challenged how rehabilitation policy viewed a person's disability and their ability to work. In 1985, Roberts cofounded the World Institute on Disability, an internationally recognized public policy think tank, and became a global leader and mentor to disability activists from many countries, including Germany and Japan, which lie at the center of this book. His legacy is preserved in the Ed Roberts Campus in Berkeley, an independent living information and community center where he is remembered for the powerful inspiration and political momentum he provided to individual activists and the independent living movement worldwide.[2]

THE DISABILITY REVOLUTION

Given Roberts's international stature and powerful charisma, it is not a surprise that he was well positioned to issue his call to unity in 1983. The passage of the Americans with Disabilities Act a few years later solidified the international reputation of the United States as a leader in disability rights. Before passage of the ADA, the United States rarely occupied a leadership role in international human rights circles. Although the United States played a key role in composing the 1948 Universal Declaration of Human Rights and other key principles that changed the nature of international human rights legislation, when it comes to signing or ratifying key international human rights instruments the United States is widely considered an outcast. The United States has failed to ratify many of the principal international agreements, most prominently the Convention on the Elimination of All Forms of Discrimination against Women (CEDAW), the Kyoto Protocol, the International Criminal Court, and the International Covenant on Economic, Social and Cultural Rights (ICESCR), commonly considered the International Bill of Rights. The ICESCR requires states to promote and protect a wide range of social, economic and cultural rights, including the right to health, to an adequate standard of living, and to education.[3] The human rights community is in general agreement that the United States prioritizes the protection of political rights and civil liberties but considers the guarantee of economic rights as incompatible with the free market economy it cherishes. And yet this chapter will show that the Americans with Disabilities Act, while celebrated as an extension of civil rights, also fundamentally affects economic rights, and therefore transcends the traditional boundary between the two. Moreover, as the first comprehensive disability antidiscrimination law in the world, the ADA has had a powerful impact on the formation of disability rights law and activism in countries across the globe. The ADA provided the first example of a disability rights model that was the envy of many disability activists at the time. It is a product of the U.S. civil rights movement, modeled after the 1964 Civil Rights Act, and as such recognizes people with disabilities as a political minority with a history of oppression. Its emphasis on equal opportunity, integration, and individually enforceable civil rights provided a powerful contrast to more traditional models of disability policy based on welfare and rehabilitation. The ADA ushered in a new generation of disability laws, reflecting a new view of disability as a social and political phenomenon, rather than as a medical problem.

Versions of this new model of disability, which I call a "rights model" of disability, have found their way into many national and international disability instruments. The disability revolution has fundamentally challenged traditional ways of thinking about disability, moving from a welfare model to a rights model. This chapter provides the theoretical background for examining the foundations of this rights model and for the subsequent journey of disability rights to countries that were deeply embedded in the more traditional welfare model. The chapter begins by looking at theoretical distinctions between the two predominant theoretical models regarding disability: a medical model, which views disability as a physiological limitation, and a social model, which views it as a form of social oppression. What are the implications of these differences for disability policy? For example, do communities respond to the universally high unemployment rates for workers with disabilities by mandating employment quotas or sheltered workshops, as proposed by the medical model, or do they guarantee equal employment opportunities and individualized accommodations of disability difference, as mandated by a rights-based model? These theoretical distinctions became key to the shift in disability policy occurring in the United States in the 1970s that offered the first rights-based alternative to the traditional welfare model. The idealistic framers of Section 504 of the 1973 Rehabilitation Act incorporated the first disability antidiscrimination mandate, consciously basing it on their experiences with civil rights law. The 1990 Americans with Disabilities Act then expanded this model into broader protections for both public and private accommodations, as well as reasonable accommodations in employment. The chapter argues that the turn to the rights model in the United States mandated a deliberate turn away from welfare. Indeed, the ADA was passed as a civil rights law by an overwhelming majority in Congress not only to combat stereotypes and expand employment opportunities, but also as a way to reduce welfare rolls and turn Americans with disabilities into productive, taxpaying citizens.

The ADA's framing of disability as a civil rights issue allowed activists to counter the paternalism and charity inherent in the taken-for-granted assumption that disability equals nonability—an assumption deeply embedded in the welfare laws of most developed nations. This framing led to a revolution in the ways disability activists organized their demands, as well as in the ways disability policy began orienting itself along a rights model. This chapter looks at the role of the United States at the forefront of this disability revolution, which shifted global attention to disability from welfare to rights-based policies. The American turn to disability rights is an instructive example to the question that animates much sociolegal rights scholarship: what is gained and what is lost when adding disability to a civil right framework, and, more broadly, when framing questions of social justice in legal terms. The ADA is deeply embedded in the American civil rights experience and as such echoes both the power and the limitations of civil rights frames documented in sociolegal scholarship (Scheingold 2004; McCann 1994).

This chapter examines the role of the United States at the forefront of the disability revolution, but also recounts the political strategies that led to the enthusiastic passage of the ADA by a government intent on reducing welfare. While the ADA connects to a powerful civil rights history, it also limits the frame of the rights model to the realm of negative rights that are emblematic of U.S. antidiscrimination law. The ADA's reasonable accommodation mandate makes some nods in the direction of positive action by requiring employers and providers of public and private accommodations to use resources in order to ensure the equal participation of people with disabilities. In that sense, disability offers a fundamental challenge to traditional assumptions inherent in the equal treatment mandate because equal treatment for people with disabilities cannot ignore disability difference. Disability equality thus demands the simultaneous recognition of equal rights and special needs. The ADA's equality mandate pushes the limits of the equality-as-sameness model by effectively arguing for differential treatment and by explicitly requiring that we not only recognize but also change norms that are based on the experiences of the nondisabled. It points to a more robust notion of equality by essentially challenging social norms to incorporate the experiences of all Americans, experiences that exist on a broad spectrum of impairments and might affect anybody during their normal life cycle.

The ADA was heralded as a tool that would "open the door" to opportunities previously denied to people with disabilities. And yet, justice would not be served if the door, both physically and metaphorically, was too narrow to accommodate the variety of bodies passing through it. The disability claim to equal treatment offers tremendous opportunities to rethink assumptions about the collective responsibility for equal opportunity and justice. It's not just a question of enabling individuals to "compete" equally but a collective responsibility to examine social environments that are created to reflect the nondisabled experience. Creating a society that is truly accessible means not only challenging individual assumptions about the meaning of disability but also reforming institutions, at a minimum of expense. This cost issue problematizes deeply held American assumptions about civil rights as individual claims to equal treatment, dignity, and respect, rather than as collective responsibilities that might entail costs. Thus, the chapter ends with an assessment of the disability rights model through the accommodations mandate and the question of costs: To what degree do we allow civil rights to come with a price tag?

MODELS OF DISABILITY: THEORIZING DIFFERENCE

The question of disability is central to our understanding of equality theory and the ways that law and public policy account for embodied difference. How do we theorize the difference that disability makes, not only in terms of our commitment to equal treatment but also in our recognition of special needs? The disability revolution has issued a profound challenge to the ways we think about the use of law and policy to create a society that is truly inclusive and reflective of the diverse ways of being in this world. How do we extend to people with disabilities the same kinds of opportunities in employment, education, housing, health care, and public services provided for the nondisabled? How do we guarantee disability equality while simultaneously recognizing disability difference? This "dilemma" of disability difference was first theorized by Martha Minow's influential book *Making All the Difference: Inclusion, Exclusion and American Law* (1990). Minow asks, "When does treating people differently emphasize their differences and stigmatize or hinder them on that basis? And when does treating people the same become insensitive to their difference and likely to stigmatize or hinder them on *that* basis?" (1990, 20).

Our assumptions about difference and how to treat people we consider "different" form a dilemma: both by ignoring and by focusing on difference we risk recreating and thus restigmatizing it. Minow's difference dilemma is based on the recognition that conventional notions of equality and difference function as comparative terms ("Different compared to whom? Equal to whom?"), which revolve around an unacknowledged norm. Differences, after all, are not intrinsic but are comparisons between people. This means that people with disabilities differ from those who are nondisabled only on the basis of an unstated able-bodied norm, which, for example, assumes that we use the voice to communicate rather than the hands, the legs to move rather than a wheelchair, the lungs to breathe rather than a respirator. Ignoring difference leaves in place a false sense of neutrality, which may recognize that people with disabilities have similar motivations to work, study, commute, and raise families, but which does not take their different needs into account. At the same time, focusing on their difference risks repeating the stigma and the limiting assumptions about disability. The problems of inequality can be exacerbated, Minow argues, both by treating people with disabilities the same as members of the nondisabled majority and by treating the two groups differently—hence, a dilemma (Minow 1990, 20).

THEORIZING DISABILITY

The disability revolution turned traditional assumptions of disability on their head and fundamentally challenged the ways that embodied difference was to be theorized and applied to public policy. Traditional ways of thinking about disability under the *medical model* focus on the disabled body and its observable deviance from a biomedical norm. The disabled person is one that needs to be fixed, cured, or at least rehabilitated to most closely resemble the nondisabled norm. Disability thus becomes a central part of the identity of the person inhabiting this body. Since disability is the direct consequence of an individual's physical or mental impairment, the disabled individual is both the source of the problem and the solution. Traditional approaches to disability are deeply rooted in modern medicine's assumptions that the body can be objectified and controlled. In this view, those who cannot control their bodies are seen as failures, both individually and as a matter of policy.

In contrast to this traditional view of disability, a *social model* has emerged to counter the medical model's focus on the disabled individual as the site of analysis, with a focus on the political response to disability. The social model of disability refuses to view disability as a stable medical category, and instead addresses it in political terms: as a product of power relations and inaccessible environments. It focuses less on the medical condition and more on the effect of that condition: exclusion from full participation in society. The social model explains the exclusion of people with disabilities from the public sphere not as a result of personal shortcomings or defects but as a direct result of inaccessible social environments. Thus, social exclusion is not to be seen as an inevitable consequence of disability. Rather, it is a result of discriminatory attitudes and a history of exclusion from institutions that have failed to adapt to the needs of people with disabilities in the same ways that they routinely adapt to the needs of the majority. So consequential was this new model that it is commonly referred to as a "paradigm shift" in the disability rights movement.

Theories of disabilities thus distinguish between two models: a *social model* that views disability as a social construct, and a *medical model* that views disability as an individual deficit. When these two models find themselves reflected in public policy, I will refer to them as either a *rights model* or a *welfare model* of disability. These two ways of thinking about disability are also reflected in theories of rights that distinguish between *positive rights* (the right to entitlements from the state) and *negative rights* (the right to be free from state intervention). Table 1 summarizes these theories and the terminology I will use for the rest of this chapter.

The first articulation of disability as emerging from social discrimination and attitudes has been traced to one of Great Britain's early, politically radical disability organizations during the 1970s, the Union of the Physically Impaired Against Segregation (UPIS). The UPIS defined disability as "the disadvantage or restriction of activity caused by a contemporary social organization," and described the medical model experience as one in which "an army of experts . . . , armed with the latest definitions and tests for measuring, will prod and probe into the intimate details of our lives. They will bear down on us with batteries of questions, and wielding their tape measures will attempt to tie down the last remaining vestige of our privacy and dignity as human beings" (UPIS 1975). The UPIS was one of the first examples of disability activists who embodied the international motto of "nothing about us without us" by defining and challenging disability policy from the point of view of people with disabilities. Michael Oliver, Great Britain's first professor of disability studies, coined the term "social model of disability" soon thereafter. In the United States, an important first articulation of the social model was law professor Jacobus tenBroek's notion that people with disabilities needed to claim their "right to live in the world" (tenBroek 1966) and call for social and political citizenship.

DISABILITY MODELS APPLIED TO POLICY: WELFARE AND RIGHTS MODELS

Translated into policy, the medical model follows a "separate treatment" doctrine, providing for the needs of people with disabilities in segregated settings, such as special schools, sheltered workshops, or assisted living centers. These social institutions are created as a separate and parallel track that provides income and services for people with disabilities, apart from the welfare institutions that serve the nondisabled. The assumption here is that rather than making mainstream institutions accessible, the needs of people

TABLE 1. Summary of Theories of Disabilities

Theoretical Model	Social Model	Medical Model
As applied to policy	Civil rights model	Welfare model
As applied to employment policy	Equal opportunity	Employment quotas
As reflected in theory of rights	Negative rights	Positive rights
Country of origin	USA/Great Britain	Western Europe/Japan

with disabilities are better served in separate facilities that can be constructed to meet very specialized needs (Waddington 1996).

People with disabilities became objects of public policy that was designed as an economic, social, and cultural response to their perceived inability to participate in society and fulfill social obligations such as working and parenting. Public policy informed by a medical model posits that the state must, out of a sense of public responsibility for helping the weak and dependent, direct resources to rehabilitation programs to help disabled people "overcome" their physical and mental problems. At the forefront of these policies—always perceived as a form of welfare—were public responses to war veterans, who generated an undeniable demand for physical and occupational rehabilitation services. The argument was that if soldiers were expected to give life and limb to their countries in battle, they could not be discarded and left to fend for themselves upon their return to civil society. In the United States, for example, the origins of disability policy were welfare measures designed to help injured war veterans returning from the Civil War. After World War I, these veterans programs were extended to incorporate the idea of rehabilitation for the general public (Stone 1984; Switzer 2003; Longmore 2001).

This parallel track became the established policy choice in most industrialized countries—until the rise of the rights model—primarily because it did not threaten existing institutions. It allowed welfare states to posit disability needs as fundamentally different from other welfare needs, knowing that these will be served in separate institutions. The segregation of people with disabilities was not seen as discriminatory, but as a natural outcome of their medical limitations. In fact, Lisa Waddington, the European Disability Forum's chair in European disability law, posits that many nondisabled policy makers, especially those in western European countries, continue to see the welfare model as generous and desirable and as a sign of welfare progress (Waddington 1996; Waddington and Diller 2000). People with disabilities may be offered income support such as public assistance or pensions, housing and schooling, and even special jobs reserved for workers with disabilities. The European disability employment quota was long considered a sign of progressive labor policy. On the whole, most European welfare states—with Germany in the lead—have established generous social security and rehabilitation provisions that allow people with disabilities to lead separate but comfortable lives in which they do not need to compete on the open labor market. In that sense, Waddington argues that disability policy based on a medical model practices a policy of exclusion, which views disability as both an excuse from the obligation to work and as an excuse for denying employment.

The "separate treatment" doctrine under the welfare model suggests that the welfare needs of the nondisabled majority are being met as a matter of good social policy, whereas disability needs are stigmatized as "special needs" and therefore not as self-evident as the "equal rights" of the nondisabled. The basis of the social model became a criticism of this automatic segregation. Instead of maintaining a parallel track, disability policy under a social model should focus on ways to make social environments accessible and reform social institutions to include people with disabilities. The assumption is that once the nondisabled majority gains increasing contact with their disabled peers, whether through integrated schools, neighborhoods, or the workplace, discriminatory attitudes and fears of the unknown "other" will disappear; prejudices will abate, and the necessity for legal intervention will decrease.

If we view disability segregation not as an automatic and inevitable consequence of embodied difference, then we must focus our attention on the very institutions that perpetuate this segregation. People with disabilities are barred from participating in mainstream institutions of citizenship, such as working, parenting, voting, or going to school, not because of their individual experience of impairment, but rather because these institutions are designed with only the nondisabled experience in mind. Since the social model locates the problem in exactly the political choices that create inaccessible institutions, the solution also lies in the reform of these institutions.

This rights model of disability posits that remedying the effects of a discriminatory society is not an act of charity or social benevolence from an enlightened majority, but a form of civil rights enforcement similar to that of other minority groups. People with disabilities claim the right to be treated as equals and participate fully in mainstream institutions of citizenship, such as education, employment, public service, voting, and parenting. In policy terms, then, the rights model replaces segregation with integration, and parallel tracks with equal opportunity and antidiscrimination mandates. People with disabilities should be considered a political minority and as such are subject to civil rights protection, similar to that accorded to other minorities. They are active rights holders, not passive patients and welfare recipients, and they should use the force of the law to protest their segregated status as a form of discrimination.

These two approaches to disability policy hold opposing views of what constitutes disability—the medical model views it as an inherent and medically determined status, while the social model sees disability as a social consequence of living in disabling environments. The medical model locates both problem and solution within the person, whereas the social model locates both in social structures and physical environments. Translated into policy, the two models embody a binary oppositions of exclusion versus inclusion, welfare versus rights, disability versus ability, employment quotas versus equal opportunities, and, most generally, different versus equal treatment. The welfare model seeks to spend resources to build better facilities to best serve the distinct needs of the disabled population, whereas the rights model demands the abolition of these facilities to integrate people with disabilities into mainstream society. Where the welfare model assumes inability to work, the rights model emphasizes capabilities and demands equal opportunities, if not obligations, to work. As theoretical concepts, then, these are opposite approaches that exist as binaries that cannot be reconciled. In their actual application, however, the differences between the two approaches tend to be much less clear-cut. Thus, despite the fact that the rights model grew both politically and theoretically out of dissatisfaction with the welfare model, few disability policies are clear-cut representatives of one model. In fact, as much as we see international excitement over the promise of the rights model—as it spreads throughout national and international disability rights instruments—we also see a growing number of countries that are working toward a coexistence between the two models.

Besides Germany and Japan, which are the focus of this book, a host of countries reformed their disability policies to reflect versions of the new disability rights model. Examples of the first wave of reforms inspired just years after the passage of the ADA are Australia (1992), New Zealand (1993), and Great Britain (1995). Since then, approximately 40 countries have made the shift from a welfare model to a rights model by passing disability antidiscrimination laws (Kanter 2003); with the passage of the United Nations Convention on the Rights of Persons with Disabilities in 2006, this number is on the rise. Although the formative role of the ADA in the disability revolution is unquestioned and uncontroversial in the disability literature, this chapter offers a critical look at the consequences of this American shift to disability rights, which included a turn away from welfare and positive rights.

THE AMERICAN SHIFT TO RIGHTS

It was the passage of a large rehabilitation funding statute, the U.S. Rehabilitation Act of 1973, and specifically a single, initially overlooked sentence in Section 504, that marked the beginning of a larger shift toward disability policy based on a civil rights framework. Section 504 is considered the first articulation of disability antidiscrimination law by forbidding discrimination against "otherwise qualified individuals with disabilities" in "any program or activity receiving Federal financial assistance." Richard Scotch offers a fascinating account of the process by which Section 504 was added to the bill at a very late stage in the legislative process (Scotch 2001). Senate aides on the Senate Committee on Labor and Welfare held a late night meeting discussing the rehabilitation bill's central promise: placing workers into vocational rehabilitation programs and then back into the labor market. They identified the central problem the law needed to address: workers with disabilities completing their vocational rehabilitation training were still being refused jobs because of employers' negative attitudes and stereotypes. The true problem facing people with disabilities, staffers concluded, was not job training or work-related disabilities, it was plain discrimination (Scotch 2001). This felt very similar to the provisions of Title VI of the 1964 Civil Rights Act—in fact, in the middle of the discussion one of the staffers rushed back to his office with the language of Title VI, which forbids discrimination on the basis of race in programs receiving federal financial assistance. Title VI became the model for Section 504, which used almost identical language to cover disability discrimination.

Passionate supporters of civil rights, these staffers were deeply disillusioned when the Nixon administration withheld funds to implement these laws. Indeed, Richard Nixon had campaigned for the presidency with pledges to turn back the civil rights advances and curb the costs of the War on Poverty initiated by President Lyndon Johnson. Scotch recounts the real sense of anger in these staffers' assessment of what they considered the Nixon administration's betrayal of the promises of civil rights legislation, coupled with an understanding that people with disabilities were included in these promises (Scotch 2001, 48). The staffers' assessment proved correct: Nixon vetoed the Rehabilitation Act twice before signing it, calling it "fiscally irresponsible" and a way of diluting scarce rehabilitation resources toward "welfare and medical goals" (Young 1997).

Thus, we see the origins of the U.S. disability rights model in race-based civil rights law, centered in the principles of antidiscrimination and equal treatment, and borrowing heavily from the experiences of the civil rights movement of the 1960s. I will explore this connection further in the next chapter, when I examine the origins and the application of the civil rights analogy in disability law. In this chapter, I will consider how a small sentence in Section 504, completely overlooked during congressional or public debates on the Rehabilitation Act, revolutionized the way the nation started thinking about disability.

The initial scope of Section 504 was fairly narrow, covering only entities that provided vocational rehabilitation services and covering only individuals whose disability affected their employment. Moreover, for the first decade following the Act's passage, Section 504 generated little litigation. Starting in the 1980s, however, the disability community began taking advantage of the antidiscrimination provision to launch legal challenges. The result was a reluctant, if not resistant, judiciary (Colker 2005). A familiar set of questions emerged: To what degree are 504-based entitlements a form of affirmative action? How much equality is really required under the law? To what degree should courts see people with disabilities as a suspect class and entitled to strict scrutiny? What does it mean to be a victim of disability-based discrimination?

The judicial discomfort with the Rehabilitation Act's antidiscrimination requirement accompanied a political struggle regarding the Act's spending promises—President Nixon vetoed the Act twice before signing a pared-down version in September 1973, and President Carter delayed implementation until 1978. The primary concerns were cost and the expansion of disability entitlements, rather than an awareness of the political and legal potential of the antidiscrimination mandate of Section 504, which I will return to later in this chapter when I consider the question of cost in civil rights law. The cost question was pertinent at this point because the late 1970s saw the resurgence of a conservative Republican Party and a larger political backlash to the entitlement programs of the War on Poverty and promises made during the civil rights era. It was a period of retrenchment in welfare politics that witnessed dramatic efforts to scale back the reach of most social programs. Not coincidentally, it is also the period in which the initial seeds of antidiscrimination that were contained in Section 504 grew into a larger, more comprehensive disability civil rights law.

THE RIGHTS MODEL HAS ARRIVED:
THE AMERICANS WITH DISABILITIES ACT

The Americans with Disabilities Act, passed by a bipartisan majority in Congress and signed by a triumphant[4] Republican president in 1990, became the world's first disability law that fully incorporates the rights model. The ADA enthusiastically defines disability as a civil rights issue and mandates equal opportunities, integration, and accommodations for difference. How did the framers of the ADA manage to sell the rights model in a conservative political climate? How were they able to challenge the prevailing medical view of disability and instead advocate for a rights-based understanding of disability that advanced both civil rights and antidiscrimination, as well as benefits programs?

There is no shortage of accounts documenting the passage of the ADA and the victory of the rights model in Congress. Joseph Shapiro's important history of the disability rights movement emphasizes the importance of a "hidden army" of lawmakers that had firsthand knowledge of disability discrimination—either personally or through the experiences of family members (Shapiro 1993). The National Council on Disability's history of the passage of the ADA tells of an unprecedented level of cross-disability lobbying and consciousness-raising by activists (Young 1997). Jane West emphasizes the urgent message about social inclusion it sent to the country: "The ADA is intended to open the doors of society and keep them open" (West 1991). Although clear divisions existed over the meaning and definitions of disability, concerns about costs to small businesses, and attempts to sideline the law by including homosexuality as a covered category, lawmakers were clear, in the end, about the ADA's basic intention: to provide a clear and comprehensive coverage against disability discrimination (Colker 2005, 65–68).

The ADA was passed by a wide majority in Congress (377–28 in the House, 91–6 in the Senate) and signed by a Republican president (George H. W. Bush). Its *Findings and Purposes* section begins with a view of people with disabilities as a "direct and insular minority" with a history of suffering discrimination. Its central mandate is to eliminate that discrimination, which it sees as a "serious and pervasive social problem" (42 U.S.C. § 12101 (a)(2)). This language anchors the ADA firmly in a civil rights paradigm, resting on the legal foundation of what are considered the "twin pillars" of civil rights and disability antidiscrimination law: Title VII of 1964 Civil Rights Act and Section 504 of the 1973 Rehabilitation Act (National Council on Disability

1997). The ADA was designed to expand the nondiscrimination mandate of Section 504 which mandated full accommodation for all facilities using public funds, to the private sector. After all, discrimination occurs in every aspect of life, be it through personal prejudices or architectural barriers. If the point of the ADA was to "open the door" and enable full participation in all aspects of society, then it must require not only that public services be made accessible but also that privately owned public places—such as hotels, restaurants, movie theaters, and shops—be accessible to all users. This point was powerfully brought home by the National Council on Disability's public forums organized in all 50 states, as well as before Congress, which invited emotional testimony by disabled Americans recounting their personal experiences with discrimination. They told powerful stories of being thrown out of movie theaters or being denied access to restaurants because managers feared the presence of the "unsightly other," providing compelling examples of the social and political exclusion the ADA was meant to remedy (Shapiro 1993, 105). The ADA covers public services and accommodations offered by both public (Title II) and private entities (Title III), requiring the provision of goods and services in "the most integrated setting appropriate to the needs of the individual" (42 U.S.C. § 12182) and the opportunity to participate in mainstream activities even if separate activities are also available.

Perhaps the most heavily debated, and subsequently the most heavily litigated, aspect of ADA is its prohibition against employment discrimination. Title I prohibits employers from discriminating against people with disabilities in all aspects of the employment relationship: in hiring and firing, advancement, job training, compensation, and all other terms and conditions of employment. This means that employers may not discriminate against qualified individuals who can "perform the essential functions of the job . . . with or without reasonable accommodations." In that sense, Title I is consistent with the general purpose underlying the ADA to "open doors," because it forces employers to include qualified workers, even if it means, in some cases, providing reasonable accommodations for these workers. However, the reasonable accommodation mandate—most commonly realized through job restructuring, creating other positions, or making minor modifications to the workplace environment—goes beyond a mere equal treatment paradigm by positing that just "opening the door" will not result in equal opportunities for workers with disabilities when that "door" is too narrow or leads to an inaccessible workplace. Failure to provide reasonable accommodations (unless employers can prove that these constitute an undue burden) is considered a form of discrimination. Employers can no longer categorically exclude disabled workers from the pool of qualified applicants if they are, in fact, qualified; the point is to focus on individual abilities rather than perceived inabilities.

The ADA's employment mandate reflects the fundamental assumption that stigma and stereotypes are primary barriers keeping people with disabilities out of the workplace. Title 1 only protects individuals who are qualified to perform the essential functions of the job, so employers can continue to hire the most qualified individual and make decisions unrelated to disability. However, they must accommodate individuals with disabilities to allow them to use their abilities to perform a job. To that end, employers are also prohibited from asking preemployment questions regarding disabilities—whether from safety fears about contagious illness or getting hurt on the job—unless these inquiries pertain to an applicant's abilities to perform job-related functions. A central concern for the framers of the ADA was to use antidiscrimination law as a way to remedy stereotypes about people with disabilities as incompetent, weak, and unemployable, and thus dependent on welfare or charity. Disability rights were to turn them from consumers of tax dollars into productive, taxpaying citizens. "Rights, not charity" became the rallying cry of the disability rights movement on the eve of the passage of the ADA. Much in the law reflects this antiwelfare sentiment, and understanding its origins will help us understand its influence on models in other countries. The next section will examine the political process that is frequently credited with paving the road for the ADA's passage in Congress.

THE ADA AS WELFARE REFORM

The continuing existence of unfair and unnecessary discrimination and
prejudice [against people with disabilities] costs the United States
billions of dollars in unnecessary expense resulting from dependency
and nonproductivity.[5]

In explaining the rationale for the ADA, members of Congress enthusiastically embraced a civil rights model of disability discrimination. The *Findings and Purposes* section, preceding the actual text of the law, calls disability discrimination a "serious and pervasive problem," explains that disability discrimination exists in all areas of public life, deems people with disabilities a

"discrete and insular minority with a history of purposeful unequal treatment," and explains that their position of political powerlessness is a result
of stereotypes and assumptions about their individual abilities to "participate in and contribute to society." The very last section shifts the focus to the
impact of this discrimination. It not only "denies people with disabilities the
opportunity to compete on an equal basis" but, perhaps more important,
costs the United States "billions of dollars." This argument is often credited
for paving the road toward passage of the ADA: not only was it a moral imperative to address the discrimination and stigma facing the country's largest minority (at the time Congress estimated there were 43 million people
with disabilities), it was good economic policy to turn people with disabilities from welfare dependents into productive taxpayers.

The origins of this argument lie in the Reagan presidency. By the 1980s,
the initial support in Congress for disability rights, as witnessed by the 1973
Rehabilitation Act, had begun to erode, and the "blank check of civil rights
entitlements had finally come up against serious political and financial constraints" (Scotch 2001, 136). The Reagan administration had promised to roll
back the development of the welfare state with a massive deregulation campaign under the auspices of the Task Force on Regulatory Relief, led by his
vice president, George H. W. Bush. Over 150 different pieces of enacted legislation were targeted for analysis, among them Section 504. When the disability community revolted against these proposed cuts, Bush agreed to meet
with representative activists, which led him to a fateful introduction to Evan
Kemp Jr. A good friend of Bush's chief counsel, Kemp came to play an important role in the development in the ADA.[6] Kemp is credited not only with
preventing the cutbacks to Section 504 but also, more broadly, for introducing what is called the "welfare argument" in American disability policy (Bagenstos 2003a). Kemp made the connection between Reagan's emphasis on
tax relief, self-reliance, and rugged individualism and the disability rights
movement's quest for independence and determination to counter assumptions about inabilities and dependency. Although Republicans and the disability community might seem "strange bedfellows," wrote Evan Kemp in a
Washington Post article, "their philosophical similarities are striking." He explained, "Both have accused big government of stifling individual initiative.
Both have advocated that only the truly needy should receive welfare and
that others should be given the opportunity to work and to become self-
reliant and responsible citizens" (Kemp 1981). As an example of excessive
government, Kemp noted that Social Security benefits for people with dis-

abilities had risen 400 percent in just seven years. If physically and mentally disabled persons became wholly or partially self-sufficient, opined Kemp, there would be "more taxpayers and fewer tax users—the ultimate Reagan objective" (Kemp 1981, as cited in National Council on Disability 1997).

The "more taxpayers, fewer tax users" argument was embraced enthusiastically by both Republicans and Democrats. The National Council on Disability (NCD), a federal agency charged with promoting and overseeing disability law, had just been created (then called the National Council on the Handicapped), and was staffed with Reaganites. In 1984, Congress issued NCD a mandate to review all federal programs relating to disability and offer recommendations on how Congress could best promote the independence of persons with disabilities and minimize dependence on governmental programs. In his extensive and authoritative history of the NCD, Jonathan Young describes the ways in which Congress made it clear that any disability law was to reflect "a whole new concept on how to decrease dependence" and that "Congress is not looking for more programs, more maintenance grants, and larger appropriations." Instead, NCD should "look for ways to convert existing maintenance dollars to help recipients achieve independence" (National Council on Disability 2010). A primary motivation of the Reagan administration was a "program that encourages people to return to work." NCD complied by not recommending any funding increases so as to "not embarrass the President." Young concludes that, from its very inception, U.S. disability antidiscrimination law "was not only about improving the lives of persons with disabilities; curtailing dependence also helped minimize the federal cost of disability" (National Council on Disability 2010).

Thus emerges a "dual concern" in American disability policy: a strong motivation to improve the lives of people with disabilities by increasing independence while reducing dependency on government. In response to the congressional mandate, the NCD issued a historically significant report, calling for the passage of a comprehensive equal opportunity law for persons with disabilities with the proposed title of the Americans with Disabilities Act of 1986. The document was appropriately called *Toward Independence*. Its central findings reflect the dual concerns outlined above. First, the report states that "federal disability programs reflect an overemphasis on income support and an under emphasis on initiatives for equal opportunity, independence, prevention, and self-sufficiency." Second, the report concludes that "more emphasis should be given to Federal programs encouraging and assisting private sector efforts to promote opportunities and independence for individuals with disabilities."[7] The message is clear: independence and equal opportunities can be consistent with fiscal conservatism.

Toward Independence is considered a groundbreaking report outlining the fundamental principles that eventually became the ADA. "If the goals of independence and access to opportunities for people with disabilities are to be achieved," it claimed, "it is essential that unfair and unnecessary barriers and discrimination not be allowed to block the way." Existing disability law was too limited in scope and application (Section 504, after all, applied only to recipients of federal funds) and did not cover disability discrimination as broadly as did existing laws covering discrimination on the basis of race, color, sex, religion, and national origin. The report specifically mentions laws on discrimination in employment, public accommodations, and housing that fail to include disability discrimination. Taking disability seriously as a civil rights issue would mean including disability rights protection under the same umbrella that Congress had already afforded to other forms of discrimination, thus firmly anchoring it in a civil rights paradigm.

The report is also groundbreaking in its embrace of fiscal conservatism, which, as many scholars of the ADA's history have noted, was crucial for securing the law's passage four years later (Bagenstos 2003a; Young 1997, 2000). Jonathan Young emphasizes the importance of fiscal restraint for winning the support of skeptical members of Congress, especially those worried about the cost of accommodations. Moreover, he suggests that "NCD rooted the ADA in Republican soil, preventing it from being discarded as a 'liberal' bill" (Young 1997). And, indeed, during congressional debates of the ADA, members of Congress were quick to pick up on the balance between civil rights and cost savings. Attorney General Richard Thornburgh, in calling the ADA "historic civil rights legislation [that] seeks to end the unjustified segregation and exclusion of persons with disabilities from the mainstream of American life," also stressed the dual nature of the law: "The ADA is fair and balanced legislation that carefully blends the rights of people with disabilities . . . with the legitimate needs of the American business community."[8] In a similar vein, Steny Hoyer, Democratic representative from Maryland, expressed his support for the ADA by embracing the dual goals of "doing the right thing" and increasing American global competitiveness by allowing every American talent to contribute to the workforce:

Many have asked: "Why are we doing this for the disabled?" My answer is twofold. As Americans, our inherent belief is that there is a place for everyone in our society, and that place is as a full participant, not a bystander. The second answer is less lofty. It is steeped in the reality of the world as we know it today. If, as we all suspect, the next great world competition will be in the market-place rather than the battlefield, we need the help of every American. . . . We cannot afford to ignore millions of Americans who want to contribute.[9]

This testimony balancing "lofty" commitments to equal treatment with the "real life" necessities of the marketplace is emblematic for the American embrace of disability rights as antithetical to welfare. It echoes Derek Bell's critique of "interest convergence" in the American embrace of civil rights law, which states that civil rights claims by African Americans will receive favorable judicial decisions to the extent that these interests coincide with the interest of the white Establishment (Bell 1979). Thus, civil rights victories in the courts were won primarily because a commitment to civil rights was seen to benefit American institutions, rather than benefitting racial minori-ties. Under this analysis, the government's dismantling of Jim Crow legisla-tion is now widely understood as a measure to improve America's foreign policy image at the beginnings of the Cold War, rather than as a simple com-mitment to ending African American suffering brought about by segrega-tion (Dudziak 2011). While the interest convergence dilemma may simplify the multiple and often contradictory commitments to civil rights in the U.S. government, it is a helpful reminder of how that same commitment—now extended to disability civil rights—captured equally complex and contradic-tory attitudes toward the role of the state in guaranteeing rights. The politi-cal currency of replacing welfare dependency with a commitment to civil rights that focuses on political and legal equality, rather than economic rights, was undeniable. More important, while members of Congress made passionate pleas for decreasing dependence on welfare rolls, disability activ-ists were making parallel arguments regarding independence.

DISABILITY ACTIVISM: INDEPENDENCE, NOT WELFARE

The ADA will empower people to control their own lives. It will result in
a cost savings to the Federal Government. As we empower people to be
independent, to control their own lives, to gain their own employment,
their own income, their own housing, their own transportation,
taxpayers will save substantial sums from the alternatives.
(Representative Steve Bartlett)[10]

The dual goal of reducing welfare spending and increasing the social and economic participation of people with disabilities resonated with the central goals of the disability rights movement at the time. Much of disability organizing during the 1970s and 1980s was energized by the idea of independent living. Centers for independent living, sparked by the successes in Berkeley, were popping up all over the country and became centers of political organizing. Independence, autonomy, self-determination, and a rejection of state paternalism were key organizing concepts, as reflected in popular slogans at the time: "when others speak for you, you lose," "nothing about us without us." Independence was initially conceptualized as the ability to live outside of institutions that leave little agency over everyday choices—when to wake up, what to wear, what to eat, what services to receive, how to receive them, and whom to socialize with. Instead, people with disabilities should be empowered to live on their own and employ personal assistants for aspects of daily living that they cannot do by themselves. The idea is that "if society is willing to pay money to keep people with impairments in institutions, it should be willing to spend that same money keeping them out of institutions" (Barnartt and Scotch 2001). The movement's goal is the provision of services that enable people with disabilities to function independently, to self-direct their lives, and to participate in the community. A common public justification for this demand is that assistance outside of institutions costs less than the same assistance when given inside an institutional setting (Barnartt and Scotch 2001). Again, we see cost cutting and economic efficiency as another argument for civil rights claims, allowing disability activists to fold their quest for independence into the government's economic interests.

The independence frame energized the larger disability rights movement and consolidated the demands of a diverse population. At the same time, it resonated well with the political climate of fiscal conservatism and welfare reduction during this period. This argument is most prominently made by legal scholar Samuel Bagenstos, who explains the tremendous value of the independence frame to disability rights advocates. "To achieve their goals," he writes, "disability rights leaders could almost endorse the wave of fiscal conservatism and opposition to welfare programs. They could say that people with disabilities do not want to be dependent on disability benefits; they simply 'want to work'" (Bagenstos 2009). The antiwelfare argument that secured the ADA's support in a conservative political climate was thus well supported by the disability rights movement's emphasis on independence.

Bagenstos suggests that "had the ADA been framed and defended differently—as a universal requirement of antidiscrimination and accommodation for any physical or mental difference—it almost certainly would not have passed" (Bagenstos 2009). Bagenstos's analysis is compelling and adds to the explanatory power of the political success of the ADA in a conservative political climate. If, indeed, Congress passed the ADA primarily as an antiwelfare bill rather than as an antidiscrimination law, and the disability rights movement made parallel arguments of independence from state paternalism, then the reach of the ADA as a civil rights law could rightly be seen as more limited than its framers envisioned. In making this claim, Bagenstos focuses on the courts' narrow interpretations of the disability category in a set of ADA employment cases that had received much criticism in the legal community. Although he tends to overstate the framing analysis of the disability rights movement's political goals (something I will address in my next chapter), his argument that the ADA is an antiwelfare bill is a central piece of this puzzle.

REASONABLE ACCOMMODATIONS
AND THE COST ISSUE IN DISABILITY LAW

We know that there is going to have to be accommodations to give us our basic civil rights. We know that. We understand that. There is a cost involved. But isn't there also a cost involved with us not being able to exercise our rights? (Congressman Tony Coelho)[11]

Although the political rhetoric surrounding the ADA clearly embraced the argument of the ADA as welfare-reduction bill that would turn consumers of tax revenues into contributors, it was also clear that the reasonable accommodations mandate would result in actual costs to businesses. The framers of Section 504 of the 1973 Rehabilitation Act had already wrestled with the question of costs. In the draft regulation, Senate staffers considered the question of cost a "non-issue." They embraced the idea that civil rights enforcement should not be dictated by costs, believing that "in civil rights law, the cost of ensuring nondiscrimination was, while not exactly irrelevant, an unreasonable excuse for condoning discrimination" (Scotch 2001, 75). This sentiment was widely held within the Office of Civil Rights at the time and was grounded in the experience of litigating desegregation in the South,

where federal courts routinely rejected southern cost concerns as an illegitimate excuse for not complying with statutory and court-ordered desegregation mandates. After all, "the very idea of a right is that it should be recognized without view to inconvenience, competing priorities, or disruptive
effect" (Scotch 2001, 75).

While the spirit of civil rights without price tags was a major tenet of
faith among the Section 504 framers, the reality of disability accessibility
prompted a more nuanced consideration of cost. After all, disability discrimination demands an approach to equal treatment that transcends notions of
simple equality; it is not enough to just "open the door," the door must be
widened enough to accommodate a variety of physical and symbolic ways of
entering public spaces. Senate staffers had to consider the possibility of financial burden on recipients of federal funds who were now affected by the
new antidiscrimination mandate. They compromised with a dual approach,
outlined in the regulation's preamble: costs would not be considered in the
question of what constitutes discrimination, only in fashioning a remedy for
it. Thus, cost deliberations were to be irrelevant in determining the standard
of discrimination, but they could matter in determining how this right
would be reached (Scotch 2001, 75).

Determining the way to "reach this right" not to be discriminated against
on the basis of disability meant that disability law had to confront the civil
rights legacy of limited, or simple, equality as mere nondiscrimination. The
framers of the ADA were well aware that a comprehensive disability equality
mandate had to account for adjustments and accommodations to the status
quo, and that these would raise the cost issue in new ways. The concept of
reasonable accommodations thus became the focal point in the law that
pushed it beyond the traditional notions of equal treatment inherent in civil
rights law.

Nowhere was this idea more contested than in the employment context.
The ADA's reach into the private sector meant that employers had to be prepared to change how an employee with a disability performs a job. The ADA
prohibits disability discrimination not only in traditional aspects of employment, such as hiring and firing, promotion and advancement, job training
and compensation, but also, explicitly, states that the failure to provide reasonable accommodations for qualified individuals with disabilities constitutes a form of disability discrimination. Reasonable accommodations under Title I of the ADA are "modifications or adjustments to a workplace
process or environment that makes it possible for a qualified person with a

disability to perform essential job functions, such as physical modifications to a work space, flexible scheduling of duties, or provision of assistive technologies to aid in job performance" (ADA Title I). The classic example of an accommodation is allowing an employee to perform a job sitting rather than standing, something that is often negotiated informally, especially when it imposes no costs on the employer. The ADA now extends this mandate to accommodations that might impose some hardship on the employer, as long as they are "reasonable" and the hardship is not "undue." The employee must prove reasonableness, that is, show how the accommodation allows him or her to perform the essential functions of the job. The employer, in turn, may use the undue hardship defense to show that this request is unreasonable. Undue hardship is broadly defined as an accommodation requiring "significant difficulty and expense" considering the nature of the task, the overall financial resources of the business, and the ways in which the accommodation may disrupt operations and other employees. In the end, however, failure to provide a reasonable accommodation—when the undue hardship test is not met—is considered a form of disability discrimination and prohibited by the ADA.

The process of negotiating reasonable accommodations is deliberately designed to be interactive, flexible, and individualistic, that is, case by case, placing employees and employers in a negotiating relationship. Employees must volunteer their disability status if they are seeking accommodations, and, if necessary, provide medical documentation outlining the scope of the accommodation requested. Employers, in turn, must show good-faith efforts to accommodate these needs, provided that they are reasonable and not too costly. This negotiation effectively creates what Karlan and Rutherglen (1996) call a "zone of bargaining," which empowers the employee to make reasonable demands, knowing that the employer is likely to offer some accommodation, even if these will tend to be less than what the employee has initially asked for. The relatively low costs of most accommodations, coupled with the fact that compensatory and punitive damages are available to workers with disabilities who can prove an employer's lack of good faith in offering accommodations, will make employers highly likely to offer at least some accommodations. At the same time, the high costs of litigation, coupled with the expenses of relocation and searching for a new job, will make the employee more willing to accept the employer's offer, however limited it may be. In these cases, Karlan and Rutherglen suggest that "employer and employee essentially share the costs of the disability" (1996, 30).

REASONABLE ACCOMMODATIONS AS AFFIRMATIVE ACTION?

The question of costs in antidiscrimination law thus remains at the center of the ADA and the rights model it represents. It has also prompted the question to what degree reasonable accommodations should be considered a form of affirmative action. Legal scholar Bonnie Tucker argues that the accommodations mandate is a central part of the ADA's civil rights framework, and should not be considered as a form of affirmative action. She makes the distinction between affirmative action, which seeks to limit the results of past discrimination, and reasonable accommodations, which seek to limit immediate or prospective discrimination. She explains that "while affirmative action gives preferential status to one group of people, reasonable accommodations do not give people with disabilities preferential status, but are provided to equalize the playing field for those requiring the accommodations" (Tucker 2001).

The ambivalence toward reasonable accommodations and the cost question reflects a "deep tension between the view of disability as a civil rights problem, and the view of disability discrimination as a social safety net issue" (Silvers 1998b). Scholarship on law and economics often frames this as a tension between efficiency and rights. The ADA's employment regulations follow well-established principles of employment antidiscrimination law: regulations are deemed necessary to equalize employment opportunities for targeted groups. For that reason, economists have criticized the ADA as yet another antidiscrimination mandate that is inefficient, unnecessary, and threatening to the country's at-will employment system.[12] This critique deems accommodations as unfair and costly, as well as inherently inefficient, because they are costs incurred by employers for workers with disabilities and not by their nondisabled workers who are arguably more efficient (Epstein 1995). Under this view, accommodations are seen as nothing more than disability subsidies, violating the rules of the free market as the costs of accommodations outweigh the benefits for both employer and employee.

There is ample empirical evidence that the vast majority of reasonable accommodations cost between nothing and $500 and that, in return, accommodations actually benefit employers by increasing job productivity, lowering job training costs, and reducing rehabilitation costs after a job injury (Blanck and Marti 1997; Blanck 2000). Moreover, these studies show the potential of the ADA to both avoid and resolve workplace conflict.[13] If accommodating workers with disabilities makes such economic sense, actually benefitting companies rather than bankrupting them, then what explains the widespread criticism of the accommodations mandate as too costly? Peter Blanck suggests that "the degree to which many companies comply with the accommodation provisions of Title I appears to have more to do with their corporate cultures, attitudes, and business strategies than with the actual demands of the law" (Blanck 2000, 217). Blanck cites studies showing that workplace accommodation strategies that were initially in place for workers with disabilities actually transcend their original purpose and result in enhancing the job productivity of large numbers of qualified workers *without* disabilities who are either injured on the job or who may become impaired in the future.

This phenomenon is well known under the term "universal design," hailing originally from architecture, which challenges the "special needs" justification of most disability-related accommodations. Instead, the argument goes, the majority of these accommodations actually benefit larger populations precisely because accommodations challenge organizations to examine taken-for-granted assumptions about working conditions and procedures. Thus, architects design buildings with wide entrances or automatic doors that now promote easy entry to all people, not only to those using wheelchairs. In universities, instructors can adopt educational modifications mandated by law for students with learning disabilities (such as lecture notes) to benefit the learning process of all students who will learn better if they can listen to lectures without having to take notes at the same time. At the workplace, flexibility in scheduling that will accommodate workers with disability-related needs can actually benefit all workers, disabled or not, by accommodating and perhaps even encouraging the multiple and complex workplace experiences of all workers, which can increase productivity and work performance.

Although the universal design strategies should bypass the need for economic justification of individual accommodations since they benefit the needs of the larger society, the defense of reasonable accommodations is still centered in bottom-line arguments. Peter Blanck points to the "the huge economic implications associated with the development of cost-effective accommodations strategies designed to prevent workplace injury and to help retain the increasing numbers of qualified employees with and without disabilities" (Blanck 2000, 223). The return to economic justifications for accommodations—in light of the growing numbers of empirical studies suggesting that the costs of required accommodations are minimal, nonexistent, or even cost-effective—should leave us wondering about the strength of social justice arguments that inspired the civil rights approach in the first place. What has happened to the idealistic rejection of cost considerations by Senate staffers formulating Section 504, the origin of the current disability rights model? Can we reject some civil rights as just too costly? To what degree should questions of economic efficiency dominate the ability of businesses to invoke an undue hardship defense?

A PRICE TAG ON CIVIL RIGHTS?

The framers of the ADA were quite clear that this kind of cost-benefit analysis should not play a role in the implementation of the reasonable accommodations mandate. The ADA's legislative history shows that factors determining whether a reasonable accommodation constitutes an "undue hardship" should not be determined by a cost-benefit analysis, but only by the nature and cost of an accommodation relative to an employer's financial capability. In this manner, the ADA codified the undue hardship regulations of the Rehabilitation Act, which stated that "deep pocket" employers may be responsible for more costly accommodations than smaller operations.[14] In the Senate debate on this issue, Senator Tom Harkin explained that a small business would have a solid "undue hardship" defense if asked to provide a reader for a blind employee, whereas "if it was IBM, maybe that would be something that could be done."[15]

The Equal Opportunity Employment Commission's enforcement guidelines for reasonable accommodations and undue hardship confirm that cost-benefit analysis should not be a part of the reasonable accommodations inquiry: "Some courts have said that in determining whether an accommodation is 'reasonable' one must look at the costs of the accommodation in relation to its benefits. . . . This cost-benefit analysis has no foundation in the statute, regulations, or legislative history of the ADA."[16] And yet, in direct opposition to this mandate, both the liberal-leaning Second Circuit (in *Borkowski*) and the more conservative Seventh Circuit (in *Vande Zande*) have ruled that a cost-benefit analysis is appropriate under both the reasonableness and undue hardship inquiries.[17] Linda Krieger's analysis of the political and legal backlash to the ADA suggests that this ambivalence toward the costs of disability antidiscrimination law is exacerbated by central characteristics of the civil rights model of disability. She writes, "Claiming a right to a needs-based allocation generates powerful normative dissonance, because where political rights are implicated, people expect allocations to be based on the principle of equality, under which everyone is treated the same" (Krieger 2003). Making a disability rights claim means arguing for equal treatment in terms of opportunities, access, and expectations, while simultaneously making difference-based needs claims. It is exactly that departure from the equality-as-sameness model that embodies the dynamic potential of the disability rights claim—and is the source of popular misperceptions of accommodations as unfair advantages. Rooted in an American tradition of equal treatment while simultaneously promising limited entitlements, U.S. disability rights find themselves at a crossroads between negative rights and the promise of positive rights.

THE ADA AT A CROSSROADS BETWEEN POSITIVE AND NEGATIVE RIGHTS

As indicated by table 1 earlier in this chapter, the ADA's heritage in classic antidiscrimination and equal opportunity doctrine points to its strong base in negative rights. We commonly distinguish between negative rights that prohibit government interference (for example, the right to free speech, to vote in elections, to practice one's religion) and positive rights that compel the state to provide the means with which to exercise the right (such as the right to an education, health, and welfare). Negative rights set a limit to invasive government action while positive rights require a certain minimal level of government intervention. In U.S. law, the prevailing view is that the Constitution is a "charter of negative, rather than positive liberties."[18] This means that the government is held solely to a negative obligation: to refrain from acts that deprive citizens of their rights. Obligations that are seen as positive, such as the duty to act or to provide, are not considered constitutional rights. Individuals thus have no right to compel their government to do anything: it must only refrain from harming or coercing them (Bandes 1990). The case of *DeShaney v. Winnebago* (1989) cemented the view of the United States as a country that celebrates negative rights. The U.S. Supreme Court ruled famously that the 14th Amendment's due process clause does not place positive obligations on the government to protect its citizens from violence. Joshua DeShaney thus had no positive right to state protection from his father's abuse, and the state social service agency could not be held liable for failing to remove him from his father's custody even when they were aware of his violent tendencies. Similarly, in *Webster v. Reproductive Health Services* (1989) the Supreme Court affirmed women's basic privacy rights to obtain abortions, but it upheld restrictions that made it difficult or impossible for poor women to exercise this right. Thus, women had the right to obtain abortions, but not the remedy (state funds) to make this right a reality.

This distinction between negative and positive rights is important as we examine the ways that countries with a strong history of positive rights ponder ways to adapt ADA-style antidiscrimination law. But it is also important to assess criticisms within the U.S. legal academy that seek to trouble the positive-negative rights distinction and the ways it simplifies the role of the state in guaranteeing even the most basic negative rights. Most prominent here is Susan Bandes's careful analysis of the historical and constitutional barriers to making the case for affirmative governmental obligations, her deconstruction of the state action-inaction distinction, and her suggestions for abandoning negative rights rhetoric (Bandes 1990). Similarly, Stephen Holmes and Cass Sunstein argue that rights are not moral absolutes, independent of government restraints, but rather "public goods" funded by taxes, administered by governments, and subject to distributive justice (Holmes and Sunstein 2000). All rights are political, and their existence is dependent upon the willingness of the community, through the government's role in raising taxes, to protect and enforce them. In other words, no right comes without costs. Even so-called negative rights, such as the right to hold property free of government interference, must be supervised and maintained by tax-funded courtrooms, police, and fire stations (Holmes and Sunstein 2000). Similarly, the right to be free from sexual harassment in the workplace might fit the classic definition of a negative right, but it is still enforced through the "non-inexpensive efforts of the EEOC [Equal Opportunity Employment Commission] and state employment agencies" (Illingworth and Parmet 2000). In that sense, disability legal scholars question the distinction between the ADA's nondiscrimination mandate and the reasonable accommodations requirement necessary to make nondiscrimination rights a reality. Disability nondiscrimination rights do not radically depart from those guaranteed by other civil rights statutes, even with the inclusion of the reasonable accommodations mandate (Stein 2000).

Indeed, Illingworth and Parmet argue that "the genius of the ADA is that it forthrightly melds positive and negative rights, creating a civil rights statute that goes beyond the simplistic equal opportunity-as-negative-rights model represented by Title VII" (Illingworth and Parmet 2000). The ADA challenges the positive-negative rights dichotomy by pushing the limits of the equality-as-sameness model. As mentioned at the beginning of this chapter, the ADA points to a more robust notion of equality by effectively challenging social norms to incorporate the experiences of all Americans and by pointing to the false neutrality inherent in social structures that reflect only the nondisabled norm.

And yet the ADA stops short of the kind of distributive justice that critics say is necessary to ensure true equality for people with disabilities (Wasserman 1998). Canadian legal scholar Jerome Bickenbach considers the ADA an individualistic, reactive, and complaint-driven system of justice that focuses on individual, rather than collective, remedies. Bickenbach points to the fact that the denial of opportunities and resources is a product of distributive injustice, a complex social phenomenon that cannot easily be addressed in an ADA lawsuit involving a single discriminator (Bickenbach 2000). The civil rights model, he argues, is not a comprehensive solution for eradicating discrimination: it might outlaw discrimination and offer legal recourse, but discrimination will continue to exist. People with disabilities face a host of nonaccommodating physical and social environments, starting with a lack of education and training, diminished job prospects, limited access to assistive technologies, and a general lack of resources to pay for impairment-related needs. People with disabilities tend to be among the poorest in a nation, and this is exacerbated in the United States, where disability poverty is worse than elsewhere in the developed world.[19] These social ills are part of a larger picture of resource distribution and power, but they are not recognized as legal harms that the state is constitutionally obligated to rectify. Rather, the characteristic feature of the inequality that people with disabilities face in the workplace and the society at large is the "unjust limiting of their equal right to participate in the full range of social roles and ways of life," which is only partially addressed by the discrimination doctrine (Bickenbach 2000, 353).

In contrast to the voices that either celebrate the ADA for taking steps in the direction of positive rights or criticize it for not going far enough, legal scholar Anita Silvers insists that the ADA should be seen as a model of "formal equality" that removes barriers to full social participation (Silvers 1998a). Silvers argues that the ADA, rather than promising material equality, promotes formal justice by requiring a "refashioning of the biased dialogical structures" that have excluded people with disabilities from exercising their rights as equal citizens by denying them access to the opportunities for social participation that the rest of the (nondisabled) population enjoys (Silvers 1998a). She contends that the ADA's reasonable accommodations mandate is not a form of positive right, but rather a form of negative liberty through ensuring freedom from past and future discriminatory workplace practices. Disability scholarship will continue to disagree on the scope of the ADA's potential and limitations and challenge the policy implications of the social model of disability. There is no question, however, that this social model, which initiated the focus on social structures and environments for their disabling qualities—and its initial application in U.S. disability law and policy—remains a powerful source of inspiration to disability rights movements across the globe.

DISABILITY MODELS AND POLITICAL CULTURE

There has always been a distinction between what we mean by IL [independent living] in Britain and what they mean in the States. IL in America is organised around self-empowerment, individual rights and the idea that in the land of the free and the home of the brave—all that crap—individuals, if they are given access under the law and the constitution, can be independent. In contrast, in Britain IL entailed collective responsibilities for each other and a collective organization. IL wasn't about individual self-empowerment, it was about individuals helping one another. (Oliver 1996, 204)

Models of disability, as well as approaches to legislating equality for people with disabilities, are deeply embedded in social and political norms and assumptions about the meanings of disability and discrimination. This is what Michael Oliver, Great Britain's first professor of disability studies, is pointing to in the quotation above. Oliver is building on a common European view of some of the basic differences in U.S. and European political cultures. The United States is seen as the country of individualism and individual rights, in direct opposition to European values of economic security and welfare rights. Oliver translates these differences into disability politics and the importance of independent living, one of the founding concepts of the modern disability rights movement. This contrast between individualism and collectivism, between autonomy and interdependence, and, by extension, between rights-based and needs-based disability policy provides an important background to the arguments I develop in this book.

This chapter has explored the different ways of legislating disability rights and the assumptions inherent in disability rights and welfare models. As the inaugural document of the rights model, the ADA has set important standards of equality and nondiscrimination and inspired movements around the globe to enact similar legislation. Using the formidable rhetoric of civil rights with its emphasis on formal equality and nondiscrimination, the U.S.-inspired disability rights model has provided a powerful example and inspiration for the framing of disability rights in other contexts. The question remains how this rights model will be translated in countries lacking such a civil rights tradition, and how much longer it will remain the international model for disability rights, especially in western Europe. Although the ADA continues to inspire movements there, it has also received its share of criticism, especially in British academic circles that have produced the bulk of theoretical work on the social model of disability. Returning to Michael Oliver's criticism, we see a growing concern over the ideal of independence and individual rights that has been promoted by the neoliberal state anxious to reduce the loads on national welfare budgets (French 1993). How can disability rights lead to more independence and self-determination without eradicating their basis in social justice?

British sociologist T. H. Marshall's classic argument in *Citizenship and Social Class* (1950) provides a useful background to the journey of disability rights from the United States to other countries. Marshall saw the history of citizenship as the achievement of three types of rights that had evolved during the last two centuries: civil, political, and social rights. Civil rights (or more appropriately, civil liberties) were the basic protections from arbitrary state power that developed in the 18th century, such as property rights, personal liberty, and the protection from arbitrary arrest. Political rights—the rights to full participation, such as voting rights, freedom of the press, and the right to demonstrate—were fought for in the 19th century. Both of these developments then culminated in the achievement of social rights in the course of the 20th century, as Marshall witnessed the development of the post–World War II British welfare state. It was in this modern period that rights came to be seen as rights to resources: to health, education, income, social security, and a general sense of welfare or well-being. Indeed, Marshal posits that notions of modern citizenship must rely on the addition of social rights as a necessary precondition to political participation. Thus, social rights are more than just the right to education and the right to be free from poverty, but also "the right to share to the full in the social heritage and to live the life of a civilized being, according to the standard prevailing in the society" (Marshall 1950).

Marshall's differentiation of social versus political and civil rights and his insistence on the sequence that rights develop in is an important part of the puzzle this chapter has tried to unravel. Applying his analysis to the development of disability rights in both Europe and the United States, we can see that the United States is following the traditional sequence of guaranteeing both political and civil rights for people with disabilities while still lacking in substantial guarantees for social rights. The European case, in contrast, has seen the development of social rights before the guarantee of full political citizenship. The European example shows that in the creation of "new" rights—such as the right to be free from disability-based discrimination—we can see potentially progressive combinations of political, civil, and social rights, which may set a new standard for disability law, guaranteeing the right to be both equal and different.

Indeed, as the rest of this book will show, there is a growing critical engagement with the U.S.-inspired social model in both Europe and Asia. European disability scholars Anna Lawson and Caroline Gooding point to the link between the social model of disability and the growth in European disability law promoting equal opportunities, which they term "emerging positive duties to promote equality for disabled people" (Lawson and Gooding 2005). The social model, as discussed in this chapter, focuses on removing the barriers created by the structures and organizations of society that prevent people with impairments from participating fully in the life around them. It is these very barriers that "positive duties" are designed to tackle. They impose obligations on those who design and operate structures and organizations to design them in a manner that keeps barriers to a minimum. Lawson and Gooding conclude that "it is fitting that, despite the fact that it was in the U.S. that anti-disability discrimination legislation first appeared, these positive duties to promote disability equality should emerge from Europe, which is the home of the social model" (Lawson and Gooding 2005).

Before we turn to the two case studies, however, there is one more aspect of the U.S.-based civil rights model to consider: the historical and cultural model that the U.S. civil rights movement has provided for the formulation of disability rights. Both U.S. policy makers and disability activists deploy civil rights analogies when making the case for disability rights. Making the civil rights analogy has provided a well-paved terrain for disability activists to negotiate their demands and inspire the legislative foundation of the ADA. It furnished a vocabulary and a frame of reference through which people with disabilities can articulate the difficulties they face in seeking full participation in society. It has enabled them to cast arguments in the form of rights—rather than needs or mere policy preferences—that resonate with fundamental values regarding equality, fair treatment, and equal opportunities. The next chapter, then, will examine the importance of the civil rights analogy for the political success of the U.S. disability rights movement, providing a cultural and political base that movements in other countries lack.

CHAPTER TWO

Disability Rights as Civil Rights:
The ADA and the Limits of Analogy

Like the African-Americans who sat in at segregated lunch counters and
refused to move to the back of the bus, people with disabilities sat in
federal buildings, obstructed the movement of inaccessible buses, and
marched through the streets to protest injustice. And like the civil rights
movements before it, the disability rights movement sought justice in
the courts and in the halls of Congress. (Mayerson 1992)

"My name is Rosa Parks." (Johnson, Shaw, and Olin 2001, 39)

MY NAME IS ROSA PARKS

The year was 1986 and Americans Disabled for Accessible Public Transit
(ADAPT), a grassroots organization widely considered the radical wing of the
disability movement, had come to Detroit to confront the American Public
Transit Association, which was holding its big trade convention there.
ADAPT had asked Rosa Parks to lead its parade through downtown Detroit.
For years ADAPT activists had been using Rosa Parks as their icon—often ap-
pearing at protests with name tags reading "My name is Rosa Parks"—trying
to make the public connect their protest with the civil rights movement. "A
civil rights movement was born when people refused to ride at the back of
the bus. We can't even get on the bus," was another well-used slogan in those
days. The analogy was meant to be poignant; unlike Rosa Park's quest to integrate the buses by moving from the back to the front, disability activists
demanded an even more fundamental kind of integration. And yet, Rosa
Parks failed to appear at ADAPT's press conference and march on October 5,
1986. In a letter to ADAPT two days before the march, Parks cited "the trau-

matic manner in which you choose to dramatize disabled Americans' lack of access to public transit" (most likely referencing ADAPT's tactics of chaining themselves to buses and disrupting traffic) as her reason for backing out. She didn't want to "embarrass the city's guest and cripple the city's present transportation system" (M. Johnson, Shaw, and Olin 2001).

Rosa Parks had long been an icon to the disability rights movement, not only because of her integration of buses, but because of her acts of courage. In the words of ADAPT activist Michael Auberger:

> Had it not been for Parks and the bus boycott, there is no question that the disability rights movement would have been light-years behind, if it would have ever occurred. Her genius was that she saw the bus as the great integrator: It took you to work, it took you to play, it took you to places that you were never before seen. We began to see the bus the same way, too, and it empowered a group of people who had been just as disenfranchised as African Americans.[1]

His colleague Bob Kafka echoes this sentiment: "Rosa Parks energized us in that she was the perfect symbol for when the meek become militant. She was someone who was willing to cross the line" (Wilson 2005).

Rosa Parks's refusal to lend herself as an icon in the disability rights movement's claim to a civil rights heritage has not deterred ADAPT from its movement tactics (which they had used to advance their new issue since the passage of the ADA: the demolition of the nursing home complex), nor did it weaken the general movement's view of itself as "the last civil rights movement" (Driedger 1989). Movement activists themselves tend to explain that Rosa Parks refused not because she rejected the disability analogy to civil rights, but because she had close ties to the city's African American establishment, whom she did not want to see embarrassed by ADAPT's aggressive tactics.[2] Neither should we see Parks's rejection of ADAPT as indicative of a larger rejection of the disability rights movement by the black civil rights movement. In fact, Sue Schweik reminds us of the central role of the Black Panthers (under the leadership of disabled Panther activist Bradley Lomax) in supporting the four-week occupation by disability activists of the San Francisco office of the U.S. Department of Health, Education and Welfare (HEW), as well as other HEW offices, after HEW secretary Joseph Califano refused to sign the Section 504 regulations (Schweik 2011). Consider also that in fashioning the NAACP's legal assault on the separate but equal doctrine, Thurgood Marshall relied heavily on the writings of Jacobus tenBroek, who was one of the earliest scholars to examine and systemically apply the 14th Amendment's equal protection clause to the area of social justice, and who later made disability history with his influential article outlining a "right to live in the world" for people with disabilities (tenBroek 1966). The disability leadership in the famous 504 sit-ins and in the struggle for the ADA had come of political age during the civil rights movement and clearly saw themselves as descendants of that movement. Their claim to a civil rights heritage was both sincere and strategically crucial and continues to be celebrated.

This chapter tells the story of the cultural turn to rights in the United States. It analyzes the tremendous political and legal power of the civil rights analogy for the formation of disability rights activism and for the framing of the legal response to disability discrimination. The analogy to black civil rights struggles allowed disability activists to frame their demands in terms of rights rather than charity, to think of themselves as a coherent movement that is united by the common experience of oppression and exclusion, and to adopt a vocabulary that allowed them to frame their experiences in a way that resonated with well-established notions of equal treatment and equal opportunities. Civil rights, as articulated by social movements, made visible, legitimated needs, and provided claims to citizenship. The point was to wage the "same struggle" as previous civil rights movements but under a "different difference." Claiming a civil rights heritage lent both political and legal legitimacy to a movement struggling to articulate notions of disability equality in a conservative political climate. As I spelled out in the previous chapter, framing disability rights as a question of civil rights rather than welfare entitlements was pivotal for generating bipartisan support for the passage of the ADA. The disability literature, both the movement literature and the legal literature, is unequivocal in crediting the civil rights movement of the 1960s, and specifically the equal rights frame it provided, for the political and legal successes in the disability case (Barnartt and Scotch 2001; Charlton 2000; Colker 2005; Driedger 1989; Switzer 2003; Shapiro 1993; Scotch 2001).

After establishing the centrality of the race analogy in the disability movement's political and legal identity, this chapter will problematize the analogy. I argue that the civil rights analogy is based on notions of simple equality—equal treatment regardless of differences—that do not always work well for the disability case. Equal treatment in the disability case demands a more complex negotiation of difference that can threaten central assumptions about the way that equality is supposed to work both politically and legally. And yet, notions of simple equality as framed by the race analogy were instrumental in securing passage of disability antidiscrimination law in Congress and gaining legitimacy in the courts. There are two areas that highlight the limitations of the race analogy for disability. The first is the ways that the legal category of disability departs from the established categories—race and sex—in regard to definitions of the protected class. As a result, the ADA introduces its reasonable accommodations mandate, which stretches notions of simple equality by recognizing that traditional notions of equality as sameness will not result in justice for people with disabilities. The second limitation is the interpretation of this disability category by the Supreme Court. I analyze the ways the court has refused to embrace the disability analogy to race and sex by ruling that discrimination on the basis of disability should not receive the same strict or heightened scrutiny that the court has used for race and sex discrimination. Many legal observers have argued that the court has not fully embraced the disability rights model as envisioned by the framers of the ADA, not only in its refusal of the disability analogy in its equal protection analysis but also in its hostility to the ADA's employment discrimination claims. In a host of ADA Title I employment cases the court has dealt significant blows to the ADA's civil rights vision by limiting the category of who counts as disabled under the law. The legal literature is replete with analysis of these cases, documenting, once again, the court's refusal to accept the analogy to race and sex in employment discrimination cases. Rather than focus on these well-documented shortcomings in the court's disability analysis, however, I have selected cases that exemplify a more drastic departure from the traditional civil rights model: cases that include forms of "rational discrimination."

Rational discrimination is a form of unequal treatment that is not motivated by traditional forms of discrimination, which are based on animus, dislike, or irrational stereotypes, and therefore considered "intentional discrimination." The traditional purpose of antidiscrimination law is to recognize and reverse this form of unequal treatment based on protected identities such as race, sex, age, or disability. More contemporary research on discrimination has pointed to a form of "unintentional" discrimination, however, that is not based on active prejudice but rather on seemingly "rational" decisions regarding the costs of hiring members of protected classes. Employers make decisions based on economic efficiency and maximizing profits that disproportionately affect members of protected classes, but these decisions are not consciously motivated by animus or stereotypes. Still, the court has ruled that Title VII prohibits these practices as unlawful forms of intentional discrimination on the basis of race and sex. And yet, when it comes to disability, rational discrimination has become a more commonly accepted excuse. While the traditional civil rights model sees costs as an illegitimate excuse to condone discrimination, in the disability case the prohibition against rational discrimination has worked very differently. Disability discrimination, I argue, continues to be seen as "rational" in ways that discrimination on the basis of race or sex never was—or at least, was never allowed to be—under the court's Title VII jurisprudence.

I conclude this chapter with insights from the critical disability literature that seeks to retheorize equality outside of the civil rights frame. This literature promotes a view of disability as a form of vulnerability that is universally shared and not limited to a legally specified minority. It locates disability outside the confines of the civil rights paradigm precisely because it recognizes the limits of the law to bring about substantive equality and true justice. I suggest that this view is both theoretically powerful and politically dangerous. A return to notions of vulnerability calls to mind a not so distant past in which vulnerability—and the accompanying helplessness and disenfranchisement—was all that defined and confined the lives of people with disabilities. Activists had marshaled the law to contest these stereotypes and gain access to institutions of citizenship. Is there room in the American politics of civil rights for a more complex understanding of disability equality? How has the civil rights movement shaped the understanding of rights and equal treatment for successive movements? This chapter tells the story of the civil rights analogy in the American disability rights movement, beginning with its inception in the American civil rights tradition.

THE CIVIL RIGHTS ORIGINS OF U.S. DISABILITY RIGHTS LAW AND ACTIVISM

The founders of IL [the independent living movement] were bright white male students of a prestigious university who grew up in homes where families could describe themselves as "comfortable." In the 40s and 50s, polio had knocked down those families' most-likely-to-succeed kids like bowling pins. America's best and brightest . . . had been transformed overnight into second-class citizens by a microscopic organism with a long Latin name. What caused them to question their second-class status? They'd hatched out of privilege and protection into

a world that was changing radically. A people's cry for liberty and justice
was visible, audible, and haunting America on its nightly news. The
nation sat witness while solemn black people stood their ground as
sheriffs set dogs on them for having the nerve to sit down on lunch
counters, go to school. Black pride arose from white oppression and
black poverty. The independent living revolution arose from among
privileged white boys. And, bless them, those boys stormed the
barricades to free us from the medical model.

LUCY GWIN (1997)

Lucy Gwin, editor of the magazine *Mouth: The Voice of Disability Rights,* re-
members the beginning years of the disability rights movement as firmly
lodged in the civil rights movement's "cry for liberty and justice" (Gwin 1997,
26–27). The first generation of disability rights activists were, indeed, "privileged white boys" who had been transformed into second-class citizens as a
result of their disabilities. The most prominent example of that generation is
Ed Roberts (introduced in the previous chapter), who is widely acknowledged
as the father of the independent living movement in the United States and
across the globe. Having spent most of his life in an iron lung, Roberts repeatedly rejected expectations that he could not finish high school, attend university, or have a family. He learned powerful lessons of advocacy and self-
determination while dealing with unrelenting bureaucracies who considered
him too disabled to go to school or hold a job—which inspired him to study
political science and to select a university not based on its accessibility, but on
its academic excellence. When UC Berkeley rejected him ("We tried cripples
before, and they don't work," he was told), Roberts decided to sue (Fleischer
and Zames 2001, 38). The year was 1962, the same year that the NAACP sued
on behalf of James Meredith to gain admission to the segregated University of
Mississippi. At Berkeley, Roberts experienced a different form of segregation:
he had to stay in the University's infirmary, the only place that could accommodate his 800-pound iron lung. The infirmary soon became the center of
early disability activism, where Robert founded the nation's first disabled students' program and the Rolling Quads, a political group that made wheelchairs commonplace in the Berkeley community.

This movement was a product of the radical politics at Berkeley, such as
the civil rights movement, the free speech movement, and the protest
against the war in Vietnam. Searching for possible candidates to work as personal assistants for the growing number of disabled students at Berkeley,
Roberts proposed using the pool of conscientious objectors from military
service, because he thought their politics were perfect for the movement.

Roberts met with a military official responsible for placing conscientious objectors and "told him about what attendants do for people with disabilities and that conscientious objectors were ideal for the job. This official was enthusiastic; he thought this was like a punishment for these people who refused to fight. So, we got them signed up. These were the kind of people we wanted to work with. We were very lucky" (Fleischer and Zames 2001, 39).

In his meetings with Stokely Carmichael and others in the black power movement, however, Roberts did not find the allies he was hoping for. "I told them that we were all fighting the same civil rights battle, they didn't believe me, they didn't understand our similarities" (Fleischer and Zames 2001, 39). Similar to the first-generation activists in the women's movement, who developed their feminist consciousness during the student protests when they realized that "we were making the coffee while the men were making the revolution" (Evans 1979, 20), disability activists realized that racial discrimination mirrored their own experiences. Just as African Americans were oppressed by prejudices surrounding the color of their skin, people with disabilities suffered discrimination on the basis of irrational fears and assumptions about their disabilities.

This is the origin story of the American disability rights movement. People with disabilities formed a social movement to protest the discrimination they faced on the basis of their disabilities and to demand equal rights and opportunities, just as African Americans had formed a movement on the basis of race to protest racial discrimination. In many ways, disability activists did not view their own situation as discriminatory until they began to see it through the lens of race discrimination. In sociological terms, the disability rights movement successfully adapted the civil rights movement's "frame" of equal treatment and equal opportunities (Benford and Snow 1998). The section that follows will describe the processes by which disability rights activists extended the equal treatment frame that has its origin in the black civil rights movement to fit the disability experience, both in generating a movement and in articulating legal remedies.

MAKING THE ANALOGY: "SAME STRUGGLE, DIFFERENT DIFFERENCE"

The extension of the equal treatment frame is best summarized by a well-known slogan that was emblazoned on T-shirts and etched into the movement's collective consciousness: "same struggle, different difference." The idea is that people with disabilities are waging the same civil rights struggle as other oppressed groups, but they are waging it under a different identity. Jonathan Young first articulated exactly how the civil rights frame extends to disability rights after purchasing a T-shirt bearing the slogan during a disability rally. He argues that the disability rights movement should be spoken of in the same breath as the African American civil rights, women's rights, and gay rights movements because these movements share four specific points of continuity: stigmatization, self-determination, collective consciousness, and a social critique of oppression (Young 1997; Stein 2004).

The notion of stigma is perhaps the most apparent obstacle facing people with disabilities. Sociologist Erving Goffman (1963) describes how a stigmatized trait, such as a physical or mental disability, or dark skin, or homosexuality, often "spoils" a person's social identity. Thus, just as blacks or gays and lesbians have been stigmatized and dehumanized for their differences, so have people with disabilities been put away in institutions, confined to the home as social outcasts, and presumed to be incapable of being productive citizens. Essays on disability discrimination have often invoked the words of Ralph Ellison's *Invisible Man* to reflect their parallel sense of being invisible as a real person: "I am invisible, understand, simply because people refuse to see me. When they approach me they see only my surroundings, themselves, or figments of their imagination—indeed, everything and anything except me" (Ellison 1974, 3). The disabled are not seen as people; they are only seen as their disability, generating unease or downright avoidance in the nondisabled. In the same sense they feel that "facing an inaccessible building is similar to encountering a *whites only* sign: the individual is denied the right to enter and participate in society" (Drimmer 1992, 1358).

An important strategy for countering the stigmatization of people with disabilities has been to assault presumptions of biological inferiority with what Jane Mansbridge (2001) terms "'oppositional consciousness': to claim a previously subordinated identity as a positive one, to identify injustices done on the basis of this identity, and to demand changes to rectify these injustices." People with disabilities are thus encouraged to embrace their identities and find pride in them, rather than hoping for a cure. This is not always a simple task in a culture that commonly assumes life with a disability is not worth living: people with disabilities often receive unsolicited advice that "I would kill myself if I were you" (Shapiro 1993).

The media coverage of prominent people with disabilities has reflected this. In 1989 *CBS 60 Minutes* asked I. King Jordan, president of Gallaudet College, if he would take a pill that would restore his hearing. Jordan responded by asking the interviewer if she would take a pill that would make her a man. He explained that he had never considered this question, and that for him this would be the same as asking a black man to take a "white pill." His deafness was a central part to his identity, not something he would want to magically cure overnight. In the end, Jordan concludes, the interviewer never understood: "She still does not. She still thinks only from her own frame of reference and imagines that not hearing would be a terrible thing" (Shapiro 1993). Cyndi Jones, editor of *Mainstream* magazine, gave a similar answer. When asked whether she would take a magic pill that would wipe away the lingering paralysis of her polio and let her walk again, "she answers quickly: No. 'It's the same thing as asking a black person would he change the color of his skin'" (Shapiro 1993, 14). Jones's and Jordan's embrace of their disabilities as a vital part of their identity and their deliberate comparison to race and gender identity underscores not only the importance of reclaiming disability as a positive form of identity but also strengthens the analogy to other identity-based movements.

Reclaiming pride in one's identity as an individual and as part of a larger disability culture rests on notions of self-determination, another point of overlap with other identity-based civil rights movements. Disability activists contend that they should run their own organizations, that they are the experts on their own needs, and that they should be the architects of their own lives. This was a radical idea growing out of a movement that had to fight hard against institutionalized forms of charity, paternalism, and policy responses to the "deserving" poor. The independent living movement, referenced by Lucy Gwin above, grew from this critique. It is through the independent living movement that people with various types of disabilities sought to develop consumer-run organizations that facilitated living independently in community settings instead of residing in institutions or with one's family. In 1988, students at Gallaudet University powerfully symbolized the claim to self-determination in their successful campaign to have a Deaf university president rather than a hearing one. Notions of self-determination are also evident in the protests against charity telethons, such as the March of Dimes and particularly in the person of Jerry Lewis, who became the disability rights movement's bête noir for misplaced paternalism and aggressive marketing of helpless crippled children to arouse viewers' pity and fear and have them open their wallets (H. Johnson 2006). The critique of telethons—and the adamant refusal to accept charity, however well meaning—is an important step in the cultural shift to rights in the U.S. disability movement.

Perhaps the most obvious parallel between the disability movement and other identity-based movements is a sense of collective consciousness: the self-conscious identification as a stigmatized group. For disability activists, identification as an oppressed group reflected a radical and powerful change in consciousness. Just as women formed consciousness-raising groups to discuss their common experiences of oppression, so did people with disabilities form "discrimination diary parties" (Young 1997) to document the various forms of discrimination they had encountered. As an example, consider Ed Roberts's explanation of the connections he made with women's groups on the Berkeley campus:

> They used to let me go to their meetings; I guess they saw a connection between our experiences. I remember them talking about how to deal with stereotypes of weakness and passivity that society placed on them. I heard women talk about how they had manipulated men by capitalizing on these stereotypes. I realized that disability is actually a strength. If someone comes up to me and doesn't look me in the eye, if all they see is my ventilator and my chair, I can tell right away. If they don't see me as a human being, if they only see my equipment, I know that I can get whatever I want out of them. As long as this is not used pathologically, but to create beneficial change for others, it is a strength. Disability can be very powerful. We used the power of disability in political strategies many times. (Fleischer and Zames 2001, 38)

Fashioning a collective consciousness on the basis of disability is commonly viewed as more complicated than generating identities on the basis of race and gender. Prior to the 1970s, people with disabilities, if anything, tended to identify with people who shared their own specific disability. As Mary Crossley points out:

> First, unlike many members of other racial, ethnic, or religious minority groups, individuals with disabilities often have grown up in isolation from other persons with disabilities and thus have had little opportunity to develop the type of group consciousness or culture that has empowered other minority groups. Similarly . . . disabled people are an extremely heterogeneous bunch. As a result, the experiences of disadvantage or subordination that individuals have encountered may be so diverse that group members may find themselves with little in common. Due to this heterogeneity, dis-

ability theorists are particularly sensitive to their inability to speak to the experience of all disabled people. (Crossley 1999)

Nevertheless, in the 1970s disability activists began to fashion the beginnings of a fragile cross-disability consciousness. The basis for this group identity, cemented by the 1978 protest surrounding Section 504, was a shared experience of discrimination on the basis of disability, rather than with shared experiences of a particular disability. Judy Heumann, one of the leaders of the 504 sit-ins, recalls that the demonstrations were successful "because the disability community was united; because the disability community absolutely unequivocally believed that 504 was our civil rights provision; because we knew if we did not fight for this civil rights provision we were in fact going to slide backwards instead of making progress" (Fleischer and Zames 2001, 54).

Heumann's celebration of disability unity comes with the recognition that the diversity of the disability category and the multiple ways that individuals experience impairments and disabling barriers has complicated attempts at fashioning group identity. Minority group models are based on identity politics and boundary-making that rely on stable categories and resist the blurring of boundaries. Civil rights law assumes race and gender to be stable categories, whereas the category of disability is particularly problematic and essentially forces distinctions between the "truly disabled" and the "merely ill." Within the disability rights movement, people with disabilities that are invisible or those whose disabilities are mitigated by medication struggle for acceptance into the disability category while simultaneously passing as nondisabled. Lennard Davis thinks about disability group consciousness in terms of coalition building with other social movements. He speculates that "while many white people have embraced the cause of people of color, and while many straight people have taken up the cause of gay, lesbian, bisexual and transgendered people, few 'normals' have resonated with people with disabilities. The reasons for this are telling. No whites will become black, few straights will become gay; but every normal person can become disabled. All it takes is the swerve of a car, the impact of a football tackle, or the tick of a clock to make this transformation" (Davis 2002).

Disability is a fluid and open category—anybody can join at any time—and it does not conform to the limitations of traditional identity categories that assume lifelong assignments to a particular race or gender. The law of disability discrimination reflects this assumption (more about this later in this chapter).

Young's first three points that allow for the civil rights analogy to be passed down from race and gender to disability—stigma, self-determination, and collective consciousness—point to a transformation in thinking about disability that parallels the development of other civil rights movements. This transformation concerns where people identify the "problem" to reside. African Americans, women, and lesbians and gays have all faced assumptions that there was the "Negro problem," the "woman question," and the "homosexual disease" (Young 1997). In each case, the individual's difference from established norms was reason for exclusion from mainstream institutions, and the responsibility for reform and life improvement depended upon the individual's ability to accommodate mainstream society. The final point of commonality, then, is the development of a social critique of oppression that would turn this assumption on its head. This critique locates the source of the problem not with the individual's inherent difference, but with the social response to this difference. In the disability case, this view was cemented by the social model of disability, as described in the previous chapter. This new way of viewing disability was revolutionary because it allowed activists to challenge assumptions that it was inherent differences that explained social exclusion and forms of discrimination, and instead focused the critical gaze on social institutions and norms that privileged particular embodied selves. Thus, both the source of the problem (the disabled body) and the location for reform (the disabled body subjected to rehabilitation efforts to resemble most closely its nondisabled counterpart) would be turned on its head. It was society that was the problem and thus responsible for the solution. Returning to ADAPT's struggle against inaccessible buses, then, the problem was not that people using wheelchairs could not board the bus because their chairs were too wide and could not fit through the doors; the problem was that the buses were not built to accommodate a wide variety of riders, including those who used wheelchairs. Relegating wheelchair users to paratransit buses was not the solution: rebuilding the buses was. Equal citizenship meant equal access to public goods and full participation, as well as visibility, in the public sphere.

CEMENTING THE ANALOGY IN DISABILITY LAW

With the civil rights analogy firmly in place, disability activists followed the civil rights model's reliance on legal remedies. Civil rights are written into law and enforced by the courts, a model set by landmark civil rights cases, such as *Brown v. Board of Education,* and the 1964 Civil Rights Act. In the case of disability rights the first articulation of the civil rights analogy was in the framing of Section 504 of the 1973 Rehabilitation Act, which is commonly considered the first civil rights statute for people with disabilities because it outlaws discrimination against "otherwise handicapped" individuals in federally funded programs (Scotch 2001). Consisting of a single sentence at the end of the Rehabilitation Act, Section 504 was added by Senate aides of the Labor and Public Welfare Committee at a relatively late point in the legislative process. It occurred during a late night meeting of Senate aides who were inexperienced with disability issues but furious at the Nixon administration's sabotaging of the Civil Rights Act. Scotch documents this meeting in fascinating detail, including when a staffer at one point raced back to his office and returned with the text of Title VI, which was copied almost verbatim, even though very little thought was given to what this antidiscrimination mandate would mean in practice (Scotch 2001, 51–54). Equally fascinating is the fact that Section 504 was virtually ignored during congressional debate of the Rehabilitation Act. Scotch speculates that most members of Congress were not aware of the fateful sentence, or just thought of it as a token gesture, something that would never be enforced since no public expenditures were projected for those regulations. Section 504, however, took center stage during the disability protests to enforce the signing of the Rehabilitation Act's regulations in 1978.

The framers of the ADA, in turn, directly copied definitions of disability from the Rehabilitation Act to signal to lawmakers and the courts that the ADA was not a radical new entitlement law, but rather a continuation of established principles that have been tested in the courts (Colker 2005). The ADA's language reinforces the disability analogy to civil rights by framing disability rights' claims "as congruent with traditional and broadly accepted values such as equality, fair play and meritocracy" (Diller 2000). The ADA's *Findings and Purposes* section identifies people with disabilities as a "discrete and insular minority who have been faced with restrictions and limitations, subjected to a history of purposeful unequal treatment, and relegated to a position of political powerlessness in our society" (ADA Section 2.7). The use of the term "discrete and insular minority" is widely viewed as a congressional mandate to the courts to embrace the civil rights analogy and start thinking about disability discrimination in ways similar to how they have been adjudicating race- and sex-based discrimination cases. Moreover, the notion that disability identity is "based on characteristics that are beyond the control of such individuals and resulting from stereotypic assumptions not truly indicative of the individual ability of such individuals to participate in, and contribute to, society" (ibid.) harks back to the notion of immutability, which is a key component of the courts' understanding of protected minorities. Although the Supreme Court in particular has refused to accept some of the basic premises of this analogy—something I will discuss later in this chapter—the advantages of the analogy for the disability rights movement are undisputed.

As mentioned in the previous chapter, the disability analogy to other civil rights movements has provided a well-paved terrain for disability activists to negotiate their demands, and it has provided the legislative foundation for the ADA. It has furnished a vocabulary and a frame of reference through which people with disabilities can articulate the difficulties they face in seeking full participation in society. It has enabled arguments on behalf of people with disabilities to be cast in the form of rights that resonate with fundamental values regarding equality, fair treatment, and equal opportunities. In particular, the civil rights vocabulary and framework have provided a means through which people with disabilities could understand their experiences and communicate them to others. In this manner, they have contributed to coalition building among different disability groups that experience different forms of impairment but are still united by the discriminatory attitudes they face. The focus on civil rights as a response to irrational stereotypes, stigmatization, and fear resonates deeply with many people with disabilities and offers a powerful vocabulary to respond to it. It has allowed them to communicate their experiences to the larger nondisabled public in ways that are familiar and understandable.

Chai Feldblum, an attorney intimately involved in the drafting of the ADA, points to the importance of continuity in the ADA's legislative language and framework. The 1964 Civil Rights Act had spelled out the basic antidiscrimination mandate to which disability "just had to be" added. Similarly, the 1973 Rehabilitation Act established this core principle with Section 504 with respect to all agencies and programs receiving federal funding. Just as the Civil Rights Act had provided the language for Section 504, so did the Rehabilitation Act's 1974 amendments provide the direct model for the ADA's famous three-pronged definition of a disability, which states that (1) disability is "physical or mental impairment that substantially limits one or more major life activity," or (2) a record of such an impairment, or (3) being regarded as having such an impairment.[3] This definition thus covers individuals with disabilities that are considered "actual disabilities," those with a history of a disability, and also those who are (falsely) perceived as having a disability (ADA Section 12102 (1)). Moreover, the ADA reflects a social model understanding of disability by viewing it as not as an individual problem but as a relationship between an impairment and the environment, that is, a "physical or mental impairment that substantially limits a major life activity." The argument here was that Congress would be more likely to endorse a definition that had fifteen years of experience and jurisprudence behind it, rather than a new and untested definition.

It was a political decision to use a familiar definition in favor of a new one that would possibly slow down passage of the bill (Feldblum 2000, 128–29). In addition to familiarity with definitions of disability, the drafters of the ADA also pointed to the three decades of case law interpreting Section 504 and its provisions. There was a strong sense that the ADA should build on the important groundwork provided by Section 504 and the courts' general acceptance of the civil rights model so far. Section 504 was considered the floor (not the ceiling) of the protections the new law provided. And the strategy paid off, at least in the sense that Congress was familiar enough with the language of disability to endorse the previous three-pronged definition. Hence, relatively little debate occurred over the ADA's definition of disability as a "physical or mental impairment that substantially limits one or more major life activity," a "history or record" of such an impairment, and "being regarded" as having such an impairment. Both houses of Congress passed the ADA with overwhelming majorities. When it comes to the question of "who counts as disabled," however, the courts have been far more restrictive in their interpretation of the ADA than they had been of Section 504. For example, the lower courts routinely included individuals with impairments that could be controlled with medication (such as diabetes, epilepsy, or heart conditions) in Section 504 cases (Colker 2005, 16 and 100). This Supreme Court interpreted "mitigating measures" differently in its rulings on employment discrimination under the ADA. Here, the court imposed a far stricter interpretation of who counts as a person with a disability by excluding those whose disabilities are mitigated by medication or devices such as eyeglasses. The host of Supreme Court employment cases that I examine later in this chapter has led many observers to declare a "backlash" against disability rights, arguing that the court does not fully embrace Congress's vision for justice for people with disabilities. I do not engage the backlash thesis, although I am critical of the court's rulings, but rather use them as examples to cast a critical glance on the assumption that disability could be seamlessly integrated into the court's understanding of civil rights law.

ANALOGIES AND SOCIAL MOVEMENTS

As I argued in the previous chapter, reliance on the civil rights model secured passage of the ADA during a period of civil rights retrenchment and welfare cuts. The civil rights analogy both unified and politicized the movement and provided opportunities to translate disability claims to the larger public. Yet, the analogy to civil rights has also been a problematic one. It has raised a host of problems for plaintiffs trying to enforce the ADA, and it has cast larger questions about the ways that disability category can fit into established equal treatment debates. Thus, in the section that follows I will problematize the analogy: first from a legal perspective, and then from a social movement perspective. I problematize the analogy not to undermine its political importance, or to suggest alternate legal or political strategies. Rather, I spell out the inherent difficulties of stretching the civil rights analogy to encompass equality issues for people with disabilities.

The disability rights movement's deployment of the civil rights analogy follows a well-traveled terrain. The argument that discrimination on the basis of disability follows a pattern similar to that of race or sex-based discrimination, and the resulting call to reclaim disability as a source of positive identity and pride, follows in the footsteps of the experiences of previous social movements. Analogical arguments are a staple in rights-based social movements, where established claims of inequality and injury become a template upon which emerging movements can build demands for rights and recognition. The African American struggle for social and legal equality became the model of equal protection analysis and the baseline against which new rights claims were to be measured. In this way, the race-based civil rights movement is commonly acknowledged for providing the civil rights "master frame" of equal treatment (Snow and Benford 1988). This frame fashioned a response to discrimination based on an equal treatment mandate, stipulating that differential treatment on the basis of race was a violation of the constitutional equal protection guarantee as well as of the statutory antidiscrimination mandate embedded in the 1964 Civil Rights Act. *Brown v. Board of Education* (1954) became the iconic case that symbolized the importance of equal treatment, the dangers of segregation, and the role of the law as an agent of social change. Fashioned on the experience of race discrimination, then, the equal treatment frame suggested a form of "simple equality"—simply opening the schoolhouse doors to children deprived of an equal education would suffice to satisfy the demands of the 14th Amendment. The reality, of course, was never that simple, but the equal treatment frame was powerful precisely because it suggested that overcoming prejudice and assumptions about the meaning of race were, in many instances, enough to combat discrimination, once *Plessy v. Ferguson* was overturned and the law "fixed" to return to its true promise of equality. Even laws that could be considered neutral and not specifically targeted against protected groups could be challenged if they turned out to have a *disparate impact* on protected groups.[4] Thus, the central idea of the equal treatment frame is the recognition that race (and by extension, other protected categories) should have nothing to do with a person's ability to perform certain job functions, be educated, or contribute to society. The "level playing field" that would result from the removal of bigotry and stereotyping would ensure that employment decisions would be based on merit rather than impermissible factors.

THE RACE-SEX (TO SEXUAL ORIENTATION) ANALOGY

The equal treatment frame was adopted and adapted in the 1960s and 1970s by feminist litigators intent on establishing formal equality between women and men. The race-sex analogy was fashioned primarily to lend the moral force and strategic expertise of the civil rights movement to the feminist cause, but it also signified an attempt to unify feminists over the Equal Rights Amendment, and to mend divisions between the black civil rights movement and the women's movement (Mayeri 2001). The analogy stipulated that sex is like race in that it is a visible and generally immutable characteristic that has been used to stereotype and classify without regard to individual merit, in both private and public life. Women, like African Americans, have been unjustly stereotyped and penalized when transgressing the boundaries of their assigned social roles. Assumptions about sex and gender, especially in the ways they shaped workplace norms, function much like those made of race, and therefore should receive similar levels of judicial scrutiny when challenged in court. The Supreme Court came close in *Frontiero v. Richardson*, holding as an empirically verified position that sex was frequently unrelated to the "ability to perform and contribute to society."[5] Moreover, the court famously recognized that the differential treatment that originated from seemingly benign protective or chivalrous concessions to women functioned more like a "cage" rather than a "pedestal."[6] This aspect of the sex-to-race analogy is important to consider here as people with disabilities have experienced similar notions of paternalistic protectiveness and assumptions that their "difference" disqualified them from equal citizenship.

The race-sex equal treatment analogy for framing a legal response to sex discrimination became strained, however, when the court had to consider the question of pregnancy discrimination. Women's biological difference to men disrupts the race-sex analogy, raising the question of what to do with women's unique ability to gestate and bear children. Simple equality—treating women like men by simply "opening the door" to professions previously denied to women—would result in unjust treatment of pregnant workers. At the same time, protective measures recognizing women's biological difference were often used as a rationale for excluding women in the first place. Feminist litigators became torn over the sameness-difference debate, specifically in framing a response to pregnancy discrimination as an equal protection violation (Williams 1984; Pedriana 2006). The goal was to convince the court to accept the race-sex analogy by elevating sex discrimination from its lowest level of judicial scrutiny (in which a mere "rational" reason was sufficient to justify unequal treatment) to the highest level of "strict" scrutiny, which the court reserved for race discrimination (where "compelling" reasons must be provided for unequal treatment). A divided court articulated its ambivalence over the race-sex analogy by compromising with "intermediate" levels of scrutiny and by focusing on the "real differences" between the sexes.[7] The common interpretation here is that American sex equality law rests on an imperfect and partial analogy to race (Mayeri 2008).

Gay rights advocates, too, have tended to make "like-race" arguments in an attempt to fit sexual orientation discrimination into the framework of race discrimination. Gays and lesbians meet the basic requirements for validation as a minority group—they are targets of discrimination and prejudice and experience unequal opportunities. Early writings in the gay rights movement emphasize the analogy to race or sex discrimination, focusing primarily on the power of the immutability argument. A well-used analogy in the struggle for marriage equality is the Supreme Court's rejection of southern antimiscegenation laws in *Loving v. Virginia*.[8] The court famously ruled that discrimination against interracial couples classifies individuals on the basis of race and thus violates constitutional or statutory provisions banning race discrimination. Relying on this "miscegenation analogy," advocates have analogized same-sex relationships to interracial ones, arguing that discrimination against same-sex couples is a form of sex discrimination because it classifies individuals on the basis of sex and, as with race, should violate provisions of law banning sex discrimination (Konnoth 2011; Clark 2002; Koppelman 1988). The *Loving* decision not only invalidated Virginia's miscegenation law on equal protection grounds, it also, powerfully, made a case for marriage rights and privacy interests under the 14th Amendment's due process clause. Both the immutability argument and the marriage rights claim have inspired the marriage equality movement to make the analogy between southern racism and heterosexism. Laws against interracial marriages, the argument goes, are analogous to laws against same-sex marriages. And yet the force of the racial analogy has been, in the words of David Richards, to "artificially compel attention to issues of immutability and salience, as if sexual orientation could only be constitutionally protected from invidious discrimination if it, like race, were an immutable and conspicuous fact of nature" (Richards 1999). This view, he argues, both distorts the case for gay rights and our view of racism. There are dangers in winning civil rights protection for gays and lesbians by using notions of immutability and focusing on the alleged biological basis of sexual orientation (Halley 1993). Such an emphasis distorts gay identity as stable and natural and fails to recognize the culturally constructed stereotypes and prejudices that make up the basis of discrimination. Although the immutability claim is a useful proxy for race and sex, the immutability story omits the real moral and ethical violence done to gay and lesbian identities.

The social movement literature has long been interested in the impact of the civil rights analogy on the political and legal formation of subsequent social movements (Skrentny 2002; Tarrow 2011; Edelman, Leachman, and McAdam 2010). In this literature, the deployment of the civil rights analogy follows a chronology that typically begins with race and then extends to gender, sexual orientation, disability, and other forms of minority identities. As much as social movements have deployed the civil rights analogy to make the case for justice and equal treatment, it is important to remember that the basic formula of "simple equality" was never fully replicated by other movements. Each movement had to negotiate notions of equality and difference to reflect the complexities of living with a particular minority identity. The disability case, as I argue below, had to stretch the equal treatment concept particularly far, with far-reaching consequences. Thus, in the section that follows I point to the spaces in the civil rights analogy that do not translate well into the disability case.

PROBLEMATIZING THE ANALOGY: WHO IS THE PROTECTED CLASS?

The first way to problematize the analogy lies in looking at the *definition of the protected class*. Traditionally, the civil rights model has been applied in situations in which the protected class is relatively easy to define. This has been the case for race and sex—both considered immutable characteristics that individuals are born with—but not disability. Under Title VII of the 1964 Civil Rights Act, an individual can bring a sex discrimination lawsuit irrespective of whether the individual is a man or a woman. Similarly, one can bring a race discrimination lawsuit irrespective of whether one is black or white. This has allowed white people to bring reverse race discrimination lawsuits, or men to sue for sex discrimination. The question is whether the employer considered an impermissible factor—race or gender—and not whether the individual is a member of a protected class.

The ADA departs from other civil rights statutes in its requirement that individuals prove that they are members of a protected class. This means that individuals must first prove that they fulfill statutory definitions of disability before they can allege disability discrimination. The question of who counts as disabled has proven to be a considerable hurdle for those plaintiffs who bring disability discrimination lawsuits.

Because the categories of race and gender are viewed as a binary, the civil rights paradigm has tended to place boundaries around the category of disability and limit it to a binary approach as well: a person is either disabled or not disabled. However, as many disability scholars have pointed out, *disabilities exist along a continuum* and are subject to change throughout a person's life. One of the central projects in disability theory has been the deconstruction of the normal-abnormal binary, placing them as points along a continuum of human functioning. Legal scholar and ADA architect Chai Feldblum asks us to

> imagine that everyone in society is on a spectrum of impairments: at the left side of the spectrum are people with calluses on their feet, in the section close

to that end are people who wear glasses or have high blood pressure; further along on the spectrum are people with cancer or epilepsy or diabetes or HIV infection, and at the right end of the spectrum are people who are blind, deaf, or use wheelchairs. The traditional view is that people at the right end of the spectrum are "disabled" with the concomitant societal view that such individuals are distinctly *different* from everyone else in society and are less likely to be able to function in the workplace and in society in general. (Feldblum 2000, 101–2)

Traditional thinking about disability will look to draw a line between the "truly" disabled (who are thus entitled to legal protection) and others with minor or temporary impairments. And yet the ADA asks us to think about disability as an interaction between body and environment, both of which are in constant flux, making it difficult to view a person's disability as a fixed trait. Robert Burgdorf, another one of the ADA's central drafters, explains it this way:

Though we are conditioned to think otherwise, human beings do not really exist in two sharply distinct groups of "people with disabilities" and "people without disabilities" . . . Disability is a natural part of the human condition resulting from that spectrum—and will touch most of us at one time or another in our lives. The goal is not to fixate on, overreact to, or engage in stereotypes about such differences, but to take them into account and allow for reasonable accommodation for individual abilities and impairments that will permit equal participation. (Burgdorf 1983)

Burgdorf points to the importance of adjusting the disability definition's focus on the provision of accommodations. Without the provision of reasonable accommodations as a legal requirement, the disability definition is incomplete. It is in its reasonable accommodations mandate that the ADA significantly departs from previous antidiscrimination legislation. This mandate, as described in the previous chapter, requires both public and private entities to make modifications to physical structures as well as to rules, policies, and practices that are necessary to ensure that people with disabilities have the opportunity to participate in or benefit from society's employment opportunities, public accommodations, and public places. Privately owned public accommodations, such as hotels, restaurants, shops, theaters, museums, lawyers' offices, and the like, can no longer be inaccessible to disabled customers. The reasonable accommodation mandate contends that, in many situations, accommodations to the built environment and to certain employment practices are necessary to ensure that disabled people have meaningful access to society. At the same time the mandate protects against unreasonable claims by allowing employers or providers of public accommodations to make an "undue burden" defense.

The ADA's reasonable accommodations mandate is a formal departure from the traditional civil rights approach that defines equality as sameness. It is an important recognition that the promise of equal treatment is meaningless for people with disabilities when their different needs are not taken into account. Thus, it makes no sense to declare equal educational opportunities for children with disabilities when equal treatment consists only of opening the schoolhouse doors when in fact those doors are still inaccessible. The disability rights argument challenges the civil rights model's notions of equal treatment not only by taking different needs into account— you cannot open the door to opportunities when the door is too narrow to fit through in the first place—but also by expanding the meaning of discrimination. In the traditional civil rights model, discrimination is a result of social and personal prejudice, but with disability the discrimination is also a result of technology, social norms, and the built environment. Under the ADA's reasonable accommodation mandate, discrimination is not only the refusal of equal opportunity because of outright disability prejudice ("we've tried cripples here and they don't work," as Ed Roberts was famously told) but also the denial of the very accommodations that would even the playing field for the disabled applicant. In that sense, reasonable accommodations can be viewed as a form of "positive rights" outside of the formal understanding of civil rights as merely offering "negative rights" to protect against discriminatory treatment.

This reframing is often perceived as undermining the legitimacy of the disability civil rights claim (Stein 2004). Thus, those supporting the civil rights model for disability are quick to point to the difference between reasonable accommodations as a remedy for immediate or prospective discrimination and the politically more contentious affirmative action policy, which is seen as addressing past discrimination (Tucker 2001, 345). This distinction is sometimes obscured because both affirmative action and reasonable accommodations were created to level the playing field, rather than as a way to confer special privileges. Therefore, it is easy to conflate the two, as legal scholar Bonnie Tucker argues (2001). Using her own deafness as an ex-

ample, Tucker explains: "If we require a provider of telecommunications services to pay for and provide me with additional equipment—not provided to
people who can hear—to enable me to understand what is said on the telephone, we are requiring that entity to take affirmative steps for my benefit. . . . We are requiring these entities to spend money and/or reorganize
their policies to treat me differently—that is, to take affirmative action on
my behalf" (Tucker 2001, 345). The question of cost is undisputable here,
however reasonable these costs may be. The "color-blind" metaphor will not
hold in the disability case—disability accommodations are a necessary step
toward a society that will not be blind to disability difference, but conscious
of the need to include disability in the ways it constructs its environment.

THE SUPREME COURT'S REJECTION
OF THE ANALOGY: EQUAL PROTECTION

Such a broad view of disability equality as part of the civil rights paradigm
has faced difficulties when being litigated in the courts. This section will examine two fundamental ways in which the Supreme Court has questioned
the civil rights analogy. The first is in its interpretation of the relationship
between disability and other suspect classes that merit heightened scrutiny
under the 14th Amendment's equal protection clause. Here the question was
whether disability discrimination could be seen as analogous to race or sex
discrimination and receive an elevated form of judicial scrutiny. We see this
most clearly in the 1985 case *City of Cleburne, TX v. Cleburne Independent Living Center,* which was one of the few pre-ADA cases to deploy the 14th
Amendment to benefit people with disabilities. In *Cleburne,* the court sided
with the disability plaintiffs, ruling that a city's requirement for special zon-
ing permits for group homes of people with mild intellectual disabilities
rested on "irrational prejudice," especially when no such requirements were
imposed on other group homes. The city had no rational basis to believe that
the proposed home posed any threat to public safety. However, despite having ruled in favor of the group home, the court took the case as an opportunity to emphasize how different people with disabilities are from other citizens, and how these differences circumscribe their right to equal protection
under the law. Thus, the *Cleburne* court ruled that classifications on the basis
of mental retardation (the term used at the time) do not require strict scrutiny because, unlike race and gender, disability was neither a "suspect" nor a

"quasi suspect" classification. The court concluded that the city's use of the mental retardation classification in treating some of its residents less favorably than others is constitutional as long as it had a rational basis for doing so, because of the *real differences* inherent in such classifications. Writing for the court, Justice Byron White spelled out these differences as "a reduced ability to cope with and function in the everyday world." As a group, then, people with intellectual disabilities are "different, immutably so, in relevant aspects," and these "immutable differences" legitimate the state's interest in providing for their welfare.

In constructing people with disabilities as a group and assuming they are more different from the nondisabled than they are among themselves, the court assumes that the boundary between the disabled and nondisabled can confidently be described as "the reduced ability to cope with and function in the everyday world." This assumption, of course, is fundamentally challenged by the ADA and the model of disability it prescribes. Under the ADA model, the boundary remains fluid, and the proper explanation of discriminatory treatment does not lie within a person's physical or mental deviance from the norm, but rather with the social perception of the value of that difference. According to the ADA, the proper place for reform isn't the person with the "reduced ability to cope and function in the everyday world," but rather the everyday world that is organized along a nondisabled norm. Congress responded directly to the *Cleburne* ruling when it designated in the ADA that people with disabilities are a "discrete and insular minority" and by detailing the various forms of discrimination that people with disabilities encounter, ranging from "outright intentional exclusion, the discriminatory effects of architectural, transportation, communication barriers, overprotective rules and policies, failure to make modifications to existing facilities and practices," and so on.

Cleburne set the stage for post-ADA decisions that limited the reach of the ADA by repeating myths and stereotypes of what it means to encounter disability discrimination. The culmination of these disappointing court decisions is seen in *Board of Trustees of the University of Alabama v. Garrett* (531 U.S. 356 [2001]). The *Garrett* decision took the position that the equal protection clause requires only "formal equality" (that is, treating similarly situated persons the same way) and that the ADA's reasonable accommodation mandate is a form of "special treatment" that is not consistent with the Constitution's guarantee of equal protection. Legal scholars Anita Silvers and Michael Stein (1999) argue that *Cleburne* falls in the same line of argument as *Plessy* (1868) and *Goesart* (1948), which denied African Americans and women, respectively, equal protection under the 14th Amendment. They analogize the court's decisions in *Plessy, Goesart, Cleburne,* and *Garrett* because in each case the court denied the plaintiffs' equal protection claim based on a "flawed conception of the plaintiffs' inferiority and subordination."

THE SUPREME COURT'S REJECTION OF THE ANALOGY: EMPLOYMENT DISCRIMINATION

The disability civil rights analogy was further limited in a group of Supreme Court disability employment discrimination cases. In 1999, the court significantly narrowed coverage under the ADA in a trio of cases (known as the *Sutton* trilogy) by ruling that mitigating measures, such as medication, hearing aids, or prosthetics, must be considered when determining whether an individual's impairment substantially limits a major life activity.[9] Congressional intent in the ADA clearly mandates the courts to view plaintiffs in their uncorrected state: the Senate Committee on Labor and Human Resources explicitly stated that mitigating measures should *not* be taken into account in determining whether a person has a "disability" for the purposes of the ADA.[10] And yet, in *Sutton* the court held that in determining whether the severely myopic Sutton twins had a substantial limitation, the courts should consider their condition in its corrected state (wearing corrective lenses). The Sutton twins had failed United Airlines' vision requirements since they were forced to take the test in their uncorrected state. When they sued for discrimination, they were deemed not disabled under the ADA because the court considered their standing in their corrected state. This created a catch-22 for plaintiffs, who were seen as too disabled by their employer, but could not use the protections of the ADA to challenge their employers' actions because the courts did not see them as disabled enough to have standing. This worked to the advantage of employers who now can reject applicants because of their condition in the unmitigated state and then succeed in defeating ADA coverage because of the applicant's condition in its mitigated state.

This decision has dealt a devastating blow to individuals who rely on medication to mitigate the effects of their disabilities. For example, individuals with epilepsy or diabetes who are fortunate enough to control the effects of their condition by medication or discipline, and thus are more independent and able to work, are conversely less protected under the law because the limitations they experience are not considered substantial enough. They would be unable to bring an ADA case, even if employers admitted that they were dismissed for their (mitigated) condition. In other words, the better individuals manage their conditions, the less likely they are to gain legal protection from discrimination. More broadly, this line of reasoning bypasses a more fundamental issue lying at the heart of the ADA. Are United Airlines' vision requirements, demanding pilots to have vision better than 20/100 in its uncorrected state, reasonable? Is it important for mechanics who repair trucks to have normal blood pressure? These are central questions, for they ask whether job requirements have a business necessity, or whether they are a form of disability discrimination. By dismissing these cases at an early stage, the courts did not have to wrestle with these important questions. They focused on the employee's condition rather than on the employer's behavior, which is the central focus of employment discrimination law.

The Supreme Court also narrowed the reach of the ADA and questioned the civil rights analogy with its narrow view of major life activities. In the 2002 case *Toyota v. Williams,* the court held that "to be substantially limited, an individual must have an impairment that prevents or severely restricts the individual from doing activities that are of central importance to most people's daily lives," referring specifically to "household chores, bathing and brushing one's teeth."[11] As a result of this ruling, lower courts began to require people alleging discrimination under the ADA to show that their impairments *prevent or severely restrict them* from doing activities that are of *central importance* to most people's daily lives. The *Toyota* ruling reflects the court's disconnect between the definition of disability and the purposes of the ADA. The fact that a person with a disability may be able to brush her teeth says nothing about whether she faces discrimination in the workplace. Moreover, the very reason that the person with a disability may be able to function independently at home may be because of accommodations and modifications. Yet, after *Toyota* this individual would be unable to challenge her employer's refusal to provide accommodations at work. The courts' interpretations of the ADA show a fundamental rejection of the original purpose of the ADA, the broad interpretation of discrimination it offers, and, fundamentally, the analogy it draws to other forms of civil rights protection.

The disability community was outraged by what it perceived as the Supreme Court's explicit rejection of the transformative potential of the ADA and the larger backlash against disability rights.[12] It didn't take long for members of the disability community to call for legislative reform to undo the damage done by the *Sutton* trilogy and *Toyota* rulings and restore the original broad reading of the ADA's coverage as envisioned by Congress. Extensive lobbying (Feldblum, Barry, and Benfer 2007) led to victory: in 2008 Congress passed the ADA Amendments Act, which explicitly urges the court to reinstate the original congressional intent of offering "a broad scope of protection" for persons with disabilities under the ADA. The *Findings and Purposes* section spells out very clearly that the question of whether a person's disability is covered under the ADA "should not demand extensive analysis."[13] Rather, "the primary object of attention . . . should be whether entities [employers, and so on] covered under the ADA have complied with their obligations."[14] The ADA Amendments Act retains the original three-pronged definition of disability, but it changes the ways these definitions should be interpreted. First, it expands the definition of "major life activity" to include activities and major bodily functions that the Equal Employment Opportunity Commission had not previously recognized (such as reading, bending, and communicating). The amended language also states that mitigating measures, including assistive devices, auxiliary aids, accommodations, medical therapies and supplies (other than eyeglasses and contact lenses), have no bearing in determining whether a disability qualifies under the law. The amendments also change the definition of "regarded as" so that it no longer requires a showing that the employer perceived the individual to be substantially limited in a major life activity, and instead says that an employee is "regarded as" disabled if he or she is subject to an action prohibited by the ADA (such as failure to hire or termination) based on an impairment that is not transitory and minor. Thus, the central purpose of the amendments to the ADA is to enable more plaintiffs to overcome the initial hurdles of establishing membership in the protected class, and thus force the courts to deal with the central questions of disability discrimination—such as what constitutes reasonable accommodations—as the original framers of the ADA had intended.

TROUBLING THE ANALOGY: THE QUESTION OF COSTS

As I argued above, the legal structure provided by the civil rights model is powerful because it casts the claims made by people with disabilities in the form of rights, rather than special needs, and of equal opportunities rather than economic redistributions or substantive equality. It is a well-accepted fact in U.S. policy making that arguments framed as appeals for equal opportunities tend to fare better in the political process and in the courts than those calling for the redistribution of resources (Diller 2000, 36). In other words, civil rights gain political legitimacy because they invoke presumably cost-free principles of equal treatment and equal opportunities, rather than the shifting of funding priorities. As mentioned previously, economic rights are not recognized as fundamental in Supreme Court jurisprudence, and the United States routinely rejects second-generation international human rights instruments that seek to establish social and economic entitlements in the form of positive rights. Although the United States is deemed "exceptional" in its nonrecognition of welfare rights, it has become a reluctant leader in international disability rights with the passage of the world's first comprehensive disability antidiscrimination law. And yet, the very basis of this law is the emphasis on equal opportunities as a cost-saving measure. As I demonstrated in the previous chapter, the ADA secured widespread bipartisan support by promising to reduce dependency on welfare and turn people with disabilities into taxpayers, rather than consumers of taxpayer funds. Thus, mandating private employers not to discriminate in hiring, firing, and benefits was to be seen, ultimately, as a cost-cutting measure.

The assumption here is that civil rights, in their ideal form, should not be motivated by questions of costs. This idea has its basis in the civil rights model's basic presumption that, in securing equal opportunities, costs are an illegitimate excuse to condone discrimination. The origins of this argument lie in the response of the federal courts to southern states making cost defenses against desegregation orders. The framers of Section 504 picked up on this tradition in refusing cost considerations as a legitimate reason for condoning discrimination. The argument was that the very idea of a right is that it should be recognized without view to inconvenience, competing priorities, or disruptive effect. In practice, however, the Section 504 framers realized that cost could be seen as a legitimate concern in fashioning the *remedies* to discrimination. Thus, in the disability case, the regulations offered the following compromise: the *standard* of discrimination was to be set regardless of cost, but the determination of how that right would be reached could include cost considerations (Scotch 2001).

This dual approach to costs was mirrored in the ADA's reasonable accommodations mandate, which places limits on the potential costs of accommodations. The question of costs is built in with business defenses: for example, accommodations may not result in an undue hardship for the employer's bottom line. Businesses were expected to shift assumptions about an employee's abilities, assist in creative ways to maximize a worker's potential with the use of inexpensive accommodations, and in the end benefit by the work of committed and capable employees. Businesses were not expected to hire employees who were unqualified: the ADA provides a defense for "qualification standards" that are "job related and consistent with business necessity." This includes a "direct threat" defense against hiring employee with contagious diseases, for example.

Thus, if disability discrimination is to be considered analogous to race and sex discrimination as prohibited by Title VII, then rational discrimination and the related issue of paternalism should be equally prohibited. In other words, employers should be sanctioned equally by the courts whether they discriminate on the basis of disability because of deeply ingrained prejudice and stereotypes *or* because of seemingly "rational" cost considerations. After all, the prohibition against rational discrimination and bottom-line defenses is deeply ingrained in U.S. antidiscrimination doctrine. The court famously ruled in *Manhart* (1978)[15] and *Johnson Controls* (1991)[16] that cost is not a valid defense to claims of disparate treatment under Title VII. Thus, if the disability analogy to race and sex discrimination is to hold, then we should see a similar rejection of cost-based rational defenses in disability cases. Legal scholar Samuel Bagenstos explains it this way: "A truer test of the theory that the Supreme Court does not understand disability rights to be civil rights would involve ADA cases that raise issues that are not unique to disability discrimination law but instead have analogs in civil rights laws involving race and gender discrimination" (Bagenstos 2003b). Bagenstos argues, convincingly, that the real evidence of the court's rejection of the civil rights analogy lies in the court's acceptance of employers' defense of rational discrimination in the disability case, when the same arguments would not been acceptable for race or gender discrimination.

When looking at ADA employment cases we see the Supreme Court being much more permissive to business defenses, even when they concern rational discrimination and forms of business paternalism. One of these is a "direct threat" case involving a worker with hepatitis C who had been fired from work that might cause a "direct threat" not to others, but to himself (*Chevron v. Echzabal* 2002).[17] This distinction is part of some administrative wrangling between Equal Employment Opportunity Commission regulations that include the threat-to-self excuse and the ADA, which expressly omits it. The ADA's legislative history shows a real concern that paternalistic exclusion from employment had been a major contributor to the disadvantage experienced by people with disabilities. For example, the *Findings and Purposes* section of the ADA lists "overprotective rules and policies" as among the forms of discrimination against people with disabilities that "continue to be a serious and pervasive social problem." During ADA testimony before Congress, the analogy to gender was made explicit: "Like women, disabled people have identified 'paternalism' as a major obstacle to economic and social advancement."[18]

The disability category is diverse, and people with similar impairments may experience radically different forms of limitations, or none at all. The ADA thus demands an "individualized inquiry" into the specific circumstances to avoid assumptions and stereotypes about what it means to live with and work with a specific impairment. The question in *Chevron* was how fast the employer "jump[ed] to conclusions" about whether this specific worker was safe to work in the oil refinery. In the analogous Title VII case concerning sex discrimination, the court has been clear that employers may not exclude protected class employees for their own safety. For example, in *Johnson Controls* (1991) the court stated clearly that "danger to a woman herself does not justify discrimination." As early as 1977 in *Dothard,* the court established the purpose of Title VII as allowing women (rather than the employer) to make the choice to elect to do a dangerous job.[19]

Another prominent example is *Albertsons v. Kirkingburg* (1999),[20] which is part of the *Sutton* trilogy mentioned earlier in this chapter. In this case the Supreme Court allowed for a form of rational discrimination by an employer who refused to rehire a truck driver who had been fired for failing the Federal Highway Administration vision requirements (he had monocular vision, meaning that he could only see out of one eye) but then had obtained a waiver that showed that he could compensate with his other eye and was a safe driver. The employer simply went by the safety standards that disqualified him without—what should have been necessary—the individualized inquiry, showing that he would indeed be unsafe and a threat to others. Here the court agreed with the employer's ability to refuse the waiver and engage in a form of "statistical" discrimination where it was easier to assume that all drivers with monocular vision were unsafe and therefore could be excluded as a group.

In these two examples of "rational discrimination," the court *unanimously* allowed employers to engage in broad stereotyping and paternalistic assumptions about disability signifying the opposite of ability and to use bottom-line financial reasons to defend their choices, which the court would not have allowed in the analogous race or sex discrimination cases. I suggest that these cases reflect the court's premise that discrimination on the basis of disability is frequently more rational (and thus condoned) in ways that sex and race discrimination never are. I would argue that while disability discrimination may appear to be uniquely rational (what employer would willingly hire a less productive employee?), many of the seemingly rational or neutral workplace rules are deeply rooted in assumptions that disability, in a fundamental way, signifies the opposite of ability, productivity, and efficiency. When considering this argument it is important to remember that the concept of disability has functioned historically not only to justify disability discrimination but also to justify inequality for women and racial minority groups, and particularly to restrict immigration. For example, women have been portrayed as "irrational, excessively emotional and physically weak," which are unacknowledged markers of mental and physical disabilities, by opponents of women's political and social equality. Disability arguments were used to explain slavery as well by claiming that African Americans lacked sufficient intelligence to participate in society, and because of their inherent physical and mental weakness they would become disabled under conditions of freedom and equality (Baynton 2013). Finally, studies of immigration law have documented not only the explicit category of "feeble-mindedness" (as well as a host of other disqualifying conditions, including arthritis, asthma, flat feet, or varicose veins) in immigration law, but also the assignment of certain disability characteristics (such as the "slow-witted Slav" or "the neurotic Jew") in debates over immigration restriction (Baynton 2013). The current debate over rational discrimination dangerously links to this past, underscoring the importance of recognizing the stereotypes of disability discrimination in all of their manifestations.

TRANSCENDING THE CIVIL RIGHTS ANALOGY

Despite the complexities of the civil rights analogy, it continues to hold an important place in the imagination of disability activists, theorists, policy makers, and legal scholars. The analogy to civil rights allowed activists to summon the power of the state to address disability discrimination and to reformulate their claims as equal rights rather than as special needs. At this juncture of movement and legislative history, however, it is imperative to reexamine the legacy of the civil rights analogy and to acknowledge important differences between disability activism and earlier movements. These movements created significant broad-based awareness of discrimination and injustice and changed public perception of African Americans and women. By contrast, it can be argued that most of the nation still remains largely ignorant of the nature and scope of disability discrimination. Joseph Shapiro's history of the disability rights movement makes this point. Shapiro writes that "disabled people got their rights without dramatic Freedom Rides, church bombings or 'I Have a Dream' speeches to stir the conscience of a guilty nation. African-Americans had changed a nation's attitudes and then won civil rights law. But for disabled Americans the reverse was true" (Shapiro 1993). Legal scholar Linda Krieger echoes this claim by arguing that "although there was certainly a disability rights movement in the United States during the 1970s and 1980s, it was neither as broad-based nor as well disseminated into popular consciousness as the black civil rights movement of the 1950s and 1960s, or the women's movement of the 1970s" (Krieger 2003, 353). This is why, more than twenty years after the passage of the ADA, activists are still working to raise awareness, to challenge attitudes, and to inform public opinion as to the civil rights foundation for laws that have been in effect for twenty years.

The disability analogy is troubled, both by the court's formal rejection of the analogy and by popular views of disability rights as special rights, partially because disability as a category refuses to behave like its civil rights precedents. But it is exactly this deviation from the civil rights norm that makes the legal response to disability so powerful. The ADA's adaptation of the civil rights equal treatment/equal opportunities frame pushes our understanding beyond just formal equality. It forces us to examine the taken-for-granted able-bodied norms that shape our understanding of social arrangements and that normalize the exclusion of people with disabilities. The ADA extends the equal treatment promise by demanding the provision of reasonable accommodations, not as special rights, but as a way of making equality meaningful for people with disabilities.

Disability rights scholarship is starting to move beyond the civil rights model and to suggest alternatives. Richard Scotch and Kay Schriner suggest a *human variation* model of disability in which "the problems faced by people with disability might be seen as the consequence of the failure of social institutions (and their physical and cultural manifestations) that can be attributed to the institutions having been constructed to deal with a narrower range of variation than is in fact present in any given population" (Scotch and Schriner 1997). They worry that common interpretations of disability discrimination under the civil rights model would have to become so stretched to encompass the wide variety of barriers facing people with disabilities that the concept would lose some of its precision and usefulness as a policy guide. Instead, they suggest that "it may be more useful . . . to look beyond discrimination to characterize the nature and consequences of a constructed environment that ignores the presence of people with disabilities."

An emphasis on *universal design* lies at the heart of these critiques. As discussed in the previous chapter, universal design is based on the concept that all products, environments, and communications should be designed to consider the needs of the widest possible array of users. Universal design recognizes that varying ability is not a special condition of the few but a common characteristic of being human and of changing physically and intellectually throughout our lives. The basic dictum is that if a design works well for people with disabilities, it works better for everyone. The classic example that dominated public discourse around passage of the ADA was the argument that while curb cuts may be a necessary accommodation for people using wheelchairs, they also help people navigating baby strollers, walkers, or those using trolleys to make heavy deliveries. Universal design has also been implemented in the development of Web-based and telecommunications technologies. More recently, universal design has made inroads into teaching methodologies, challenging teachers and professors to teach in ways that accommodate different learning styles. The literature of educational accommodations has long recognized that guided notes, lecture notes, or slides during lectures, which are mandated for students with learning disabilities, can help all students learn better. Advocates for universal design are careful to reject special rights arguments; instead, they emphasize the ways that accommodations will benefit the larger public. Universal design approaches look for reasonable accommodations that make the world more accessible for everybody rather than offer adjustments on an individualized basis. When social and physical environments are created in a universally accessible manner, the need for individualized retrofitting becomes unnecessary, and the stigma associated with such accommodations disappears.

Disability scholar Ani Satz has used notions of *vulnerability,* inspired by Martha Fineman's argument that vulnerability is universal and constant, as yet another way to address the limitations of the civil rights model (Satz 2008). Vulnerability and interdependence are part of the human condition, and our vulnerability to *disability* is both universal and constant in that we are one curb step away from disability. And yet the ADA focuses on independence and asks us to look past individuals' disabilities, treating them, with the aid of reasonable accommodations, like their nondisabled peers. The argument is for the law to move past identity categories and antidiscrimination mandates toward addressing shared and constant vulnerabilities. These vulnerabilities may be biological, social, or economic, and require social supports.

Appealing to universal vulnerabilities removes the stigma of needing assistance and improves protections for all. In the workplace, for example, powerful analogies can be made between officially vulnerable and therefore "protected" workers with disabilities and workers whose impairments do not rise to a level of disability, or even workers without impairments who are still vulnerable to at-will employment, health issues, or family crises. As Matthew Diller (2000, 47) reminds us, "If differential and individualized treatment under the reasonable accommodation mandate is necessary for the establishment of equal opportunities for people with disabilities, it may also be necessary for other groups." Finally, the vulnerability argument will allow disability scholarship to refocus attention on the role of the state (rather than on employers) in addressing the vulnerability of disabled workers. Critics of formal equality have long argued that formal equality results in a "withering state" as corporate and other private interests limit the role and ability of the government to address inequalities. Consider the fact that there is no federal funding for reasonable accommodations; the ADA relies exclusively on private parties to fund this mandate.

The power in the disability deployment of the civil rights analogy lies in its ability to connect politically to legally recognized modes of making demands. For a movement that has fought hard against notions of vulnerability and interdependence, these arguments appear politically dangerous and suggest a return to welfare and charity models that the movement worked hard to replace with the ADA. And yet, the civil rights model has become established in national and international instruments—the subject of the rest of this book—where it has become retheorized in sophisticated ways that transcend traditional binaries between positive and negative rights. It seems that the American basis for this model, which relies heavily on analogies and identity categories, can give way to more nuanced approaches that merge civil rights with social welfare.

CHAPTER THREE

"Dreamland USA": *American Disability Rights Travel to Germany*

Ein Stuhl
Genau besehen
Ein Stuhl ist ein Stuhl ist ein
Rollstuhl
Ein Urteil ist ein Urteil ist ein
Vorurteil
Eine Behinderung ist eine Behinderung ist eine
staatlich geförderte Maßnahme.[1]

[A chair
looking carefully
A chair is a chair is a
wheelchair
A judgment is a judgment is a
misjudgment (prejudice)
A disability is a disability is a
state-sponsored measure.]

"A CHAIR IS A WHEELCHAIR"

This poem circulated in German disability circles in the fall of 1997 as an expression of outrage against a ruling by Germany's Federal Constitutional Court that students with disabilities do not have a right to an integrated education and may be forced to attend a segregated school for disabled children.[2] The case involved a thirteen-year-old girl who had successfully attended an integrated elementary school until the fourth grade. She was using a wheelchair and was fully integrated into all subjects except for math, where she received special education. When she prepared to transfer to a new school for her next level of schooling (as is the custom in Germany), the new school's administration refused her request to continue her education at a "regular" school. The reason given was that because her disability-specific needs could not be met by the existing teaching personnel, it was in the girl's best interest to attend a segregated school for students with disabilities. The court sided with the school, ruling that the administration had acted in accordance with German disability education law. The law allows such a judgment as long as the reasons are pressing, the school does not have the ability to address disability needs, or it is in the best interest of the child.

This judgment came at a time when the German disability movement was fully mobilized, empowered by the recent passage of a constitutional equal rights amendment and working toward a comprehensive disability antidiscrimination law. This "resegregation case" (De-Integrationsurteil)—as it became known in movement circles—was seen as an example of how poorly the constitutional equality amendment protected basic civil rights, and, by extension, how much further the movement still had to go to raise awareness about disability discrimination. Activists considered the court's message to be clear: when a school is ill-equipped to educate a student with a disability—whether due to financial constraints or lack of trained teachers—the school can order a student to be transferred to a segregated school.

Despite the constitutional antidiscrimination mandate, children with disabilities would never be able to claim their integrated education as a basic civil right if a school's administrative needs could so easily trump a child's rights. Andreas Jürgens, a legal expert for the German independent living movement (Interessenvertretung Selbstbestimmt Leben), argued in a press release that "[t]his decision is as incomprehensible to us as a potential decision relegitimizing corporal punishment in schools for the sake of administrative ease. We cannot have our basic rights denied for financial or organizational reasons."[3] The ruling by Germany's highest court mobilized Germany's growing disability rights movement and crystallized a consensus in favor of legal change that would challenge Germany's persistent disability segregation policy and replace it with a comprehensive disability equality law.

This chapter examines the evolution of German disability law and activism, and the influence of the American-style disability rights model. It explores the ways that this "imported" model took hold in German disability law and policy after German disability activists had their first contact with the American disability rights model in the 1980s and 1990s. German disability policy, especially prior to contact with the American model, was deeply committed to a medical or welfare model of disability—a model that views disability as a medical problem that needs to be fixed or mitigated by rehabilitation and welfare. German disability policy had long been recognized for its well-funded and extensive welfare and rehabilitation system that takes care of disability special needs in sophisticated, albeit segregated, settings. In the early 1980s disability activists began mobilizing and criticizing the welfare approach and segregation of German policy and looking abroad for alternative examples. The declaration of the UN's International Year of Disabled Persons in 1981 and the passage of the Americans with Disabilities Act in 1990 were important external developments that pushed the German movement to confront deeply held assumptions regarding the nature of disability and the traditional welfare-based policy responses. In addition to these external models, the politics of German reunification in 1989 after the fall of the Berlin Wall gave the movement an unexpected boost to focus its efforts in the legal arena: a reunited Germany needed a new constitution. Activists focused on the general antidiscrimination mandate of Article 3, and in 1994 they were successful: the German Bundestag (lower house of parliament) amended Article 3 of its Basic Law to read: "Nobody may be discriminated against on the basis of disability." This expansion of the constitutional antidiscrimination clause came after extensive lobbying by disability groups demanding that the Constitution include disability as a protected category, along with race, gender, and national origin. The intellectual model for this lobbying effort, and for the 2002 Disability Equalizing Law (Behindertengleichstellungsgesetz), was the political organizing of the American disability rights movement and the Americans with Disabilities Act, both of which played a powerful role in the political imagination of German disability activists.

The politics surrounding the 1994 constitutional amendment symbolizes a shift in German disability activism. It organized and radicalized the German disability movement and placed it on a path toward rights-based activism. Theoretically, it was a shift from the medical model, which emphasizes rehabilitation and welfare, toward a social model of disability, which focuses on civil rights, equal opportunities, and disability pride. The efforts to amend the constitution also represent a political milestone for the German disability movement, turning it into what prominent disability rights scholar Theresia Degener calls "Germany's last civil rights movement" (Degener 1996). The move from welfare to rights allowed German activists to define disability as a category of positive identity and pride, to create a political movement, and to generate public awareness of disability discrimination.

The German struggle for a disability antidiscrimination law was directly inspired by the ADA and the mobilization strategies of the American disability movement. A new generation of German disability activists traveled to the United States as "rights tourists" to learn about the empowering effects of disability rights. Arriving back home from "Dreamland USA," these rights tourists launched an unprecedented and widely successful media campaign to generate disability rights awareness. This chapter is the first comprehensive analysis of this media campaign, which generated support for a constitutional antidiscrimination amendment and a German version of the ADA. Despite strong ties to American colleagues and mentors, German disability activists remain critical of what they consider the limitations of American notions of equality. The German Disability Equalizing Law of 2002 combines antidiscrimination mandates with positive equality rights and rests on German traditions that posit the state as a provider of basic social rights. Like their American counterparts, however, German activists use rights talk to define disability as a category of positive identity and pride, and to shift the national conversation on disability politics away from special needs and entitlements. Ultimately, this chapter suggests how the ADA became a symbol of the ways that legal mobilization can transform people with disabilities from objects of charity and welfare into equal citizens, even where the original model does not provide a blueprint for legal change.

Although the importation of an American-inspired rights discourse has powerful implications for movement strategies and identity politics, I argue that rights discourse is a difficult tool to transplant successfully in a different political and social context. American disability rights discourse is based on a civil rights framework that has no parallels in the German legal and political imagination. Moreover, American disability rights law—most prominently the ADA, which served as the initial model for German legal reform efforts—is based on limited notions of equality that do not resonate with the more progressive guarantees of the German welfare system. Nonetheless, the German movement has deliberately turned toward American-inspired rights-based activism and the political promise it holds. This chapter asks two questions that arise from this new development: How are disability rights mobilized in the German context, and what policies will result from an imposition of rights-based equality legislation in a policy setting based on special needs and welfare?

I begin with a summary of German disability policy, which should be read in light of the different policy approaches outlined in the first chapter ("legislating disability rights"). The German policy against which activists are mobilizing is based on a difference model, on what I call a "parallel track" of welfare institutions for people with disabilities. The next section examines the development of German disability activism as it shifts from a focus on welfare and special needs to a focus on equal rights and antidiscrimination. I trace the events leading up to the constitutional amendment and discuss its impact, using the Aktion Grundgesetz media campaign as a case study. The chapter concludes with an analysis of the 2002 Equalizing Law and the accompanying reforms of rehabilitation law (Neuntes Buch des Sozialgesetzbuches, or SGB IX) that integrate notions of independence and self-determination into German welfare law.

GERMAN DISABILITY POLICY: THE PARALLEL TRACK

As outlined in the first chapter, Germany's approach to legislating disability rights falls squarely into the welfare model. German disability policy has traditionally followed a difference or special treatment doctrine, providing for disability needs in segregated settings, such as separate, disability-specific schools, sheltered workshops, and assisted living centers. This has led to the establishment of one of the most comprehensive and extensive rehabilitation systems in the postwar period, rivaled only by those in Scandinavian countries. The German welfare system is internationally recognized for its extensive benefits and sophisticated rehabilitation measures, which offer educational, vocational, and residential services providing cradle-to-grave care for people with disabilities.

Like most welfare states, the origins of German disability policy lie in policies geared toward the rehabilitation of war veterans. Assistance to war veterans generally precedes civilian welfare policies, tends to be more generous, and is governed by different principles. As David Gerber reminds us, public assistance to disabled veterans is typically not conceived of as charity or welfare but as a reward for, and implicitly as an incentive to inspire, military service, as well as repayment for a soldier's grave personal sacrifice to the state (Gerber 2000, 11–12). Beyond the political imperative for supporting veterans, it was also active and effective lobbying by veterans themselves that has historically made governments more willing to provide assistance to disabled veterans than to some other groups. As the welfare state expands, the assistance once offered to veterans gradually becomes available in some measure to the civilian population. Similarly, many of the medical and surgical developments and rehabilitation practices initially developed to serve veterans are later extended to the civilian population. Thus, Gerber suggests that the evolution of public policy for the disabled veteran has served as a model for social policy and practice toward all disabled men and women.

The return of disabled soldiers from the battlefields of World War I gave rise to the first disability-specific laws in Weimar Germany: in 1917 the Reichstag established the first employment quota for businesses over 50 employees to hire severely disabled war veterans. This regulation was later expanded into the 1922 Law for the Severely Damaged (Schwerbeschädigtengesetz), which extended coverage to people disabled by industrial accidents and included a special protection from dismissal that survives to this day. The rhetoric during the political debate for passage of this law made it clear that speaking out against disabled war veterans—whether from the Left or the Right—would be considered unpatriotic and politically unwise (Jackson 1993, 428–29). Likewise, the 1920 Cripples Welfare Law (Krüppelfürsorgegesetz) guaranteed not only medical treatment but also education and vocational training to young people (under 18 years) with physical disabilities. The German emphasis on rehabilitation and work was considered quite progressive at the time, and soon the German rehabilitation system, with its mixture of church-run and state-sponsored institutions and clinics, became known as "the most advanced and best-organized rehabilitation system in the world" (Poore 2007, 9).

German disability policy under the Nazi regime is well known for its gruesome extermination of what was considered "unworthy life." People with disabilities were declared to be "useless mouths to feed" (Mostert 2002). There is an exhaustive and important literature tracing the history of racial hygiene in Germany, examining the ways that methods used for mass extermination in the Nazi death camps originated and were perfected from earlier methods used against people with physical, emotional, and intellectual disabilities.[4] In direct contrast to its view that disability contaminated the body politic, Nazi policy also venerated war veterans and elevated the disabled soldier to hero status as "first citizen of the Reich" (Poore 2007, 69). Consistent with the Nazi favoritism toward veterans, the disability employment quota under the Law for the Severely Disabled was actually strengthened, resulting in dramatic reductions in veteran unemployment rates (Jackson 1993, 447).

Caught between policies of forced sterilization and extermination, on the one hand, and public veneration, on the other, official Nazi disability organizations for deaf, blind, or physically disabled civilians negotiated a precarious space between collaboration and advocacy. The key was to emphasize the potential for rehabilitation and participation, however marginal, of the disabled labor force in the service of the national community (Poore 2007, 68). Although disability organizations rightly pointed to their status as victims of the Third Reich in the postwar period, their negotiation between official recognition and veneration and the simultaneous fear of extermination was an indicator of the complicated politics of negotiating survival during the Nazi era.

Postwar disability policy faced a new wave of both disabled veterans and civilians disabled as a result of the bombing campaign during World War II. Within just a few years of the creation of the postwar (West) German state in 1949, the new federal government created laws to both compensate war victims and reintegrate war veterans. The 1950 Federal War Victims Benefit Law (Bundesversorgungsgesetz) was one of the country's first major pieces of social legislation. It granted pensions to all victims of the war, not just to disabled soldiers. The 1953 Federal Law on the Employment on the Severely Disabled (Bundesgesetz über die Beschäftigung Schwerbeschädigter; Schwerbeschädigtengesetz) mandated hiring quotas for all but the smallest employers.[5] Unlike the prewar law, it was not limited to persons with the right to a pension: the law covered anyone whose disability (of 50 percent or more) was caused by military service, the Nazi regime, injury under the postwar Occupation, or industrial injury. Most notably, the reach of the disability hiring quota was expanded to cover all businesses with seven or more employees to account for the large number of people emerging from the war with disability-related needs. The employment quota was raised to 10 percent for bodies of public administration, insurance companies, and private banks, which were considered more suitable for employing workers with disabilities (Jackson 1993, 451). The law also provided disabled workers with special protections against dismissals and additional numbers of paid vacation days. From the sense of public duty during Weimar to protect disabled veterans who had served the "fatherland" now emerged a more general and broadly defined right to employment by a traditionally disenfranchised group of workers.

Through the evolution of German disability law and policy, disability employment remained a form of social welfare—initially as a reward for patriotic

duties, and then emerging as part of a public consensus that work had thera-
peutic and social value. By transferring the responsibility for employment
from what was traditionally considered a state responsibility to private employers, Germany led the way in making the disability employment quota a
staple of the postwar welfare state. Protection for disability difference became
a central part of the growing German welfare state, which became legitimized
in the German national identity. The 1949 postwar Constitution defines the
German state as a "democratic and social" state (Article 20.1) that must both
guarantee formal rights and liberties *and* develop material, or positive, rights.
As a "social" state (*Sozialstaat*), the state must guarantee a decent standard of
living and social justice, including both income and employment security.
Germany's rapid postwar economic expansion was based on a "social market
economy" (*Soziale Marktwirtschaft*), which is predicated on the basic compat-
ibility of a free market with a socially conscious state. That meant the social
market had to combine free enterprise with strong unions, which had a vested
interest in economic expansion through their codetermination in management, in combination with the state's responsibility to secure the basic needs
of the population. Thus, Article 28 (1) spells out the "principles of a republican, democratic, and social government based on the rule of law." The German Constitution thus combines civil rights and liberties with positive rights
to social justice (Kommers 1997, 241). The focus on employment—as a primary activity of citizenship and as a central hallmark of postwar prosperity—
carried with it the protection of workers with disabilities and the general social responsibility toward individuals not competing in the open labor
market. As a result, disability status in Germany has never been an indicator
of poverty like it remains in the United States.

GERMAN DISABILITY ACTIVISM

Just as disabled veterans provided the impetus for German disability law, it
was disabled veterans who formed the first disability organizations. These
first disability groups also included civilians, because the postwar Occupation authorities did not allow associations that consisted solely of war veterans. The largest of these was the VdK (Verein der Kriegsbeschädigten und
Kriegshinterbliebenden), founded in 1950 initially as an "association of the
war damaged." Today the VdK is Germany's largest social service association
and political interest group, representing the interests of people with dis-

abilities, retirees, and those with chronic illness. Its political counterpart is the Sozialverband Deutschland, founded by war veterans in the post–World War I era but dissolved during the Nazi era because of its political Left-leaning tendencies. Resurrected after the war, it is now another umbrella organization addressing a variety of disability needs. Other disability-specific organizations formed to lobby for disability-related needs in the growing network of social welfare and rehabilitation policies. Among those were associations of the deaf (Deutscher Gehörlosenbund, founded in 1927), blind (Deutscher Blindenverband, dating back to 1912), and people with multiple sclerosis (Deutsche Multiple Sklerose Gesesllschaft, founded in 1952). Many of the disability associations were founded before World War II, and like the Sozialverband Deutschland they reconvened during the Occupation. During the 1950s, parents of children with disabilities also gathered to advocate for their children and to create support structures for families, such as the Lebenshilfe (Life-Help), which was founded in 1958 by parents of children with mental disabilities. A focal point for the parents' activism was the inclusion of their children in the highly segregated German education system, which strictly tracks students according to abilities (and disabilities).[6]

The thalidomide scandal of the early 1960s strengthened the disability movement, which was still heavily divided by disability-specific groups. Developed by a German pharmaceutical company as a "safe" sleep aid and morning sickness drug, thalidomide was found to cause severe birth defects, most prominently lack of limbs. The resulting scandal brought tremendous media attention to disability issues that, for the first time, brought serious attention to the question of rehabilitation and education. The "thalidomide children" grew into adulthood and became active members of a movement criticizing the continued segregation and medicalization of disability issues.

A new generation of disability activists would also come of political age during the 1960s. The German "economic miracle" was in full bloom, unemployment was low, and people were looking for a more critical engagement with the country's Nazi past, which had been discouraged during the conservative postwar years. Willy Brandt had just been elected chancellor in 1969 with the slogan of "daring more democracy," and both the student and women's movements were beginning to form their platforms for social justice and progressive change of German society. Inspired by the demands for equality being made by both of these movements, people with disabilities began to form their first "clubs of the disabled and their friends" (Clubs Behinderter und ihrer Freunde, or CeBeeFs) to foster communication and to make connections to nondisabled groups. These clubs, formed initially as social clubs, soon realized that socializing was difficult in nonaccessible buildings, in pubs without accessible restrooms, and with a public transportation system club members could not use. As a result, these clubs would be the first to protest against physical barriers and inaccessible public spaces (Kommers 1997, 241). The protests soon grew into organized movements with letter writing campaigns, sit-ins, and demonstrations.

The passage of the 1974 Schwerbehindertengesetz (Law of the Severely Disabled) included the lobbying of disability organizations for the first time. The law removed the term "damaged" to denote disability and covered all those who were considered severely disabled, regardless of the cause or nature of their disability. The term *severely disabled* covered those whose ability to secure an income was 50 percent or less than that of equally qualified nondisabled persons. Although not as pejorative as *damaged,* disability was still seen as a comparison to a nondisabled norm. The law imposed a 6 percent employment quota, covering all employers with 16 or more employees, and increased the levy against businesses that failed to meet the quota (originally 100 DM per month, raised to 200 DM in 1986). The law also strengthened the special protections against dismissals, requiring the corresponding disability welfare office (*Hauptfürsorgestelle*) to approve every dismissal.[7] In addition, people with disabilities were issued a "disability ID card" (*Schwerbehindertenausweis*), which they could use for discounts in public transportation, admissions, and especially lower tax rates.[8]

Although many considered these changes to be relatively marginal, the 1974 law was widely considered a big advance in social policy because it removed the "causality" principle from legal coverage. The cause or nature of the disability no longer mattered; instead, the social effect of the disability, specifically the reduction in earning power, provided the basis for benefits. The number of people benefiting from the law rose dramatically. Employment rates did not rise as dramatically, however, as businesses tended to pay a levy in exchange for not hiring disabled workers, which, in turn, was used to fund the vast expansion of rehabilitation and welfare resources. Political approval of the employment levy remained strong among all parties, not only those friendly to labor issues; it became an indirect tax on businesses to continue funding Germany's growing but still segregated "parallel track." As a result, Germans with disabilities experienced very little income deprivation on account of their disabilities, especially in comparison to the United States during this same period (Burkhauser and Daly 1994).

Given this progressive, supportive climate, what were the grounds for early demonstrations by CeBeeF groups and others? People with disabilities lived economically secure but still segregated lives. They were, in the words of Horst Seifert, "cared for but infantilized" by a state that took care of all their needs but did not consider them equal citizens (Seifert 1991).[9] Most of all, they were dissatisfied with the work of the large disability organizations, which were led by nondisabled people, who were all well trained in the traditional politics of focusing on the expansion of welfare facilities and protective measures. During the 1960s and 1970s, disabled members of these organizations became increasingly dissatisfied with what they perceived as the patronizing attitudes of the nondisabled leadership and their continued focus on the "parallel track." They began to challenge their segregation—which they saw not as the natural consequence of their disabilities, but rather the result of a *disablist* society.[10] Gradually, these groups shifted the focus of their lobbying from welfare benefits to the rights of inclusion, integration, and barrier-free environments. With this shift in focus came a shift in name. Activists insisted on calling themselves "cripples," developing "crip consciousness," and excluding nondisabled members to demonstrate their commitment to a more radical disability politics.

The 1970s also witnessed the beginning of a movement by parents to integrate their children who were attending special schools into regular schools. As mentioned above, parents' groups had been largely responsible for post–World War II reforms in special education that created a highly developed system of "special" schools (called *Sonderschule* at the time, now called *Förderschule*) and apprenticeship programs, as well as for legal reforms creating compulsory universal education in the 1960s. A decade later parents organized again, this time forming local working groups to establish programs that would allow more regular contact between disabled children and their nondisabled peers, such as during recess, or in music classes, or on field trips (Heyl 1998, 695). Their lobbying was successful initially because parents limited their advocacy to specific local projects and did not threaten the special education structure. The success of these programs, however, led to more fundamental demands for integrated education, as seen in the experimental projects (*Schulversuche*) in Berlin and Bonn during the 1980s. This was the beginning of a split in parental activism between those who continued to work within the existing *Sonderschulen* system to ensure the provision of services to their children and those who began to challenge the special education structure in favor of integration.

The UN's International Year of Disabled Persons in 1981 and its promise of "full participation and equality" launched the second phase of post–World War II disability activism. Although disability movements in Japan and other Asian countries greeted this year with enthusiasm, in Germany it generated protest and launched what movement activists call their first "paradigm shift" (*Perspektivenwechsel*). German activists were very critical of the UN Year and Decade, viewing its adoption by the government as a form of political posturing belied by the lack of commitment to real reforms. People with disabilities watched as politicians made political promises to improve employment opportunities, make public transportation more accessible, and increase social integration. These promises sounded hollow to disability activists. They felt that, once again, the discussion marginalized and objectified them as "those who must be integrated" rather than focusing on ways to make the environment more accessible (Heiden 1996). Instead of allowing the government to use the UN Year as a platform to sing its own praises, activists decided to use the UN Year for their own publicity purposes. For example, they interrupted the official opening event in Dortmund in 1981, chaining themselves to the stage to prevent the federal president from delivering his official speech. Activists took over the stage, calling for "no speeches, no segregation, no violation of human rights." The president, in turn, had to give his formal speech in a side room, where he emphasized everything the activists were rallying against: a call for charity, welfare, and social responsibility for the less fortunate (Steiner 2003).

As a larger counter-event, activists staged a Cripples Tribunal (Krüppel-Tribunal) in which they turned the tables and charged the government with discriminatory policies that keep people with disabilities from, as the UN motto called for, participating equally in society. Activists demanded the right to an integrated education and pointed to the ongoing inaccessibility of public buildings and buses. Activists spoke of human rights abuses in institutions and group homes and the "double discrimination" experienced by women with disabilities. These protests politicized the movement, and thus 1981 is remembered less as the UN Year and more as the beginning of the "crip movement" (*Krüppelbewegung*).

The change of government after elections in 1980 meant a turn toward more conservative economic policies. A calculated economic and distributive policy to reduce government spending included reduced state quotas and wage quotas, cuts in social security, and dwindling real wages. The legislative activism of the 1970s was over. As general unemployment levels rose, less legislative attention was placed on disability employment policies. However, the conservative government did make two contributions to disability politics during this period: it established the office of the "disability liaison" (*Behindertenbeauftragter*) and decided to publish a disability report once every five years on the state of disability policies.[11] In 1986, it reformed the 1974 Law for the Severely Disabled to erase some of its stigmatizing terms: the law now categorizes disabilities according to "degree" (*Grad der Behinderung*) rather than by "reduction in work capacity" (*Minderung der Erwerbsfähigkeit*). Benefits are now called a "leveling of disadvantage" (*Nachteilsausgleich*) rather than "privileges" (*Vergünstigung*). Although most activists saw this legal reform as a positive measure, they remained critical of the office of the disability liaison, which, as a political appointment, hardly seemed likely to become a source of advocacy and reforms.

German disability politics during the 1980s can be well summarized by Udo Sierck and Nati Radke's provocative book title, *Die Wohltätermafia* (The Mafia of benefactors). The authors criticize the German welfare state's patronizing and paternalistic caregiving, pointing to medical experts, large disability organizations, welfare offices, and politicians who "speak of integration and living together, but who refuse to acknowledge the direct and indirect discrimination against disabled people" (Sierck and Radtke 1988, 26). A new generation of activists was moving away from traditional German disability politics, which focused on the expansion of benefits, and instead was turning to a more radical understanding of disability as a social construction. With the discourse shifting from welfare to discrimination, the time was ripe for employing models that embodied a rights approach to disability. German activists had long been following the political maneuvering of their American counterparts, watching the politics surrounding the implementation of Section 504 of the 1973 Rehabilitation Act, which had mandated full accommodation for all facilities using public funds, and, of course, the historic passage of the 1990 Americans with Disabilities Act. Looking across the Atlantic to the development of disability rights as civil rights, German activists wondered, "Is this the land we are dreaming of?"

"DREAMLAND USA"

"Is the United States truly *the* dreamland for people with disabilities?
More and more of us traveling in a wheelchair or using a cane return
from our trips to the U.S. with eyes glazed over, oohing and aahing that

life there is so much better for disabled people—because an antidiscrimination law has enabled broad participation for people with disabilities in all areas of public life." (Hermes 1998, 5)

"For German wheelchair users a trip to the United States is like a *trip to a better world*. Airports, hotels, restaurants, movie theaters, the post office, any kind of state office—all are accessible without problems." (Brückner 2000, 4; emphasis added)

The United States became a "dreamland" for the new generation of German disability activists. As Gisela Hermes mentions in the citation above, activists became curious about a country that had, in their eyes, embodied the paradigm shift from charity and dependence to equal rights and self-determination. Many German disability groups traveled to the United States to learn about the movement there and returned full of enthusiasm and optimism about what might be possible in a land of disability rights. It is safe to say that all the leading figures in Germany's contemporary disability movement have made at least one trip to the United States, most commonly to Berkeley, the origin of the American independent living movement, and to Oregon, the origin of the people-first movement for people with developmental disabilities. International exchanges became a common way to experience the land of rights, especially for students spending a semester abroad. German students with disabilities, such as Dominik Brückner cited above, were in awe at the ease with which their American counterparts could navigate college campuses, catch a movie in town, or meet friends for a beer afterwards. All of these activities would require careful planning in Germany where wheelchair accessibility was spotty or nonexistent, preventing spontaneous outings like the ones he experienced during his visit to "a better world."

Trips to the "dreamland" of disability rights invoked much enthusiasm among disability activists and envy of their American counterparts. At the same time, Germans kept a critical awareness of the shortcomings of the American welfare system. A book whose translated title would be *Dreamland USA* (Hermes 1998) has the provocative subtitle *Between Anti-discrimination and Social Poverty*, indicating that the siren call of the ADA did not come without reality checks. Right from the beginning of the book, the authors concede that American laws and conditions cannot simply be transferred from one cultural context to another. They remind us that the United States has a reputation for little to no state intervention concerning the well-being of its citizens, which translates into poor medical care, joblessness, and poverty. Nonetheless, the reality of an antidiscrimination law is seductive. People with disabilities no longer need to ask or beg for services; they are rights holders, confidently demanding that existing antidiscrimination laws be respected and complied with.

The confidence and sense of entitlement afforded to a rights holder, according to the German authors, has also affected the attitudes of the nondisabled population. In the United States, they claim, disability has become a normal aspect of everyday life; it is an equal way of living. Nondisabled Americans hold fewer disabling stereotypes and fears than their German counterparts, because they are more likely to attend schools with disabled children or to have disabled colleagues at their workplaces. The American self-confidence that the German activists wanted to take back with them is also evident in language. English language terminology such as "peer counseling," "antidiscrimination," and "independent living" found their way into the German movement. Ottmar Miles-Paul suggested adopting the word "empowerment" without translations because its German equivalents (*Ermächtigung* or *Befähigung*) sound too passive, apolitical, and, well, not empowering enough (Miles-Paul 1992 in Hermes 1998, 11). Miles-Paul speaks passionately about the transformation he has experienced ever since he got infected with the "empowerment virus" during his frequent visits to the United States.[12]

An example of the German love affair with American-style disability rights is an essay by journalist Sigrid Arnade, who embodies a fairly common skepticism of American culture and politics. A progressive Left-leaning journalist, Arnade outlines her critical distance to the United States, a country that, in her eyes, had lost all political credibility during the McCarthy and Vietnam eras, and symbolized a superficial and naïve engagement with the world. She admits that it took her years to finally take a trip to the United States, preferring instead to visit Canada or Australia. However, after having reluctantly visited "Dreamland USA," she could not help but acknowledge the contributions of the U.S. rights model. Her essay concludes with the admission that "I have never experienced a place with as few barriers as here. It's not that I could walk again—that hasn't changed—but I felt less disabled because I *was* less disabled" (Arnade 1998, 67).

Arnade, an avid camper, loves the American national park system. Her essay describes her sense of freedom at being able to count on accessible toilets wherever she went, even in parks out in the wilderness. At one campsite she found an exception, where the bathroom and shower weren't accessible. She decided to educate the park ranger about this violation of both Section 504 of the 1973 Rehabilitation Act and, of course, of the 1990 ADA, and she was determined to pay only half of the campsite fees as a public recognition of that violation. The ensuing conversation with the park ranger symbolizes what she describes as the "ADA effect": the ranger apologized and reduced her fees, telling her that the park is in the process of becoming accessible, and calling it inexcusable that this beautiful park cannot be equally enjoyed by people with disabilities. In this interaction, Arnade had become a rights holder, empowered by having the law on her side. She imagines how this conversation would have occurred in Germany: she would have had to plead rather than demand or get angry, and she would have had to face arguments such as "but we've already done so much for the disabled; besides, there's just no money" (Arnade 1998, 69).

All the contributors to the *Traumland USA* (Dreamland USA) collection describe a sense of freedom and self-confidence that they took back to Germany. Their engagement with the U.S.-inspired disability rights model ushered in the next phase of the German disability movement, which looked toward the establishment of similar equality-based disability laws in Germany. They began to have meetings to discuss the implications of the ADA for German legislative reforms. Most important, activists also realized that they had to begin working in coalitions rather than in disability-specific groups. One coalition, the Initiative for Equality of the Disabled (Initiativkreis Gleichstellung Behinderter) (henceforth, Equality Initiative), was formed by the larger, well-established disability groups reaching out to the smaller, radical groups and to politicians. The Equality Initiative set the goal of introducing a law similar to the ADA in Germany and planned more media work and public consciousness-raising. Two other disability groups formed with a sole focus on the law. Netzwerk Artikel 3 (Article 3 Network) focused on the constitutional amendment, and the Forum behinderter JuristInnen (Forum of Disabled Jurists) focused on disability rights. That same year, 1990, marked the birth of the German independent living movement (*Interessenvertretung Selbstbestimmt Leben*), headed by an activist who spent a year in training at Berkeley (Miles-Paul 1992). Two years later, the first national women's network (Weibernetz) emerged, pointing to the connection between sex and disability discrimination.

The Equality Initiative won its first political victory at the 1991 meeting of international rehabilitation experts (REHA Hilfsmesse) in Düsseldorf, one of the largest conferences in the field. The Equality Initiative used this setting to organize the first roundtable with people with disabilities and representatives from government and industry to discuss rehabilitation issues. Planned as a friendly roundtable, activists soon took over the discussion and challenged the government liaison in particular to respond to their stories of everyday discrimination, stigma, and unequal opportunities. The result was a document entitled the "Call of Düsseldorf" (Düsseldorfer Appell), which was signed by more than 130 disability organizations and ten thousand individuals. It outlined detailed demands to combat discrimination and ended with a demand for a comprehensive equalizing law (citing the ADA as an example) and for the expansion of Article 3 of Germany's Basic Law. In 1993, the signatures collected were formally handed over to the Bundestag vice president as a mass petition.

DISABILITY EQUALITY IN THE GERMAN CONSTITUTION

The timing was perfect. In 1992, prompted by German unification, the Bundestag had begun its revision of the German Constitution. Members of the Equality Initiative strategized quickly, deciding to focus their energies on the constitutional demand first. They pushed for a hearing with the Constitutional Commission on their proposal modeled on the ADA, the antidiscrimination mandate in the State Constitution of Brandenburg, and the Canadian Charter of Rights and Freedoms, which had added a disability discrimination clause as early as 1982. Their public reading in front of the commission was especially powerful because they represented a tightly knit, unified network of groups, ranging from the usual suspects (the smaller autonomous groups from the crip movement) to the larger social welfare organizations, such as the conservative VdK and the War Victims Association (Kriegsopferverband). This unprecedented view of disability organizations as a united front convinced even the government liaison to change his opposition to the constitutional amendment, an opinion he had held as a political appointee of the conservative governing coalition.

A constitutional amendment requires the approval of a two-thirds majority of the constitutional commission. The progressive opposition parties, such as the Social Democratic Party, the Greens, and the Party of Democratic Socialism,[13] were in favor of the amendment; the governing coalition of conservatives and liberals, the Christian Democratic Party and the Free Democratic Party, was not. Indeed, they were not even present at the hearing. The conservative consensus was that the rights of people with disabilities were adequately covered through "the principle of the social welfare state"[14] and that the new Basic Law should not "degenerate into a constitutional shopping catalog" (Heiden 1996, 33). The head of the conservative faction, Wolfgang Schäuble, who uses a wheelchair, was one of the amendment's staunchest critics.

In preparation for the commission's vote on June 17, 1993, the Equality Initiative expanded their political lobbying by flooding the commission with postcards and petitions and by staging nationwide demonstrations. Despite this effort, the vote in June failed to get a two-thirds majority. Rather than giving up, however, the Equality Initiative used the annual meeting of rehabilitation experts (REHA Hilfsmesse) in Düsseldorf to publicize their proposal and to call attention to the last possibility for adoption: both houses of the German parliament would have to vote on the commission's draft constitution.

Here, again, timing was of essence. The campaign period for Bundestag elections kicked off in May 1994, giving the Equality Initiative another opportunity to question candidates about their stand on equality legislation for people with disabilities. This was the moment, according to many activists, when Chancellor Helmut Kohl suddenly recognized people with disabilities as potential voters. In an assembly organized by the VdK on May 20, 1994, Kohl surprised everyone by declaring that he, too, was in favor of an antidiscrimination clause in the Basic Law. This forced the ruling coalition to change course. Only six weeks later, on June 30, the new Constitution with the amendment was adopted almost unanimously (with only three dissenting votes and four abstentions) in the Berlin Reichstag. It had taken two years to fight for the inclusion of a seven-word sentence, "*niemand darf wegen seiner Behinderung benachteiligt werden*" (nobody shall be discriminated against because of disability).

The new Basic Law took effect on November 15, 1994. Article 3 now reads as follows:

1. All human beings are equal before the law.
2. Men and women have equal rights. The state shall promote the actual implementation of equal rights for women and men and take steps to eliminate disadvantages that now exist.
3. There shall be no discrimination based on gender, birth, race, native

and social origin, beliefs, religious belief or political opinion. *Nobody shall be discriminated against because of disability.*

The choice of Article 3 is significant: when Germany wrote its Basic Law in 1949, it chose Article 3 to acknowledge those persecuted during the Nazi regime on the basis of "race, native and social origin, beliefs, religious belief or political opinion" (Section 3) and enacted an equal rights amendment (Section 2). The absence of disability, even though it had been a category of extermination, was painfully evident. The history of Nazi persecution of people with disabilities did not receive serious academic consideration in Germany until the late 1970s.[15] In 1994, disability activists thus felt that finally they had taken their rightful place in Article 3.

The constitutional amendment was celebrated as a political victory after an intensive, two-year struggle by a movement that had never acted in unison before. It symbolized an important first step toward legitimizing people with disabilities as equal citizens and political subjects, rather than as objects of welfare. The amendment led to federal states adopting similar language into eleven of the fifteen state constitutions. Some state constitutions simply repeat the nondiscrimination mandate; others went even further and mandated equal treatment (Theben 1999). The constitutional approach, however, has its limitations, whether as an antidiscrimination or equality mandate. It protects disabled persons against discrimination by state entities only and not by private employers or private providers of goods and services. It functions as a "standard of value" only in private law (*Wertentscheidung*). Furthermore, constitutional provisions are by necessity broad and vague. Neither disability nor discrimination is defined in any of the constitutional provisions, thus leaving vast discretion to the courts. It is not surprising that, immediately following the victory celebration in 1994, activists gathered for the second round of the struggle: the fight for an antidiscrimination law, similar to the ADA, that would spell out a German understanding of disability rights and disability discrimination.

CAMPAIGNING FOR EQUALITY: "OPERATION BASIC LAW"

The second round of the Equality Initiative's struggle was to give the constitutional amendment the political and legal teeth necessary to become an effective tool against disability discrimination. The Equality Initiative decided that the first step toward this goal was to recognize the importance of educating the larger population about the presence of the constitutional equality mandate and its implications. A 1994 survey showed that 79 percent of respondents had never even heard the sentence "nobody shall be discriminated against because of disability," and fewer than 10 percent knew even approximately when it had been added to the Basic Law.[16] The same poll showed that 71 percent of respondents thought Germany was "not disability friendly" in terms of its public transportation system, employment opportunities, and housing. Finally, only 19 percent of respondents thought that people with disabilities received some form of equal treatment by their nondisabled peers (Mittler and Zirden 1997).

Based on these sobering statistics, Germany's largest and most prominent charity organization, Aktion Sorgenkind, organized an extensive media campaign, Operation Basic Law (Aktion Grundgesetz), to educate people about the meanings of the nondiscrimination mandate. Aktion Sorgenkind (lit. Operation Problem Child) was selected because of its background in communications, name recognition, and, of course, its vast funds in case corporate sponsorship fell through (which, not surprisingly, it did). As the name suggests, this is a classic feel-good charity, banking on images of helpless disabled children who need your financial support. It began raising money in 1964, initially for children affected by thalidomide, but soon extended its mission to disabled adults. The Aktion Sorgenkind's hugely popular lottery had funneled billions into disability-related projects and enjoyed high levels of public support. Disability organizations, however, rejected the label of "problem child" and openly criticized the organization for its patronizing stance, as well as for its exclusive support of sheltered workshops rather than integrated facilities. They have argued that while the Aktion Sorgenkind raises much-needed funds, it does so at the expense of creating images of disabled people as helpless, needy, and objects of charity.[17]

Accordingly, many of the autonomous disability groups initially opposed Aktion Sorgenkind's leadership in the Aktion Grundgesetz project. They feared that the organization's traditional apolitical stance would influence the operation's very political agenda (Mittler and Zirden 1997, 21–22). In the fall of 1997, after nearly a year of negotiations, more than 90 disability organizations (growing to 130 in 2001) were united behind Aktion Sorgenkind in a media campaign to educate the general population about the meaning of the constitutional amendment. This was the largest political campaign ever launched by the disability community.

The campaign was limited to two months—October and November of 1997—to heighten the impact of both the variety and the sheer mass of materials flooding the country. Twelve different ads appeared in all major German newspapers and magazines, and six different billboard ads graced every twelfth billboard in the country. Every German television station ran advertisements. Posters, buttons, beer coasters, stickers, and postcards bearing 125 different slogans were disseminated in almost every neighborhood. Street theater, conferences, community meetings, talk shows, and public demonstrations were held throughout the country.

All of the materials had the same characteristic look: a bright green background with a few poignant slogans and the characteristic red logo of Aktion Sorgenkind. Like a well-run public relations campaign, organizers knew that name recognition, or in this case color and logo recognition, would add to the success of the campaign. They wanted the public to start associating what they called the "campaign green" with the sentence "nobody shall be discriminated against because of disability." To heighten the impact of the slogans they also decided against the use of photos or pictures.

The media campaign operated on two levels: on a macro-level via billboards, TV commercials, and advertisements in the public sphere, and on a micro-level for every individual via stickers, buttons, and postcards. Activists ordered packages of buttons, stickers, postcards, and posters that featured a variety of slogans (all created by the membership of the disability organizations involved in the campaign). Every participant, disabled or not, could use these materials to draw attention to what organizers called "points of discrimination" in everyday life and make their environment, if not disability friendly, then at least disability aware. All of the materials listed the website of Operation Basic Law[18] and most of them prominently featured the text of Article 3(3) to increase its visibility.

The campaign encouraged participants to distribute materials liberally in their neighborhoods, with only token warnings to stay within the limits of the law. For example, they might point to inaccessible buildings by placing stickers on stairways saying, "Thank you! Your wheelchair users." Inaccessible public telephone booths were plastered with stickers saying, "Unfortunately, not everybody can use the phone here." Unfriendly neighbors or sales clerks might find themselves with notes saying, "Why don't you get to know me? You might lose your fears" or "Now you know why we are called 'the disabled'—because people like you disable us." When public assemblies, theaters, or movie houses failed to provide sign language interpreters or hearing aids, activists could send them postcards saying, "We would like to have participated, too! The Deaf and Hard of Hearing." Restaurant guests or beer drinkers in pubs might find their drink sitting on a green coaster, saying on one side, "Dear guest, your chair might be a bit damp . . . (p.t.o) [please turn over]," and reading on the other side, "unfortunately there was no accessible bathroom" (see figs. 1–2).

While the postcards, stickers, and buttons used humorous and provocative slogans to jolt the reader into awareness, the posters invited more thoughtful reflection. They featured original quotes from people with disabilities, telling stories about the discriminatory attitudes and stereotypes they face in their everyday lives. The stories were authentic, giving the name of the person telling it, except for a few who used pseudonyms. The poster topics covered the common range of central issues in the disability movement: human rights, self-determination, bioethics, health care, women's issues, integration, invisible disabilities, sign language, and assistive technologies. As an example, consider a poster that addressed the issue of dignity. It featured a prominent title, "Human Dignity Is Alienable" (*die Würde des Menschen ist Antastbar*), referring to the well-known First Article of the German Constitution, which states that human dignity is inviolable. The following three quotes placed the topic in the perspective of people who experience daily assaults on their human dignity:

"They think that I can't think. But my head is not disabled, my body is." (Anja Maiwald)

"At the nursing home I'm told when to go bed, when to come home, and what to eat. I have no control how I get washed, dressed, or moved." (Roman Deserno)

"It makes me mad when movies show those of us who stutter as stupid and clumsy. As if stuttering has anything to do with intelligence." (Konrad Schäfers)

Closely related to the topic of dignity, the notion of self-determination and independent living are addressed in a poster with the self-explanatory title, "I Know What I Want." Unlike the previous posters, this one does not reveal the person's identity.

Fig. 1. *Beer coaster, front side:* "Dear Guest: your seat might be a bit damp. . . . (please turn over)."

Fig. 2. *Beer coaster, back side:* ". . . Unfortunately, there was no accessible bathroom."

"You can't tell us what to eat or drink, even if we live in a nursing home." (Sven P.)

"Despite my Down syndrome I can see, hear, walk, and read. I am now learning how to write and do math. Am I disabled?" (Bernard Moser, name changed)

"When I got an apartment in an assisted living facility in 1986, I felt that I was truly living for the first time. I was doing things I never thought I could do, things I forgot even existed." (Andrea K.)

Another poster addressed the subject of prenatal testing for birth defects. This is a heated topic in the disability community, not in reference to abortion rights as it is in the United States, but because of Germany's history of forced sterilization and abortion during the Nazi regime. The following poster, entitled "Mother and Child Are Healthy?," shows the stigma of knowingly giving birth to a disabled child rather than choosing abortion:

"It's a boy, severely disabled, the nurse told my mother. Do you even want to see it?" (Tillmann Kleinau)

"After folks found out that Timo has a disability nobody came by to congratulate us anymore. Nobody was happy for us—they just felt sorry for us. But having pity robs others of their strength. Instead of receiving their pity, I would have loved having their help." (Judith von dall'Ami)

"When I cross the street with Leah, a child with Down syndrome, I hear them say, but this could have been prevented, it should have been detected before birth. So I ask myself, yeah, but then what?" (Tina Winter)

Another important subject the posters addressed concerned integrated education and employment. Several posters featured the isolation of students ("Why are none of your fellow students disabled?") and workers ("Why don't you have a disabled colleague?"). For example,

"When I passed the test to advance to the next level school, my father was called in to the principal's office. Your daughter poses too much of a burden to the class, they told him. All my girlfriends went to that school. Now I had to go to boarding school for physically disabled girls, far away from my family and friends." (Marita Boos-Waidosch, Mainz)

"Nobody thinks a person with a disability can do the job. Even if we prove them wrong, there are a thousand reasons why we can't be hired—they can't build an elevator, the building is too old, the hallways are too narrow for those of us using wheelchairs, they worry that colleagues will feel over-whelmed with a sense of responsibility to help us. I have heard every one of these arguments, and as soon as they saw me in person, I never got the chance to prove myself." (Tilmann Kleinau, Stuttgart)

Yet another poster addressed the issue of invisible disabilities, a growing topic in the disability rights movement. People with invisible disabilities had to wage a long struggle to become accepted in a movement that, for both political and ideological reasons, relies on a disability identity that is visible. The very ability to "pass" as nondisabled that allows people with invisible disabilities to avoid the more obvious consequences of stigma and public discrimination also denies them the legitimacy of making disability needs-based claims. This poster is entitled "I Have Something You Don't See," a pun on the German phrase of the "I Spy" game.[19] Perhaps not surprisingly, the first of the three quotes on this poster comes from an American source and the other two are pseudonyms:

"One day I had to give a current events report in school. I stood in front of the class, but couldn't get a word out. I wanted to say, 'the,' but all that came out of my mouth was 't . . t . . t.' I broke into tears and went back to my chair, cov-ering my head in shame." (John Scatman, Los Angeles)

"Why will nobody believe me when I say I have to use the bathroom, I really have to go? It's bad enough having to worry about getting to the bathroom on time when you have Crohn's disease." (Maike Wangenhein, name changed)

"When I ask for directions, or how much something costs, I expect a serious response, rather than having the bus driver or sales clerk tell me, "it says so right there." I'm not asking for the fun of it, I'm asking because I can't read." (Hannelore Losen, name changed)

Finally, the experience of dual discrimination by women with disabilities was of great concern to Operation Basic Law, no doubt in part due to the vocal presence of feminists in the autonomous disability groups. A poster with the title, "Sex: female [with the word *female* crossed out]—disabled" sought to address some of the public misconceptions of motherhood, sexuality, and disability. Considered asexual beings and unfit mothers, women with disabilities have to fight for the right to be seen as women, while at the same time challenging gender stereotypes:

"As a single woman with a disability and a child I always drew attention. At times it was encouragement, other times it was rejection. My daughter dealt with this on a daily basis. It wasn't easy for her to have a disabled mother. People thought I wasn't capable of giving her the love and care she needed." (Ingrid Schmidt, name changed)

"'I can't ask my colleagues to deal with someone like her!' This is how my application for a receptionist job was rejected." (Elke Krinke, Mannheim)

"I noticed that I had to assert my wish for a child even in front of my doctor. I had to be careful not to let her talk me into having an abortion." (Vera Marx, Bottrop)

MOBILIZING DISABILITY RIGHTS, GERMAN-STYLE

The media campaign represented an innovative form of rights mobilization that not only raised disability awareness in German society but also helped build a new disability movement. To the general public, the posters and other action materials conveyed a very simple but poignant message: disability rights distinctly affect everyday life in ways the nondisabled had not previously imagined. Disability rights are not just something the Bundestag might declare and bestow in a constitutional amendment; they are central to people's self-understanding as equal citizens. By telling their stories and sharing their experiences with disability and with the public's misperceptions, people with disabilities used the language of rights as markers of humanity and respect, which powerfully resonated with the public. Indeed, the public response to the campaign was overwhelmingly positive. Opinion polls of the general population showed very positive results: 80 percent of respondents judged the campaign as "very good," 85 percent saw it as "important," and 87 percent as "necessary." Elderly respondents especially connected with stories of rights violations in nursing homes and slogans surrounding human dignity (Mittler and Zirden 1997, 23).

Just as important as the campaign's effect on public opinion and awareness, however, was its effect on the members of the 90 participating disability organizations. Perhaps the most powerful lesson was that of unity between groups that "used to fight each other all the time." For the first time, the younger, autonomous groups had worked together with the more established and conservative networks. In a 1999 meeting on Operation Basic Law's impact, one participant stated: "I noticed a feeling of unity and connection, which made me very optimistic. Rigid organizational structures are finally beginning to break down a bit. I think things will get better, and I credit the Operation."[20] The charity organization Aktion Sorgenkind itself felt the effect of this new political cooperation very profoundly: in June 2000, it announced that it had changed its name to Aktion Mensch (Operation Human Being) to signal its new understanding of people with disabilities as human beings rather than as "problem children." The notion of considering people with disabilities as humans or people, before considering their disabilities, is a direct nod to the impact of the U.S.-developed people-first language, which the Aktion Mensch directly acknowledges in its discussion of the philosophy behind its name change.[21]

This new sense of solidarity also addressed internal hierarchies in the movement. As one participant pointed out, "The 'wheelchair users' are always out in front, and the so-called mentally disabled are pushed to the back, never getting the same resources. Operation Basic Law showed that it is possible for all of us to work together: the wheelchair users, the blind and the mentally disabled. If we keep this up, I think we can build a disability movement that is unique, just like the student movement we had."[22] The hierarchy between the physically and developmentally disabled was, for once, pushed to the background, as, at least according to the movement literature, every group had an equal say in the discussions surrounding the choice of slogans and events.

Issues surrounding rights and rights consciousness played a central role in participants' assessment of the campaign's success. One participant commented, "I'm with the self-advocacy movement, so my approach is one that enables people with disabilities to demand their rights and learn how to talk about them in the first place. The Operation helped us do this by providing financial assistance: we could hold meetings and publish pamphlets to educate people about their rights."[23] On a philosophical level, the media campaign prompted activists to identify disability discrimination as a civil rights issue not only for the purposes of public policy and legal reforms but also for the evolution of their own understanding of what it means to be disabled and experience discrimination. Whether through the stories told in the posters or the points of discrimination in the action materials, the campaign made the different forms of oppression apparent. Current and future movement members were able to see that despite the diversity of the disability category, the experience of discrimination and stigma is equally devastating. Activists learned to identify the experience of discrimination not as an inevitable outcome of having a disability but as a product of public ignorance, misconceptions, and fear. This recognition engendered a feeling of common identity, which forms an important basis for a social movement. More important, however, the shift of attention from personal shortcoming (I cannot climb these stairs because I use a wheelchair) to social discrimination (this building is not wheelchair accessible) points to a parallel shift from welfare to rights.

Attention to rights consciousness often included references to the United States, which is still considered the country of origin when it comes to disability rights. As one participant summarized:

> The Operation has started important discussions regarding integration as a civil right, not as something given out of pity. This shows that we are in the process of a paradigm shift. This includes the disability organizations: we all had to work together, traditional associations and newer ones, working on a common platform. When I heard about the Operation I had just returned from the U.S., experiencing the civil rights approach there, and I thought that we should be doing the same thing in Germany. So, I was so happy that now things are getting started here.[24]

PUBLICIZING DISCRIMINATION IN THE COURTS

As a separate but related mobilizing strategy, activists focused public attention on lawsuits that demonstrated the unjust and discriminatory treatment of people with disabilities. The literature on rights mobilization points to such publicity as an effective tool. In *Rights at Work,* for example, Michael McCann cites one activist declaring that "a lawsuit is a marvelous occasion for a press conference" (McCann 1994, 62). McCann clarifies that the target for this publicity was generally the attentive audience of fellow and potential movement activists rather than the public at large. "As such, national media coverage was only one stage of a much broader effort to disseminate legal knowledge for movement building purposes" (McCann 1994, 63).

For example, a 1980 court case generated intense publicity and sparked indignation in the movement. In what became known as the "judgment of Frankfurt" (*Frankfurter Urteil*), the Frankfurt District Court ruled in favor of a family demanding a 10 percent reduction in the price of their vacation package. The hotel where they had stayed had hosted a group of severely disabled children whose "sight and sounds" were so upsetting and "disgusting" that the family felt the value of their vacation experience had been severely compromised.[25] The ruling sparked such indignation in activist circles that a mass rally was planned—5,000 demonstrators from all over West Germany gathered for what was considered the largest political rally of the disabled at the time. Along with the protests against the UN Year of Disabled Persons a year later, this protest was considered one of the founding moments of modern disability activism in Germany. In 1992, the Federal Constitutional Court, Germany's highest court, upheld the ruling of the lower court.[26]

A related and equally well-publicized case, mentioned at the beginning of this chapter, was the 1997 judgment against a disabled student's request for an integrated education. For activists, the court's ruling made clear that the constitutional antidiscrimination mandate did not provide for integrated education as a basic civil right. The third prominent disability judgment emerging from the courts has become known as the "muzzle" case (*Maulkorb Urteil*). On January 8, 1998, the high court (*Oberlandesgericht*) of the state of Cologne ruled that the occupants of a group home for people with mental disabilities could be prohibited from having conversations in their garden during restricted hours. Their neighbor, a composer and piano teacher, sued because he felt "bothered and disgusted" by their "inarticulate sounds, screams, and moans." The problem was not the noise level, but the "inhumanity" (*Artfremdheit*) of their sounds. The court ruled that such sounds constitute an unacceptable burden even for open-minded people. Moreover, because the sounds could not be considered a "language," they did not fall under "the protection of the sphere of privacy" (Theben 1999). This ruling, in effect, denied one of the most fundamental rights of personal communication, language, to people with mental disabilities.

Activists publicized these cases to create both public and personal outrage, similar to the politicizing effects of the Aktion Sorgenkind media campaign. There was an acute recognition within the movement that it was time to move away from the "business as usual" politics of lobbying the government of the welfare state, which had separated the movement into disability-specific lobbying efforts. The legitimizing powers of the German welfare tradition on social movements underscore the importance for disability groups of being seen as part of the larger society, rather than as a "minority group" asking for special rights. In their search for a politicized and radicalized understanding of disability discrimination, German activists turned to the American model, which symbolized the move away from welfare and toward equality, rights, and empowerment. The U.S. rights model, however, is solidly built upon a civil rights tradition that has no counterpart in German politics. Thus, rather than asking for separate group status, the German movement asked for an expansion of the categories of political citizenship, which would equalize them with the rest of society. In that sense, German disability activism straddles a difficult divide of advocating for rights and empowerment without losing gains already established under the welfare model. The section that follows will show how the German interpretation of disability rights departs from its American inspiration.

MERGING RIGHTS AND WELFARE MODELS:
THE 2002 DISABILITY EQUALIZING LAW

After the media campaign, the logical next step on the activists' agenda was the passage of a new law, an "equalizing" law (*Gleichstellungsgesetz*) that would go beyond the constitutional antidiscrimination mandate.[27] A new Center-Left government prevailed in the September 1998 election, ending almost two decades of conservative rule. In their coalition contract, the Social Democrats and the Green Party had promised to expand the constitutional mandate to include a separate, equalizing law. The final round of the Aktion Grundgesetz media campaign included a set of billboards on busy intersections reminding drivers of this promise.

The Center-Left government held a Bundestag session on May 19, 2000, declaring that current German disability politics should center not on the care and protection of people with disabilities, but rather should focus on their "self-determined participation in social life and the removal of barriers toward their equal opportunities."[28] In October 2000 the government's disability liaison organized a conference in Düsseldorf, Equalizing Law *Now!*, to promote the first nationwide meeting among activists, politicians, and representatives of the business community, and through them to agree on the membership of the project groups assigned to draft the law. Although this meeting signaled political will for eventual passage of the law, the movement did not take any chances. Once again German disability activists turned to organizing and lobbying practices they had learned from their American peers, such as circulating flyers outlining "tips for successful lobbying" and instructing citizens to contact their elected representatives and push for disability rights. These flyers were direct translations from the U.S. disability movement literature.[29]

The movement also began using the yearly European Day of Protest for the Equality of Disabled People (May 5) to publicly remind the government of its promise to expand the constitutional mandate to include a separate, equalizing law. Another media campaign was launched, similar to the one in 1997 but on a much smaller scale. The campaign was headed by the "new and improved" Aktion Sorgenkind under its new name Aktion Mensch. The campaign placed large-scale ads in all the major newspapers and bought airtime on large TV networks featuring images from the previous year's protests. Individuals could request "action materials" from Aktion Mensch, consisting of postcards and stickers with demands for an equalizing law. The Operation's website featured suggestions for individuals to launch their own demonstrations and street theater. For example, a skit entitled "Have You Researched Today?" involved people with disabilities wearing white lab coats, examining doctors (dolls) in their hospital beds.[30] The purpose of this research, they would claim, was to examine how such questionable bioethics— which allowed physicians to treat patients as manifestations of disease rather than as real people—had entered the doctors' heads. The researchers would encourage bystanders to do their own examinations, assuring them that this was a good opportunity—after all, the subjects were physicians who wouldn't understand what was being done to them anyway.

Another skit was intended to draw attention to physical barriers in public buildings. It called for the use of lots of yellow construction tape to rope off the stairs leading to the main entrance to a marriage license bureau with a big sign saying that the entrance was blocked for fire safety reasons. All applicants had to use the wheelchair accessible backdoor. The Operation also had a grand unveiling of its "info bus" in front of Berlin's city hall. Painted on the side of the bus was a background of the eye-catching "campaign green," the slogan "A Promise Is a Promise" (*Versprochen ist Versprochen*), and a calendar counting down the number of days the government had left to keep its promise.

The German government finally made good on its promise and passed the Disability Equalizing Law (Behindertengleichstellungsgesetz, BGG) in 2002.[31] Because it had also promised to reform social welfare legislation (Sozialgesetzbuch IX)—which includes the bulk of all rehabilitation legislation—at the same time as the equalizing law, the justice ministry had asked the Forum of Disabled Jurists to prepare a legislative draft. This was an unprecedented move by the state to acknowledge the expertise of movement activists and to have a disability law drafted by people with disabilities themselves.[32] A central question for the new law concerned the definition of disability and who counts as disabled under the law. Forum members were determined to move German disability law away from medical definitions and insisted on using the World Health Organization's International Classification on Impairments, Disabilities and Handicaps. These classifications distinguish the medical condition of a disability ("impairment"), for example, a broken back after an accident, from the functional limitation this causes ("disability"), for example, the inability to walk, and the social barriers that limit that person's mobility ("handicap").[33]

DEFINITIONS OF DISABILITY

Accordingly, the 2001 Rehabilitation Law (Sozialgesetzbuch, SGB IX) and the 2002 Disability Equalizing Law (Behindertengleichstellungsgesetz, BGG) both define a person with a disability as someone whose "physical functions, mental capacities or mental health are highly likely to deviate for more than six months from the condition which is typical for the respective age and whose participation in the life of society is therefore restricted" (§ 3 BGG).[34] The definition outlines three requirements, which are related by cause: a deviation from the "typical" state of an individual of the same age (deviation principle), a limitation of function, and a limitation of a person's life chances. Although the German definition stresses the importance of social participation, it still reflects a biomedical understanding of disability by orienting disability as a deviation from the nondisabled norm (Geist, Petermann, and Widhammer 2002, 577).

German disability law also distinguishes between "disabled" and "severely disabled" individuals. People are considered severely disabled if their "degree of disability" (*Grad der Behinderung*) is at least 50 degrees (SGB IX). The degree of disability measures the "physical, mental, emotional and social" consequences of a functional limitation due to disability. It is measured in degrees, rather than percentages, and can vary between 20 and 100 (measured in units of 10). Once a degree of disability is medically certified to be 50 or more, a person is entitled to a disability ID card (*Schwerbehindertenausweis*) and the accompanying protective rights and benefits. The cause of a severe disability is irrelevant; German law removed the causality clause in 1974. Thus, a severe disability differs from a "simple" disability only in degree, not in kind. The term *severely disabled* is unique to the SGB IX (neither the Constitution nor the BGG contains the term) and is only binding for the SGB IX—almost all of the provisions pertaining to severely disabled individuals are located in the SGB IX. Primary among these provisions are employment rights and benefits outlined in the next section.

DISABILITY RIGHTS AND WELFARE

It is significant that the paradigm shift toward equality in German disability law occurred through welfare reform first. It was the enactment of the SGB in 2001 that marked the shift from material provisions to self-determination and equal participation in social and working life. Thus, it is welfare reform that first embodies the constitutional equality principle guarantee by focusing its legislative efforts on the removal of all obstacles hindering equal treatment (Schimanski 2008). In substance, the SGB IX combines the most important legal codifications in disability law (the employment provisions outlined in the Schwerbehindertengesetz and the more general welfare and rehabilitation provisions) into one central code. The new law was the first to combine rehabilitation and employment rights, thus disrupting the traditional separation between disability special needs—the traditional focus of rehabilitation law—and disability equal rights, as mandated by the paradigm shift. The law prioritizes the integration of people with disabilities into the regular labor market, rather than into workplaces specifically created for disabled workers. The law outlines three groups of benefits: medical benefits (Sections 17-21), income supports (Sections 44-54), and employment participation benefits (Sections 33-43). Until the passage of the 2001 SGB IX, the term "discrimination" did not exist in German law outside of the constitutional mandate in Article 3. Now, under Section 81.2, "Employers may not discriminate against their severely disabled employees on the basis of disability." This means that the employer cannot refrain from hiring the disabled applicant *because* of his or her disability. If the employer violates this obligation, the rejected disabled applicant has the right to sue for monetary damages, but cannot claim employment. However, the employer, bearing the burden of proof, can prevail by proving that the selection of a nondisabled candidate was based on performance and suitability, rather than disability (Section 81.2-1). It is important to note that, in line with the traditional emphasis on protecting the employment rights of severely disabled employees (*Schwerbehinderte*), the antidiscrimination mandate only covers employees with severe disabilities who are certified as such (i.e., those who can demonstrate a degree of disability of 50 or more).

Along with the disability antidiscrimination mandate, the law continues the tradition of a disability employment quota in Section 71.1. Every private and public employer with at least 20 employees must fill a disability quota of 5 percent. Noncompliance is penalized with an "equalization contribution" (*Ausgleichsabgabe*) or levy payable every month the reserved post remains unfilled (Section 77.1).[35] The levies are collected by the integration office and then used to fund vocational rehabilitation measures and employment benefits for severely disabled employees. Disabled employees maintain the special protection from dismissal they had received under the provisions of the previous Schwerbehindertengesetz and enjoy an additional week of paid vacation. When it comes to disability employment policies, disability quotas and equal employment measures are traditionally viewed as polar opposites. Quotas emphasize disability difference and special treatment and are considered a hallmark of the medical model, whereas antidiscrimination mandates emphasize equal treatment and opportunities under the rights model. The passage of SGB IX—along with the corresponding Equalizing Law—suggests that the two models could be combined, and that the integration of equality and antidiscrimination measures into welfare benefits law is not a contradiction in terms.

One year after the passage of the SGB, the Disability Equalizing Law (BGG) came into force on May 1, 2002. It was celebrated as a milestone in the disability movement's fight for equality (Degener 2006). The law's central focus is the social integration of people with disabilities made possible by equal access to transportation, buildings, and communication services. The law has two stated goals (BGG Section I): "freedom from barriers" (*Barriere-freiheit*) and antidiscrimination, both to ensure equal participation and social integration. Paragraph 8 mandates barrier-free access to public buildings, public spaces, and public transportation. Paragraphs 9, 10, and 11 focus on nonmaterial barriers, such as means of communication (which include the use of sign language and Braille), and alternate access to information. Sign language is now an officially recognized language with the accompanying right to interpreters (paragraph 6). In terms of the second goal, paragraph 7 establishes the antidiscrimination provisions covering the public sector. Private enterprises are not explicitly covered by the law—a separate law is required for the private sector—but the antidiscrimination mandate has had a significant impact on places of public accommodations such as restaurants and inns.[36] Disabled women are mentioned as needing special recognition and additional support for the double discrimination they face (paragraph 2), although the special quota for women with disabilities as envisioned by the Forum drafters did not make it into the final law.[37] The GBB (paragraph 13) also provides for a *Verbandsklagerecht* ("power of attorney for disability organizations and right of action"), which allows organizations, and not just individuals, to sue under the law. Disability employment discrimination is not covered in the BGG, as it is completely covered by the rehabilitation law SGB IX. Finally, the law adjusted 52 existing federal statutes to bring them in line with the new equality mandate.

The Disability Equalizing Law represents the first step toward integrating German disability law into a broader antidiscrimination framework while maintaining a commitment to welfare rights. The law does maintain aspects of the biomedical model in its definition of disability as a divergence from medical norms. Moreover, one must wonder about the wisdom of applying an identical definition of disability to two laws with different functions. Accordingly, legal scholar Theresia Degener posits that the definition of disability should vary according to the legal context and purpose of the law. She suggests that "while a social (welfare) law that provides disability related benefits might serve only a small group of severely disabled persons, a discrimination law must cover a much larger group and, thus, include a more comprehensive definition of disability" (Degener 2006). The employment discrimination provisions of SGB IX cover severely disabled employees only,

and neither the BGG nor the SGB IX cover persons with past, future, or im-
puted disabilities. Furthermore, neither family members nor associates of
disabled persons are included in these laws. In the end, she finds that both
the BGG of 2002 and the new Rehabilitation Law (SGB IX) of 2001 have a
ways to go to truly embrace the paradigm shift to a social model of disability.

THE DISABILITY RIGHTS MODEL IN GERMANY

The literature on rights mobilization in the United States shows that rights
discourse in the American setting can provide activists with "a compelling
normative language for identifying, interpreting, and challenging the unjust logic of discrimination" (McCann 1994, 48). Rights discourse allows activists to identify and criticize hierarchical relations and to recognize the
importance of collective action in the struggle for a good cause. In the case of
the disability rights movement, questions of definition are especially important, both in the movement-building stage (who counts as disabled and thus
is part of our movement?) and in the policy-making stage (who counts as
disabled and thus is entitled to benefits?). Rights discourse builds movements by encouraging a common identity and providing a vehicle for collective effort. On a personal level, activists can derive powerful personal and
political meaning from their involvement in struggles that will fundamentally change the way they think of themselves as, in this case, disabled, workers, and rights-bearing individuals.

The U.S. literature also points to the notion that the call for rights should
work differently in different stages of movement activism—from movement
building, to policy formation, to implementation. The German disability
rights movement is still in its initial phases of building movements and formulating policy demands. Thus, the rights mobilization strategies chosen,
the media campaign, and, to a lesser degree, the publicity over the Supreme
Court cases focused on the importance of public awareness and consciousness raising, both within the disability community and in the society at large.

It is significant that the German disability movement chose an advertis-
ing campaign to introduce notions of disability rights to the general population. They made the analogy of civil rights to a commercial product for which
marketers wage an advertisement campaign, thus leading to the question,
"How do we sell disability rights?" Do we sell them as products that will benefit everybody ("curb cuts also help the elderly and families with baby car-

riages") or do we sell them by asking others to "put yourselves in our shoes and then you'll understand" (the inaccessible bathroom example). This might transform the struggle for special disability rights into a struggle for universal rights to help create a more open and accessible society for everybody. It might turn a civil right into a marketable product, appealing to notions of fairness, justice, and community. Rather than advocating for "special" rights limited only to people with disabilities, which the disability quota clearly is, the media campaign framed disability rights as civil rights that concern everybody and become a measure of a society's political progress.

Rather than adopting a complete paradigm shift toward an ADA-based rights model, disability rights in Germany seek to blend the two approaches of welfare and rights. The ensuing legislative reform sought to combine what are considered binary opposites: employment quotas (special treatment) and antidiscrimination mandates (equal treatment). The law also differs from the ADA in that it contains affirmative action policies for women.[38] Equality and equal treatment resonate differently in Germany. Germany's constitutional equality article (Article 3) is instructional here. It not only spells out an antidiscrimination mandate for protected groups but also adds an affirmative command of equal opportunity (*Gleichberechtigungsgebot*) that extends to social realities (*gesellschaftliche Wirklichkeit*) (Article 3.3). Thus, the provision for equal treatment does not only lead to the removal of discriminatory practices that base advantages or disadvantages on prohibited categories. In the gender case, it seeks to promote equal opportunities for women and men in the future, securing equal earning opportunities for women. Moreover, the German understanding of equality includes a strong affirmative command for the state to promote positive rights in the sense of not only protecting against discrimination, but to be actively involved in making equal opportunities a reality. Accordingly, Article 3 (3) commands the state to "promote the actual implementation of equal rights for women and men and take steps to eliminate disadvantages that now exist."

Germany's broader understanding of equality goes beyond the right not to be discriminated against, which is a limitation of the American legal approach to equal treatment. It is the beginning of a more robust understanding of equal treatment that does not shed the recognition of different needs and that actively enlists the state in making equal treatment a reality. Inspired by a U.S. model of disability rights, German activists felt drawn to the political and strategic power of rights discourse, both as a way to shift the emphasis away from welfare and segregation and as a way to cement a rights model into a special needs approach. Rights function as a commodity that can buy freedom and equal access to participate in both the political process and the economy. Perhaps it is the relatively privileged status of disability rights activists vis-à-vis the German welfare state that allows them to embrace the rights model so uncritically. With their special needs safely secured, the demand for equal rights becomes politically and strategically possible. At the same time, German disability activists struggle with this relatively new emphasis on the law. They acknowledge common notions that "laws don't change reality," yet they still see them as a necessary part of organizing. They compare their struggle with that of women's suffrage in Germany, arguing that women would never have achieved the right to vote with mere appeals to goodwill and moral righteousness:

> We [from Netzwerk Artikel 3] aren't real fans of the law. We would be happy had there been a big bang after the constitutional amendment that would have changed the consciousness of the general population in regard to disability, and that would have caused the government to make some real political change to end discrimination. But history has shown, not only in our country, that progress always has to be fought for, and that laws do have the ability to change consciousness. We therefore believe that we need laws in the short run to be able to change attitudes in the long run. (Heiden 1996, 9)

CHAPTER FOUR

From Welfare to Rights: Disability Law and Activism in Japan

In my years in the United States I never thought of myself as a disabled person. But when I came back to Japan I suddenly felt that I was disabled. In Japan, different is bad. I'm telling people, "Different is not bad, it's just different. (Yasuhiro Yamazaki)

"DIFFERENT IS JUST DIFFERENT"

Yasuhiro "Mark" Yamazaki, wheelchair manufacturer and champion Paralympic swimmer, tells this story, which began during his high school exchange year in the United States when a fall out of a window left him suddenly paralyzed.[1] In his home country of Japan, he says, such an accident would have meant a three- to seven-year hospital stay, but in the United States he was out and about in just four months. "Will I be able to swim again?" was one of his first questions for his rehabilitation counselor. "Of course" was the answer, and he threw himself into his rehabilitation to relearn how to lead an active life. Mark, as he was called by his American friends, ended up completing both high school and college in the United States—only to return to Japan to experience full culture shock about what it meant to live as a person with a disability. "When I was in a wheelchair in the U.S., people would look at me and say, 'Oh, you're a college student.' Here, when I came back and was a businessman, people would look at me and say, 'Oh, you're a disabled person.' Always the disabled part came first."

Yamazaki's experience of culture shock echoes that of the German disability activists traveling to the United States and experiencing the power of the disability rights model. Yamazaki acquired his impairment at a time when U.S. attitudes and thinking about disability had experienced a paradigm shift toward independence and pride, fueled by a political movement that posited disability as a civil rights issue. Thus, Yamazaki got the kind of counseling that both gave him an honest assessment of his condition and encouraged him to lead the kind of life he wanted without letting his paralysis define him. Such counseling, he argues, was virtually nonexistent in Japan at the time. The type of counseling he received in the United States was heavily influenced by the independent living philosophy, which posits that the freedom to make choices and the ability to live independent lives in the community is a basic civil right. People with disabilities don't need "to be taken care of" but rather need to be empowered to make their own choices and manage their own lives. As described in chapter 2, the independent living philosophy grew out of a political movement that originated with Ed Roberts's time at the University of California at Berkeley, where he fought for admission in 1962 and, ten years later, founded the first Center for Independent Living. The independent living (IL) philosophy traveled to Japan with Ed Roberts as well. In 1981, as part of the UN's International Year of Disabled Persons, Ed Roberts and Judy Heumann traveled throughout Japan, giving presentations about the IL philosophy to an enthusiastic and receptive audience. Five years later, in 1986, Japan's first independent living center (ILC), Human Care, opened in Tokyo (S. Nakanishi 1997).

KEEPING UP WITH THE UNITED STATES AND EUROPE

This chapter will provide an overview of Japanese disability politics and the Japanese engagement with the disability rights model. To understand Japanese disability politics it is important to get a sense of the degree to which both Japanese activists and policy makers deploy national comparisons regarding the status of Japanese disability law. There is a keen sense that Japan tends to "lag behind" the West, not only in terms of policy but also in terms of general attitudes toward disability rights.[2] This often results in generalizations that exaggerate the power of the rights model, especially in the United States, which becomes a "dreamland" for people with disabilities, similar to the imagination of German activists described in the previous chapter. It also leads to a general sense of "we in Japan are behind the West and need to catch up." As I will argue in a later chapter, this international comparison is based on a deep sense of Japanese national identity as an

Asian country exemplifying Western values. For now, however, it is important to consider the power of comparison and the Japanese self-awareness
of their standing in the international community regarding their commitment to disability rights.

As an example of the Japanese tendency to look westward for inspiration,
consider a program aired on the Japanese public television station NHK (Japan Broadcasting Corporation) in December 2000, "My Life Supported by
Hi-Tech: New Disability Policies in the United States." It featured new work
opportunities using high-technology devices that would enable workers
with disabilities to rejoin the work force in fulfillment of the equal opportunity and integration mandates of the 1990 Americans with Disabilities Act.
The program offered high praise for such innovations, as well as for the ADA,
emphasizing three times that the ADA has led to a tripling of employment
figures for Americans with disabilities—a number that is not borne out by
U.S. labor market statistics. Accurate or not, the program caused a stir in the
Japanese disability movement.[3] Long enamored of the equal treatment
promise of the groundbreaking ADA, the Japanese movement rarely hears
such high praise by a government organ such as the NHK. Moreover, it con-
firmed the sentiment that Japan continues to lag far behind the West in disability policy and rehabilitation measures. Those in the movement still see
the ADA as a powerful tool against discrimination. Its promise of equal rights
and integration is considered an enviable alternative to the Japanese disability policy emphasis on special needs and segregation. In 2000, a *Japan Times*
newspaper article about discrimination against the blind, for example, cites
a blind activist describing the situation of blind people in Japan as "leading
sad lives. . . . There are no jobs for the blind except massage and acupunc-
ture." She believes the cause of this is because Japan does not have the equivalent of the ADA, which she believes has vastly improved the employment
situation of disabled Americans. In fact, she goes on to declare that "in
America there are 600 blind lawyers, but not one here."[4]

With American disability policy—or more exactly, the ADA—becoming
such common knowledge for the Japanese disability community, it is not
surprising that the NHK broadcast on employment technologies made a
deep impression. As in Germany, Japanese employment policy for disabled
workers focuses on employment quotas, in contrast to the integration and
reasonable accommodation mandate of the ADA. The fact that the NHK offered such high praise for American employment policy for people with disabilities was seen as a sign of hope for Japanese disability activists. If the ADA

approach has proven so successful, they wondered, perhaps the Japanese government will finally hear their calls for a policy change that would address notions of stigma and disability discrimination.

Japanese disability activists had harbored similar hopes two decades earlier, when the United Nations declared 1981 the International Year of Disabled Persons to mark the beginning of the International Decade of Disabled Persons (1983–92), both using the motto of "full participation and equality." The International Year of Disabled Persons came at a time when people with disabilities all over the world were starting to form political and social movements to draw attention to the ways societies stigmatize embodied difference and discriminate against people with mental and physical disabilities. It pointed to the shift in international thinking about disability policy away from welfare and medicine and toward independent living and equal rights. The UN motto symbolized this shift by emphasizing the importance of equal opportunity, social integration, independent living, and government responsibility to combat discrimination against people with disabilities.

The UN Decade led to some legal reforms in Japanese disability law, which I will outline in this chapter, but it did not result in the kinds of sweeping reforms activists had hoped for. When the U.S. Congress passed the Americans with Disabilities Act in 1990, the world's first comprehensive antidiscrimination legislation, another ray of hope broke through. Japanese disability activists came to see the ADA as a shining symbol of the power of the law to ensure equal treatment and social justice. The ADA example prompted conversations about the meaning of the antidiscrimination principle in Japanese law and inspired Japanese activists to move legal reform to the next level—toward the enactment of a "Japan Disabilities Act." Twenty-some years after the passage of the ADA, this might actually become a reality, but not without another push from the international sphere: Japan enthusiastically signed the UN Convention on the Rights of Persons with Disabilities in 2006 and promised to ratify the treaty by 2013.[5] With ratification the Japanese Diet must pass some form of disability antidiscrimination law to align Japanese law with the mandates of the Convention. This means that Japanese reformers are grappling anew with the promise of equal treatment and antidiscrimination—something I explore in more detail in the book's final chapter. This chapter will focus on the initial process of importing a disability rights model, inspired by the American example and strengthened by Japan's adoption of UN human rights instruments.

MOBILIZING DISABILITY RIGHTS IN JAPAN

This chapter follows the journey of the disability rights model to Japan and asks: What are the promises and challenges of transplanting notions of rights, equality, and independence into a Japanese setting? To what degree can Japan incorporate U.S.-inspired ideas of independent living, autonomy, and disability rights consciousness into a country that values family interdependence and eschews using the law as a tool for social change? In charting Japan's journey from welfare to rights this chapter identifies two central waves of reform, both inspired and strengthened by international developments. The first is the UN's International Year and Decade of Disabled Persons starting in 1981, followed by the passage of the 1990 Americans with Disabilities Act. These two developments inspired a new generation of Japanese disability activists to radically rethink and reframe the basis of their activism. They also culminated in Japan's enthusiastic participation in the 2006 UN Convention on the Rights of Persons with Disabilities, which will eventually lead Japan on the path toward disability antidiscrimination legislation.

This chapter argues that the ADA and the UN human rights instruments (specifically the International Decade of Disabled Persons) provided a powerful template for the Japanese disability movement's activism for political and legal reform. They inspired a new generation of Japanese activists to replace traditional organizing tools with rights talk, rights consciousness, and disability pride. The new emphasis on rights and discrimination allows Japanese disability activists to frame their political demands as a human rights issue, using Western terminology of self-determination, independent living, and advocacy that remains foreign to the Japanese political and cultural context. This use of such imports is strategic: it frames disability rights as a progressive and Western project that Japan must embrace to be considered truly international (*kokusaika*). At the same time, transplanting a rights model that is deeply rooted in American civil rights approaches poses unique challenges to Japanese disability activists. The assertion of rights and independence is considered fundamentally incompatible with Japanese political, legal, and social norms. Legal remedies traditionally hold less power for Japanese social movements than they do for their American counterparts. Disability laws and policies reflect specific historical, legal, and cultural assumptions about the meaning of disability, equality, and the law as a tool for social change. The American-inspired disability rights model provides tremendous inspiration for Japanese activists but poses tremendous challenges when they seek to implement the model into law and policy.

JAPANESE DISABILITY POLICY:
SPECIAL NEEDS OVER EQUAL RIGHTS

The Japanese Constitution famously guarantees the "right to maintain the minimum standards of wholesome and cultured living" and spells out the government's duty to provide social welfare (Article 25). This guarantee is a product of the American New Deal reformers assigned to the Allied Occupation's government division charged with rewriting the Japanese Constitution and establishing democratic norms (Ward and Sakamoto 1987). While the idea of a positive right to a decent standard of living didn't take hold in the United States, it certainly became a central part of the Japanese postwar understanding of government obligations and modern citizenship. A minimum standard of living is widely considered a fundamental entitlement, resulting in the establishment of an extensive welfare and rehabilitation system that rapidly became a model for other Asian countries (Hayashi and Okuhira 2008). Article 25 is frequently cited by disability activists as the inspiration for seeking disability benefits as a public benefit that should be funded by tax revenues, rather than as a private or family matter funded through social insurance.

Japanese law defines a person with a disability as someone "whose daily life or life in society is substantially limited over the long term due to a physical disability, mental retardation, or mental disability" (*Shōgaisha kihonhō*, the Disabled Peoples' Fundamental Law of 1993, Article 1 (2)).[6] This definition closely follows the first prong of the disability definition of the ADA, which states that "a disability is a physical or mental impairment that substantially limits one or more of the major life activities of such individual." Significantly, the Japanese definition ignores the other two prongs of the ADA's definition, which gesture to the fact that disability discrimination also occurs when people have "a record of such an impairment" or when they are merely "being regarded as having such an impairment." Subsequently, the official number of Japanese who qualify as disabled under the law is seven million people or 6 percent of the total population, which is low in comparison to the United States or European Union countries. The Prime Minister's Office publishes yearly census surveys in a white paper on disability (*shōgaisha hakushō*). In 1998 it counted a total of 7.24 million disabled Japanese, of which 3.66 million have a physical disability (*shintai shōgai*), 547,000 have an intellectual disability (*chiteki shōgai*),[7] and 3.3 million have a psychiatric disability (*seishin shōgai*) (Shōgaisha Hakusho 2005). This is considered to be a low percentage of the general population in comparison to other countries (10 percent in Germany and the United Kingdom, over 30 percent in Sweden), mainly because Japanese law strictly limits the types of disabilities it recognizes. The types of disabilities recognized by law are itemized by type and severity (on a grade level from one to six) on a closed list attached to the legal text. Most significantly absent from the list are AIDS or HIV infection, alcohol or chemical dependency, epilepsy, rheumatism, and learning disabilities.[8] Furthermore, official surveys include only those people carrying a disability handbook or certification card (*shōgaisha techō*), which lists the name, type, and severity of the individual's disability. Carrying this card is not a requirement, but it is the only way to receive a host of welfare and tax benefits. These include reductions in income tax and exemption from other taxes, subsidies for electronic or mechanical aids, discounts on postage, public transportation, public housing, and public assistance, among others. Many disability activists see this card as reproducing the stigma associated with having a disability, and some refuse to carry one for that reason, but many cannot afford to forfeit the benefits associated with it. Students attending special schools are encouraged to apply for a handbook, as are job seekers at their local public employment security office because only handbook owners can officially claim to be disabled and thus count for a company's legal employment quota.

The stigma associated with having a disability is based on Japanese cultural beliefs about *kegare*, or impurity (Iwakuma 2000). People with disabilities (and by extension, their families) were considered polluted and kept out of public view. A notable exception here is the historical role of blind people as healers, massage therapists, and singers (Fritsch 1996). While the social role of disabled Japanese has changed considerably, aspects of stigma and shame persist. People with visible disabilities are often not invited to participate in auspicious occasions, such as weddings or New Year's Day ceremonies out of fear that their *kegare* might spoil the good fortune of the married couple or the new year. Another example is the use of accessible toilets. While there is a growing number of accessible public toilets in Japan's largest cities, many of them have signs declaring them "for the disabled only," and they are universally avoided by able-bodied users.[9] In fact, many of them are not even located in the same bathroom area, so it is rare to see disabled and nondisabled people waiting in line for the bathroom together.

A related cultural norm surrounding disability is protectiveness. Japanese law has traditionally designated families as official protectors of their disabled family members, both in taking care of their needs and protecting society from their potential harm. This sense of community protectiveness is now considered patronizing and infantilizing by many disability activists. While many train stations are now declared "barrier free" (more about this at the end of this chapter), it is still a common experience for wheelchair users to have to be carried up and down several flights of stairs by train station attendants. Travelers who use wheelchairs often cannot rely on elevators, and even when elevators are present they are used by all travelers not wishing to navigate stairs and generate long wait periods (Stevens 2007). Station attendants will direct wheelchair travelers to designated train compartments and then phone the next station attendant to help make the next transfer. "Who will learn how to negotiate the train system this way?" activists complain. "We are not allowed to make mistakes and then learn from them. They treat us like children."[10] The sense of being in a childlike position of dependence is echoed in Atsuko Kuwana's experience of her "homecoming stress" (*satogaeri sutoresu*). In an essay of the same title, Kuwana, who now lives in the United States, tells of her cultural readjustment after returning to Japan as a person with a disability who needs to be "protected by the able-bodied" (Kuwana 1997). When she missed her regular train one evening to attend an office party, for example, the station attendants were so concerned about her that they phoned her office and her transfer station to inquire about her whereabouts. Kuwana likens this to the treatment of a "missing child" at a station who needs to be protected and can't be expected to make independent choices (Kuwana 1997, 118). Such attitudes of benevolent paternalism and segregation are characteristic of Japan's postwar disability policy. However, they also stem from a cultural norm of protecting the disabled. The sense of protecting the community is now considered insulting, while the sense of needing protection is considered patronizing and infantilizing by many disability activists, for example in the disability employment and education systems.

JAPANESE DISABILITY EMPLOYMENT POLICY

The Japanese government has instituted a sophisticated network of rehabilitation and welfare benefits to serve people with disabilities. Its vocational rehabilitation system is internationally recognized for the way it operates vocational training and placement services at the public employment security offices (Ison 1992, 4). Japan is now widely considered a leader in vocational rehabilitation in Asia and provides much financial support and research aid for the establishment of similar systems throughout the region.[11] Following the Recommendation on Vocational Rehabilitation made by the International Labor Organization (ILO) in 1955, which became the internationally recognized guideline for vocational rehabilitation and spurred appropriate legislation in most member nations, a coalition of disability groups led by the Japanese Society of Disabled People for Rehabilitation (Nihon Shōgaisha Rehabilitation Kyōkai), one of the first-generation disability organizations formed by disabled war veterans, demanded that the Japanese government take concrete action.

As a result, in 1960 the Physically Disabled People's Employment Promotion Law (Shintai Shōgaisha Kōyō Sokushinhō) was enacted as the first employment law for people with disabilities, changing the status of their assistance from social welfare to improving their employment opportunities. The law first instituted an employment quota system of 1.3 percent for private companies and 1.6 percent for government organizations, a grant program, and extensive vocational training and placement services at the public employment security offices. The quota remained a moral obligation for employers, rather than a legal requirement. Despite the lack of enforcement, however, the employment rate of persons with physical disabilities in private enterprises increased from 0.78 percent in 1961 to 1.10 percent in 1965 and then to 1.25 percent in 1970. By 1976 the target rate was actually surpassed by 0.6 percent, to 1.36 percent (Matsui 1994, 368). This increase, however, cannot be credited to the law but to Japan's high economic growth in the 1960s and early 1970s. This period offered employment opportunities for people with light disabilities, especially in small or medium-sized companies that had difficulties recruiting nondisabled workers from the labor market (Matsui 1994, 368).

All this changed with the 1973 oil shock, which severely hampered the Japanese economy. At the same time, government surveys were showing an increasing number of elderly people, elderly disabled people, and people with severe disabilities. The welfare approach was no longer enough. People with disabilities had to be able to support themselves, and in 1976 the law was revised to make the employment quota a legal requirement. The quota itself was raised to 1.5 percent (1.9 percent for government bodies), and severely disabled persons counted double under the quota. The 1976 Revision also requested that employers report to their local public employment security office the number of physically disabled persons that they employed. Employers not complying with the quota would have to draw up a plan for such employment and would be "urged" to follow it. Such plans might require employers to adapt existing facilities, build new facilities, or provide extra supervision and training. The costs that this might entail were to be covered by grants, which, in turn, were to be provided by the monthly levies collected from employers who did not comply with the employment quota. Noncompliance with these plans would place companies on a list published yearly by the Labor Ministry, and they could face additional fines of up to ¥200,000. The 1976 Revision also established the National Association for the Employment of the Physically Handicapped (Nihon Shintai Shōgaisha Sokushin Kyōkai) to oversee and administer the levies and grants system. The Association was also mandated to organize educational programs to raise public awareness, offer counseling to management, and operate 55 vocational rehabilitation centers around the country.

The UN mandate for full participation and equality and the 1983 ILO Convention Concerning Vocational Rehabilitation and Employment of Disabled Persons, which was geared primarily to expand employment opportunity, forced Japan to revise its employment law once more in 1988. The main focus of this revision was the inclusion of people with mental disabilities. The quota was raised again, to 1.6 percent for private enterprises and 2.0 percent for public enterprises, but most important both the quota and the levy systems could now also be applied to people with mental disabilities without, however, making their employment a legal obligation (Nihon Shōgaisha Sokushin Kyōkai 1998, 12). This happened ten years later, on July 1, 1998, when the quota was raised one more time to 1.8 percent (private enterprises) and 2.1 percent (public/government affiliated organizations). Since then the quota has been raised one more time to its current level (as of 2013) of 2.0 percent for private enterprises. The Japanese government changes the quota system every five years by considering the relationship between the total number of employees and the total number of (registered) persons with disabilities. Table 2 summarizes the evolution of the Japanese employment quota for private companies.

Companies that fall short of the employment quota are levied ¥50,000 (approximately $500) per employee per month, but for now only companies with 300 or more employees are actually levied. However, awards are given to every employer exceeding the quota. Companies with 300 employees or less are awarded ¥27,000 per person per month that they exceed the quota, and companies with 300 or more are awarded ¥21,000 ($337). The money levied is pooled into a rehabilitation foundation that is chiefly used to provide employment subsidies and grant aid to companies striving to achieve the quota. The money also funds the vast system of rehabilitation centers headed by the National Institute for Vocational Rehabilitation (Shōgaisha Shokugyō Sōgō Centā). The Institute conducts surveys and research, trains rehabilitation counselors, collects and distributes information concerning the employment and rehabilitation process of people with disabilities, and gives advice and technical assistance to employers. In that sense, there is wide consensus that the levy should not be considered a "fine" but rather a cost-sharing tool that encourages the labor force participation of workers with disabilities (Tokoro 2013). It allows companies actively working to hire disabled workers to offset the potential costs of arranging workplaces—what are considered reasonable accommodations in the American context. Another enforcement measure is public humiliation: companies that continue to fall short of the quota have their names publicly listed by local labor bureaus. The levy-grant system fills the dual purpose of promoting disability employment and of recognizing and equalizing the potential financial burden borne by firms for employing persons with disabilities.

EFFECTIVENESS OF THE QUOTA SYSTEM

The employment rate of workers with disabilities has been growing steadily since the quota was first introduced in 1976, but it still falls short of the legally required rate. Table 3 shows the gradual rise of the employment rate for disabled workers along with the rise of the legally mandated employment rate. In 2012, only 47 percent of all private companies covered by the employment quota were in compliance, which means that approximately half of all enter-

TABLE 2. Evolution of the Japanese Employment Quota

Year	Quota	Ratio of Disabled/ Nondisabled Employee
1976–85	1.5%	1/67
1986–97	1.6%	1/63
1998–2013	1.8%	1/56
2013–	2.0%	1/50

prises do not reach the quota. Company size clearly matters in compliance with the quota system: generally, the larger the company, the higher the actual employment rate. A 2012 Ministry of Health, Labor and Welfare survey shows that, when it comes to quota compliance, small and medium-sized companies lag the furthest behind. The actual employment rate is at the lowest level in companies employing 56 to 99 employees (1.42 percent).[12] Large companies with over 300 employees (to whom the levy system applies) have developed a way to comply with the quota by establishing special "barrier-free" subsidiary companies (*tokurei kogaisha*) that function as separate units from the parent company. These separate companies primarily hire people with disabilities who then count toward the parent company's employment quota.[13] This de facto resegregation into separate workplaces falls short of the UN integration mandate, but it is seen by many companies as the ideal way to comply with the law without having to alter workplace norms. The Japanese government also promotes the *tokurei kogaisha* system as the preferred means to boost the employment of people with disabilities.

Despite the quota system, then, which was designed to integrate people with disabilities into regular companies, the Japanese workplace remains highly segregated. Sheltered workshops remain a vital source of employment for Japanese people with disabilities. The majority of these are private community workshops that exist as extralegal facilities outside of the authorized workshops by the Ministry of Health, Labor and Welfare. The first workshops started sporadically in the 1950s, focused primarily on people with mental disabilities whose employment needs were ignored by the law, but by the late 1960s they had spread as an organized, nationwide movement. By the 1990s, there were approximately 4,000 community-based workshops—four times the number run by the Ministry of Health, Labor and Welfare (Fujii 1994, 146), and by 2004 the number had risen to over 6,000 private workshops (in comparison to 2,400 government-run workshops) (Matsui 2008). The Japanese government has officially acknowledged that the increase in commu-

TABLE 3. Employment Rates

Year	Legal Employment Rate	Actual Employment Rate
1977	1.5%	1.09%
1982	1.5%	1.2%
1996	1.6%	1.47%
2012	1.8%	1.69%

nity workshops is due to the shortage and uneven distribution of government-run facilities, but it effectively has come to rely on this private network to provide essential services for people with disabilities.[14] With only 1 percent of persons with disabilities finding employment in the open labor market annually, sheltered workshops have become de facto places of employment rather than places of training and vocational rehabilitation as envisioned by law. People working in sheltered workshops typically work without employment contracts, get paid less than one-tenth of the minimum wage, and are not protected by labor laws. The Japanese government has announced its intentions to reorganize these facilities back into the time-limited training facilities they were originally intended as, and to shift the emphasis back to placement into the open labor market (Matsui 2008).

Disability activists and legal scholars vigorously debate the future of the Japanese employment quota. There is widespread agreement that the Japanese disability employment system remains segregated and is in need of reform, but the question remains about the degree to which the employment quota itself can be reconciled with notions of equality and integration. While quotas are typically seen as fundamentally incompatible with equal treatment in the Western legal tradition, Japanese scholars have sought ways to rethink this dichotomy and theorize the Japanese employment quota as part of a larger commitment to equal opportunities. There are normative arguments based on political philosophy that call for radical types of positive action to balance out able-bodied advantages (Hoshika 2012). Other scholars make more pragmatic arguments, pointing to Japan's leadership role in Asia and to the consequences of abolishing the employment quota, which would lead to unacceptable levels of unemployment, with a corresponding increase in welfare payments.[15] They see the quota system as a tax subsidy, in which the levy works as a tax against underemployment. Companies that fail to employ workers with disabilities pay a fine, which in turn funds the adjustment allowance as a kind of subsidy given to employers who exceed the quota. In theory, both the levy and the adjustment allowance should reduce the marginal costs of employing workers with disabilities and provide enough financial incentives for employers to overcome whatever levels of prejudice and stereotypes prevent them from hiring workers with disabilities (Kawashima and Matsui 2011). The Japanese quota system, similar to its German equivalent discussed in the previous chapter, has become an integral part of the welfare system that funds the vast network of rehabilitation facilities and services. The question remains to what degree this system is sustainable in light of the international focus on equality and inclusion that increasingly views quotas as incompatible with the principle of equal employment opportunities. Japanese policy makers are now debating the impact of the antidiscrimination mandate of the 2006 UN Convention on the Rights of Persons with Disabilities —discussed in the second part of this chapter—and the future of the Japanese quota system. The section that follows gives an overview of the Japanese disability education system and the attempts, similar to those in Germany, to expand educational access and equal treatment for students with disabilities in a highly segregated system.

JAPANESE EDUCATION POLICY FOR STUDENTS WITH DISABILITIES

The Japanese education system for students with disabilities is highly segregated. The vast majority of students with disabilities are educated in special education schools (*yōgōgakkō* or *tokushugakkō*). Parents and teachers fought a long and ultimately successful struggle for basic education rights in the postwar period when the 1947 Education Law (*kyōiku kihonhō*) failed to provide state support for the establishment of special education. A coalition consisting of the newly founded Association of Teachers at Schools for the Deaf, along with other special education teachers and parents organizations, lobbied the Ministry of Education to establish a national network of special education schools. The fiscal foundation for the nation's special education system, however, did not occur until 1956 with the Special Education School Establishment Law (*kōritsu yōgogakkō seibi tokubetsu sochihō*), which also established compulsory education (until junior high school) for all children with physical disabilities. Only blind or deaf children were subject to compulsory education before 1956 due to the relatively early establishment of blind or deaf schools in the 1870s. Special education for children with mental disabilities did not become compulsory until 1979 (Mogi 1992, 442).

The Japanese special education system is fiscally and politically separate from the "regular" education system.[16] There are three types of segregated schools: schools for the blind (*mōgakkō*), schools for the Deaf (*rōgakkō*), and schools for students with developmental disabilities, physical disabilities, and health impairments (*yōgakkō*). Most children with disabilities will attend one of these schools in their prefecture, unless their disability qualifies them to attend their local public school's special education class (*tokushu gakkyū*). In the late 1990s another reform was enacted: the resource room (*tsukyu*) in regular schools. This came about because an increasing number of children had managed to enter regular schools as "exceptions." Besides the special education classes that had been established in a select number of regular schools, the resource rooms now provided additional space to teach children with disabilities in the regular schools. These classes are also subdivided by disability category: vision impaired, hard of hearing, physically disabled, mentally disabled, ill and weak, behavior impairment, and speech impairment. They are held in separate classrooms and are established by the individual school based on need and teacher availability. Since Japanese compulsory education does not include high school, special education classes tend not to exist in most high schools.[17] This means that most children with disabilities will at some point in their education attend a segregated special school, or spend the majority of their educational experience in a separate classroom.

The very early separation between a disabled and a nondisabled world has become a source of intense criticism by parents of disabled children who might receive a pedagogically sound and disability-appropriate education in special schools but in the process remain segregated from the children of their neighborhoods. Parents argue that the interaction between disabled and nondisabled students is a basic requirement for future success in the workplace, which relies heavily on interpersonal relations and adherence to social norms. Parental activism today is mostly focused on the right to access high school education, something that is often denied to students who are academically qualified but whose inability to fulfill physical education requirements or access school grounds is often used as a reason not to admit them. A typical case involved a student with muscular dystrophy who scored in the upper 10 percent on the entrance examination of Agagasaki Public High School. The school principal refused to enroll him for not being able to fulfill the gym requirement and because he might endanger himself using a wheelchair on school property. The case went to court in 1991, and the student was admitted to the school (Mogi 1992, 443).

Until 2007 Japanese law did not recognize learning disabilities as official disabilities. This means that children with learning disabilities would receive neither special attention nor an appropriate education in Japan's public school system. Parents of children with learning disabilities united in 1990 to form the National Parents' Association of Children with Learning Disabilities to lobby for the inclusion of the category. Other disabilities that had been excluded until the 2007 reform were attention deficit hyperactivity disorder and autism. Children would struggle in regular classrooms, which were often comprised of 40-some students and a single teacher, and they were generally expected to perform along their nondisabled peers. There is a strong ethos of equal treatment in the Japanese classroom that values uniform expectations and resists the recognition of special needs. Students with disabilities—even those that are officially recognized—would have to perform in class on an equal basis, and they will not be provided with personal assistance or special attention from teachers. It is still common procedure for a classroom teacher to accept a child with a disability only if the mother or another family member will promise to serve as a full-time personal assistant.[18]

A compelling example is Ototake Hirotada's experience attending mainstream schools, captured in his best-selling autobiography *Gotai Fumanzoku*.[19] Born without his four limbs, Ototake would have been a natural candidate for a *yōgogakkō*, but his parents insisted he be mainstreamed. After being turned away from countless public and private schools with the explanation that there were special schools for "children like theirs," Ototake's parents finally had to lobby the local board of education, which controls the admission process (Ototake 1998, 91). They brought their son to the meeting to demonstrate how he had learned to feed himself and to write by holding a pencil between his shoulder and his cheek. Finally, after demanding that a caretaker (his mother, naturally) would be with him at all times, the board of education finally approved his attendance at a regular elementary school. "My own parents," Ototake writes, "felt that getting me into elementary school was more difficult than penetrating a fortress" (Ototake 1998, 18).

Once mainstreamed, Ototake was treated like all other students with no consideration for his disability. He spent weeks learning to jump rope for his gym class requirement and was not excused from his fourth-grade class excursion up a mountain. He, too, was going to "hike" Mount Kōbō, but only with the help of his classmates who all insisted that it would be "unfair" to let him use his disability as an excuse to get out of a strenuous hike. Thus, his classmates alternately pushed or pulled his heavy wheelchair up the mountain (Ototake 1998, 50). Ototake himself does not criticize or even regret his complete lack of accommodations: to the contrary, he celebrates his teachers' and classmates' refusal to recognize his disability difference as a victory for the Japanese education system's equal treatment doctrine: every child works under the same rules and expectations for success, even if some will have to work harder to master the curriculum (Heyer 2008, 48). Ototake excelled in school and was universally liked by his classmates, but he still had to work hard to offset his poor grades in physical education since no allowance was made for his disability.

Not all Japanese parents pursue their children's mainstreaming as relentlessly as Ototake's did. There is considerable parental activism focused on what they consider more pragmatic goals of working within the segregated school system, which they see as the strongest advocate for their children's educational needs, and, perhaps more important, for job placement. For example, while not officially mandated, it is considered a matter of honor among special education teachers to find some form of employment for every one of their students. These teachers will develop extensive personal networks, often on their own time, with local firms, employers, and sheltered workshops, to guarantee their students' economic future.

The debates on how best to accommodate a child's disability-related educational needs are framed by Japan's postwar commitment to an educational meritocracy, which promises equal educational opportunity through a single-track system that provides remarkably similar classes to every child in the nation. Japanese schools implement a national curriculum emphasizing the importance of every student mastering the same curriculum regardless of educational abilities and talent. Tremendous attention is paid especially in the lower grades to students assisting one another in mastering this curriculum, with the underlying expectation that eventually everybody can succeed without the need for specialized instruction. Once inside this system, students like Ototake are afforded equal chances as long as students and their families are willing and able to personally provide the accommodations they need. Ototake takes great pride in his accomplishments—he graduated in political economy from Waseda, one of Japan's elite universities, and became a successful sports journalist—but he does not fundamentally challenge the homogeneous system, asking only that the system be broadened to allow more disabled students to participate (Ototake 1998, 72) Ototake has recently begun teaching in an elementary school, and it will be interesting to see to what degree he will practice the spirit of equal treatment he received as a student.

In 2007 the Japanese government amended its School Education Law to include a new special education system entitled Special Support Education (*tokubetsu shien kyoiku*). The Ministry of Education cited a commitment to the normalization principle in promising "equal opportunity for children with disabilities . . . by providing individualized educational supports . . . to promote their autonomy and participation in all aspects of society" (Goto 2008). The idea was to recognize that special education needed to serve students' individual needs, rather than think about special education as being provided only by special schools that are segregated by disability type. With this individualization also came the official recognition of learning disabilities, attention deficit hyperactivity disorder, and "high-functioning autism" (Goto 2008, 3). Many parents' groups view this as the first step toward full inclusion, which is guaranteed by Article 24 of the UN Convention that Japan has signed but not yet ratified. They welcome the official recognition of students with disabilities that require academic interventions, but the provision of educational accommodations is not yet mandated by law. Moreover, the 2007 reform maintains the segregated school system, but its future is being questioned as the Japanese government works toward ratification of the Convention.

JAPANESE DISABILITY ACTIVISM

The Japanese disability employment and education systems exemplify the persistence of disability-based segregation: people with disabilities lead protected but separate lives. It is not surprising, then, that the Japanese disability rights movement is enamored with (what they consider) the successful American example of integration, equal rights, and the general visibility of people with disabilities in public life. This section will outline the profound impact of two distinct moments in international disability politics: the UN's International Decade of Disabled Persons (1983–92) and the passage of the Americans with Disabilities Act in 1990. I argue that the Japanese disability movement split into two generations in response to these international developments: a "first generation" of activists who lobbied for extending benefits within a segregated system, and a "second generation" of activists who have fundamentally challenged segregation and look toward implementing U.S.-inspired disability rights.

The traditional, or "first generation" of disability organizations consisted primarily of national associations of physical and psychiatric therapists and social workers that emerged in the immediate postwar period and responded primarily to the medical needs of their patients and clients. The country's large network of physical and occupational rehabilitation centers was founded and operated by these groups. They successfully organized them-selves around the assertion of "special needs," which resulted in welfare pol-icies based on well-developed but still segregated facilities. Organizations such as the Japan Federation of the Deaf (Nihon Rōa Renmei), the Japan Fed-eration of the Blind (Nihon Mōjinkai Rengō), the National Federation of Families with Mentally Ill People (Zenkoku Seishin Shōgaisha Kazoku Kai Rengokai; Zenkaren), and the Japan Federation of Disabled Peoples Associa-tion (Nihon Shintai Shōgaisha Dantai Rengōkai; Nisshinren), all founded during the immediate postwar period, focused their activities on gaining services and protective legislation by lobbying the appropriate ministries. Nisshinren especially became a powerful political force in the postwar pe-riod. Founded in 1958 by disabled war veterans, Nisshinren has successfully lobbied the labor and welfare ministries and was instrumental in passing the 1960 Employment Law. Nisshinren is known in activist circles as a politically conservative organization, characterized by *amakudari* (networking and po-litical favoritism), that will not push government doctrine beyond politi-cally comfortable limits.[20]

POLITICAL ACTIVISM IN THE 1960S AND 1970S

This national network of disability organizations can be credited with laying the foundation of the rehabilitation and welfare institutions, but it fell short of recognizing the very real needs of families struggling to choose between caring for their disabled children at home or having them institutionalized. As I described earlier, care for disabled family members was traditionally seen as a private responsibility, which included shielding the person from the stigma and shame associated with disability, and even more so when the per-son had a mental illness. Parents who did not want to send their children to institutions were not supported in their efforts to take care of their children's special needs at home. They needed to be trained in the daily medical needs of their children, find appropriate schooling, and, perhaps most important, assure them a future occupation and community that would support them as the parents themselves grew older. In response to these needs parents formed local support groups that grew into a nationwide network. These groups are largely responsible for the large network of community sheltered workshops.

Parental activism was born out of the direct needs of their children but also reflected the political activism of other movements of the time, primarily that of the Buraku movement, the student movement, and the women's movement. The Buraku Liberation League framed its activism in terms of discrimination and human rights in fighting against their status as outcasts during the feudal period, which had left a social stigma and social status discrimination to this day. Parents' groups drew their own parallels to the stigma attached to their disabled children, and as a result the Kansai Region, where the Buraku movement was strongest, holds the largest number of children attending regular school in the country (Roeder 2001, 103). Activists in the student movement became important allies as well, providing personal assistance to the first generation of disabled activists struggling to leave the institutions to live on their own.

A national association of people with cerebral palsy, Aoi Shiba no Kai (Green Grass Club), assumed a leading role in Japan's political disability movement during that time. Children with cerebral palsy were typically confined to their homes, but the founding members of Aoi Shiba came from affluent families that could afford to send their children to residential rehabilitation facilities. A lucky few even got to attend college. Once they graduated, however, they faced an increasingly hostile world that was utterly unprepared for their disability. Even established disability organizations did not welcome them (Hayashi and Okuhira 2001, 860). They founded Aoi Shiba as a social club but soon began to formulate policy platforms that called for permanent residential facilities for people with cerebral palsy, something that the movement today vehemently rejects, but that represented the only form of freedom imaginable for group members at that time. Aoi Shiba's 1961 meeting with representatives of the Ministry of Health and Welfare, in which they successfully lobbied for the disability welfare pension, is still considered a milestone in Japanese disability history.

The group reached national prominence in 1970 during the public debate over an infanticide: a woman had killed her two-year-old disabled child as a form of "mercy killing." Such infanticides were reported in the media almost every year, with much sympathy for the mother's difficult decision to "end her child's misery." Parents' groups would sign petitions supporting the mother and blaming her decision on the lack of adequate facilities. In a politically bold move, Aoi Shiba publicly criticized such parents' movements and the general sympathy for the mother. It protested the lack of sympathy for the disabled child and drew attention to what it termed a "eugenic ideology of an able-bodied society" (Tateiwa 1990). The group successfully petitioned the prosecution to file murder charges, while the woman's neighbors and friends petitioned for leniency. The infanticide case provided the impetus for Aoi Shiba's subsequent radical activism. The group would attend rallies, demonstrations, and sit-ins, and engage in civil disobedience activities such as occupying as many as 78 city buses in Kawasaki after the bus company had refused to transport wheelchair passengers.[21] Aoi Shiba sees its activism is a form of "aggressive self-assertion" against common notions that people with cerebral palsy constitute "an existence which should not exist." They reject the "love and justice" of the able-bodied society, which they interpret as pity and oppression, and see themselves not as problem-solvers, which only leads to easy solutions, but as those exposing the problems (Tateiwa 1990, 179; Nagase 1995). This was a far cry from the helpless, passive, and compliant behavior commonly expected of people with disabilities.

Aoi Shiba's turn to aggressive activism has alienated others in the disability community. When parents killed their disabled children the group focused their criticism on the mothers (rather than the fathers or other family members) and waved signs imploring, "Mothers, don't kill." While deploring any form of infanticide of disabled children, many women in the movement began to question Aoi Shiba's lack of awareness of the social stigma women bear once they give birth to a disabled child (Hayashi and Okuhira 2001, 862). A Japanese woman's social role is traditionally tied to producing healthy (and preferably male) children for her husband's family, and once she fails that endeavor by having a disabled child, she faces shame and alienation. An awareness of the ways disability and sex discrimination intersect would have allowed Aoi Shiba to not only denounce infanticide but also the oppression of mothers with disabled children.

Another form of internal strife concerned Aoi Shiba's relationship with allies on the left and in the student movement, many of whom had become the first unpaid personal attendants in the movement. In order to maintain their disability authority and draw attention to structures of oppression and subordination, Aoi Shiba members insisted that able-bodied allies be nothing more than the "arms and legs" of the movement and acknowledge their responsibility as oppressors. They were called to provide free labor as volunteers but would have no voice in the movement. While it is a common complaint that many disability organizations are controlled by well-meaning able-bodied allies, Aoi Shiba antagonized potentially powerful allies and failed to capture an important moment in the development of the movement for independent living. A key to the independent living movement, which developed in Japan a decade later, would be the acknowledgment of the important role played by professionally trained and compensated personal attendants. Despite these criticisms, it is safe to say that Aoi Shiba's unapologetic and passionate activism helped pave the way for a new generation of rights-based disability activism brought forth by the UN's International Decade of Disabled Persons and later by the passage of the ADA.

INTERNATIONAL INFLUENCES: THE UN DECADE OF DISABLED PERSONS, 1983–1992

Unlike their German counterparts who viewed the UN's International Decade of Disabled Persons with suspicion, Japanese disability activists enthusiastically embraced the UN Decade and the equality principles it promoted. The Japanese government responded to the UN equality mandate by adopting the "normalization principle" (*nomarizēshon*) as the guideline to reform its disability law and policy. The normalization principle was first developed and implemented in Sweden during the late 1960s. It offered the first fundamental critique of the treatment of people with mental retardation and their segregation in hospitals, where they were denied the most fundamental rights to privacy, personal possessions, and communication, and the right to fully express their individuality. Beignt Nirje (1969) first theorized that people with disabilities had the right to live lives under conditions that were as close as possible to the norms and patterns of the mainstream of society, thus the emphasis on "normal."[22] The standards of self-determination and self-advocacy that developed from the normalization principle have profoundly influenced the course of the developmental disability rights movement and the provision of services. What seems self-evident today was a revolutionary concept in the 1960s when people with developmental disabilities were assumed not to be able to make even the most basic life choices for themselves. Self-advocacy movements found their strength in the simple but powerful concept that people with disabilities could, and should, have a voice in determining the course of their lives and could be expected to share what could be considered "normal" needs for privacy, intimacy, connection, and fulfillment.

When Japan chose the normalization principle to reflect its commitment to the UN mandate of full integration and equality, it spent considerable time and effort explaining how the term was going to apply to Japanese society. The Prime Minister's Office immediately became the International

Year of Disabled Persons headquarters and established a Central Council on Measures for Mentally and Physically Disabled People to formulate an action program to implement the UN mandate in the areas of education, health, employment, recreation, housing, welfare, and public awareness. A 1982 Ministry of Health and Welfare report defined normalization as "the creation of a society in which all people can lead ordinary lives in their communities, regardless of the presence of any disability," and emphasized the importance of people with disabilities leading "ordinary lives in their homes and communities" (Ministry of Health and Welfare 1982, 2). The purpose of rehabilitation services, it concluded, should therefore go beyond medical technology and provide "technology that aims for the restoration of rights as a full citizen for those alienated from human living conditions for reasons of disability, and a comprehensive system for social and political measures."[23]

While this report emphasizes rights and social inclusion it did not lead to substantive policy reforms that would suggest a shift from welfare to rights. However, the emphasis on normalization brought, for the first time, attention to the fact that much of Japanese disability law had ignored the very existence of people with mental disabilities. Adopting the normalization principle, then, meant that Japan had to update the language of its disability law and broaden the meaning of the term "disability," which until then had been limited to "physical disability" in Japanese disability law and policy.

LEGAL REFORMS AFTER THE UN DECADE: EXPANDING DEFINITIONS OF DISABILITY

The first evidence that the Japanese government elected to show its commitment to the UN doctrine was a 1984 revision of the 1949 Law for the Welfare of Physically Disabled Persons (Shintai Shōgaisha Fukushihō). This was the first postwar disability law and had primarily responded to the needs of the large number of disabled war veterans. It provided for basic services and assistive technology, such as prosthetic appliances, wheelchairs, canes, hearing aids, and artificial limbs. Most important, it laid the foundation for the vast rehabilitation network, consisting of physical and occupational rehabilitation centers as well as community centers and counseling services. It mandated the issuing of disability handbooks for those with legally recognized physical disabilities, as well as the provision of technical aids for daily living, such as bathtubs, toilets, beds, and communication aids.

This law was revised in 1984 to showcase the Japanese government's commitment to incorporating the normalization principle. In its opening section, the law states that the revision was made to "integrate full participation and equality, the guiding principle for the International Year of Disabled Persons, into the law." This was accomplished by changing the language of the law: the term "rehabilitation" was replaced with "independent living and provision of opportunities" (Article 2). It also defined "full participation and equality" to mean that "all physically disabled persons, as constituent members of our society, are entitled to the opportunity of participating in social, economic, cultural, and other aspects of all fields of endeavor" (Article 2 (2)).

The expansion of the term "disability" was settled in the renaming of the 1970 Physically Disabled People's Fundamental Law (Shintai Shōgaisha kihonhō), which had used the term for "physically disabled person" (*shintai shōgaisha*) to designate all people with disabilities (*shōgaisha*). In 1993 the law was renamed Disabled People's Fundamental Law (Shōgaisha Kihonhō) to reflect the expanded legal definition: "disabled persons are persons whose daily life or life in society is substantially limited over the long term due to a physical disability, intellectual disability, or mental disability" (Article 2). The law was drafted in the wake of the ADA but is far more limited in scope. It neither defines nor prohibits discrimination on the basis of disability, but rather "clarifies fundamental principles of services" and outlines state responsibilities (Article 1). A central part of these responsibilities was to recognize the importance of independence and participation in society, both fundamental aspects of the normalization principle: "Disabled persons shall endeavor to participate actively in social and economic activities by making effective use of the abilities they possess. The family members of disabled persons shall endeavor to promote the independence of disabled persons" (Article 6). This last sentence is significant because it recognizes the complicated relationship between people with disabilities and their families in matters of independence, something I will discuss later in this chapter.

The legal definitions of the three disability types—physical, developmental, and mental—are found in the corresponding welfare laws: the Physically Disabled Persons Welfare Act, the Act for the Welfare of Mentally Retarded Persons, and the Mental Health Act, all of which include a disability classification system that is based on certification by medical experts.

The definition of physical disability is classified along physical impairments and functional limitations, according to the medical model's understanding of disability that hails from Japan's prewar years. The five legally recognized types of physical disabilities are based on impairments that are visual, hearing, speech/oral, or internal. These are then further classified by six degrees of severity, ranging from the most severe (grade one) to the least severe (grade six). These definitions and grades of severity are crucial for the issuing of the disability certification handbook that grants holders income support, welfare services, rehabilitation services, and discounts in public services such as transportation. Neither mental nor developmental disabilities have legal definitions in the Fundamental Law—these are to be found in the corresponding welfare laws. For example, the term "mental disability" is broadly defined in the Mental Health and Welfare Law as including schizophrenia, dependency on psychotropic substances, psychosis, or mental illness (Article 5). Mental disability, too, is divided into grades of severity (*kyū*) from one to three, for the purposes of determining state support and services. Services for people with developmental disabilities are covered by the Law for the Welfare of Mentally Retarded Persons, which has been amended several times since its passage in 1960, and which applies the definition used by the criminal justice system—an IQ of less than 75—to determine the provision of services and benefits.

MENTAL HEALTH REFORMS: THE UTSUNOMIYA CASE

While the revisions to address the UN mandate amounted to mere changes in terminology, it was the field of mental disability law that demanded true reform. The devastation of World War II had made the need for comprehensive mental health legislation very pressing. There was a desperate need for beds in psychiatric hospitals, and fewer families could now take care of their mentally ill family members, as prewar legislation had mandated. Prewar public policy toward mental illness mandated that those whose mental illness was seen as a threat to public safety were confined and isolated from the community, with the family holding the initial responsibility for confinement. The 1950 Mental Hygiene Law (Seishin Eiseihō) reflected these attitudes: while it outlined the treatment and protection of mental patients, it also provided for the protection of the society at large. There were many aspects of this law that violated basic human rights principles, the most striking being compulsory hospitalization. Over 90 percent of all hospitalizations occurred without the patient's consent under a system (misnamed "consent admission") that allowed either a physician or, in most cases, a family member to order the hospitalization without any possibility of appeal by patients and with little to no possibility of external review (Salzberg 1991, 148). In many cases doctors were required to notify local police when the patient was deemed to be a danger to society. Moreover, the Mental Health Law prohibited the incarceration of those who had committed a crime because of insanity, and instead mandated their indefinite hospitalization in a psychiatric hospital (Article 29). Along with the passage of the 1958 National Health Insurance Act, which created a boom in the private provision of heath care, privately owned psychiatric hospitals became a lucrative industry that was well represented by a powerful lobby, the Japanese Association of Psychiatric Hospitals.

The system of involuntary hospitalization reflected not only the tremendous stigma associated with mental illness but also the expectation that families would institutionalize their mentally ill family members as a form of social responsibility for public safety. Media reports on the "inherent danger" of persons with mental illness soared in 1964 when U.S. ambassador Edwin O. Reischauer was attacked and seriously wounded by a young Japanese man with schizophrenia. The incident prompted the first live telecast from Japan to the United States with Japanese prime minister Ikeda Hayato issuing his sincerest apologies for the acts of the "deranged" youth (*Nashua Telegraph,* March 24, 1964, 9). The media later became an important force for reform as it began publishing reports on the physical abuse and wide-scale human rights violations of patients inside Japan's psychiatric hospitals. The case that drew international attention was the infamous 1984 Utsunomiya case, which revealed that patients in a locked ward in Utsunomiya Psychiatric Hospital north of Tokyo had been beaten to death by hospital staff in full view of other patients, and their families were told the deaths had been caused by epileptic seizures. Media investigations revealed a large number of deaths within this privately owned hospital, very few of which had been investigated by the authorities. Utsunomiya was not an outlier: the majority of psychiatric hospitals operated under a system that denied patients the right to communicate with their families, kept patients sedated with massive doses of psychiatric drugs to keep them quiet, subjected them to degrading and inhumane treatment, and generally lacked any rehabilitative or adequate therapies.

The Japanese story took a turn when political efforts to remedy the situation in Utsunomiya were deflected by the traditional political channels. The

Ministry of Health and Welfare merely issued "administrative guidance" for the prefectural governors, urging them to tighten supervision of psychiatric hospitals and to establish guidelines regarding patient communication with the outside world (such communication had been intercepted and destroyed in the Utsunomiya case). However, when the issue was raised before the United Nations Sub-Commission on Preventing Discrimination and Protection of Minorities, the Japanese government denied that widespread abuses had taken place and insisted that the rights of psychiatric patients were adequately protected by the 1950 Mental Hygiene Law (Salzberg 1991).

Professional organizations, such as the Japan Federation of Bar Associations and the Japanese Society of Neurology and Psychiatry, had been keenly aware of human rights abuses but were not prepared to challenge the ruling conservative government and call for fundamental legal reform of the Mental Hygiene Act (Totsuka 1990, 196). The National Federation of Families with Mentally Ill People (Zenkaren) would have been a natural ally, but they, too, were not prepared to fundamentally change their political lobbying from a focus on social welfare benefits to human rights. Moreover, many family members felt conflicted challenging a system that obliged them to consent to the hospitalization of their mentally ill family members and then held them "hostage" (Totsuka 1990, 196). The reluctance of local organizations to depart from traditional political action under the social welfare model of disability, which focused on expansion of welfare benefits in a segregated system, created the space for a new generation of Japanese disability activists led by DPI Japan and the Japanese Fund for Mental Health and Human Rights to radically change the approach to the problem. Inspired by a rights model of disability, these activists decided to alert the international human rights community and shame their government as laggards in the human rights protection of the mentally ill. Japanese activists called on the International Commission of Jurists and the newly formed International Committee of Health Professionals to investigate the situation in Japan. In May 1985 a joint delegation from both organizations conducted on-site investigations and released a highly critical report that condemned the Japanese mental health system and recommended a complete overhaul of the Mental Hygiene Law (Harding, Schneider, and Vistotsky 1985, 81). The report pointed to fundamental problems that had been surfacing at Japan's psychiatric hospitals but that had not received political attention until international eyes were on Japan. Besides the fundamental problems surrounding the practice of involuntary hospitalization, the report highlighted the fact that Japanese psychiatric hospitals tend to be seriously understaffed (in comparison to general medical treatment).

The Utsunomiya case demonstrates the impact of domestic and international pressure on legal reform in Japan. Disability activists activated what Keck and Sikkink (1998) have termed the "boomerang effect," which worked in that activists circumvented a recalcitrant national government, activated international attention and investigation, and then used these international norms to pressure their government to make reforms. It was DPI's contacting the United Nations, which then resulted in the International Commission of Jurists and International Committee of Health Professionals mission, rather than the Japanese government's formal commitment to the normalization principle, that caused the government to implement legal reforms. These reforms replaced the term "hygiene" with "health," renaming the law Mental Health Law (Seishin hokenhō), and instituting stricter treatment standards for patients. The law introduced, for the first time, a legal form of voluntary hospital admission and established psychiatric review boards as a mechanism to monitor the need for the continuing hospitalization and treatment of patients who were involuntarily hospitalized. It set limits on the use of physical restraints and established patient communication rights (Salzberg 1991, 163). Another important aspect of the revision was its emphasis on community-based social rehabilitation, establishing facilities (such as halfway houses and sheltered workshops) to ease reintegration into society. The law, however, still ignored central issues of self-determination that were now being discussed in the mental disability rights movement, and it has not prevented further rights abuses in mental hospitals.[24]

The employment needs of people with mental disabilities also took a long time to achieve legal recognition. As mentioned earlier in this chapter, Japan instituted one of the more sophisticated employment quota systems. Its main weakness, however, was its negligence toward people with mental disabilities and their employment needs. The 1960 Physically Disabled Persons Employment Promotion Law (Shintai shōgaisha koyō sokushinhō) was the first law directly targeting the employment status of people with disabilities through a voluntary quota aimed at ensuring employment opportunities in regular workplaces. People with mental disabilities were not included in the quota until 1988 when the law was renamed Law for the Employment Promotion of the Disabled (Shōgaisha no koyō no sokushinto ni kansuru hōritsu). This legal change marked the official recognition of people with mental disabilities as members of the labor force.

A NEW GENERATION OF DISABILITY RIGHTS ACTIVISM

The UN equality and integration mandate also affected the Japanese disability movement, although in different ways than it influenced Japanese disability law. It gave birth to a new generation of disability activism that is moving away from a welfare-based model and frames itself in the context of rights, equal access, and disability pride. An immediate consequence of the UN Decade was the founding of the Japan Council for the International Year of Disabled Persons in 1981, which was then renamed Japan Council on Disability (Nihon Shōgaisha Kyōgikai), or JD, in 1983. JD began operating under the UN theme of "full participation and equality," focusing its efforts on lobbying the government to promote normalization plans.

A prominent disability organization of the new generation is the Japan branch of Disabled Peoples International (DPI Nihon Kyōkai), founded in 1986. DPI itself was founded during the International Year of Disabled Persons in 1981 and represents the first international human rights organization led by people with disabilities, and not by nondisabled allies. It was a remarkable shift in the world of disability organizing not *for*, but *of*, people with disabilities. In its relatively brief history, DPI's influence in international disability policy has been remarkable. It provided a catalytic role in the formation of national disability movements, particularly in developing countries through the training of national leaders. It was influential in the writing of UN policy documents, such as the 1982 World Program of Action Concerning Disabled Persons, and in pushing for the swift passage of the 1983 ILO Convention Concerning Vocational Rehabilitation and Employment of Disabled Persons. In Japan, DPI was instrumental in bringing the Utsunomiya incident to the attention of the world community and coordinated the International Commission of Jurists fact-finding mission, which eventually led to the revision of the Mental Health Law described earlier.

Like their German and American counterparts, Japanese disability activism centers on a broad list of issues that affect people's daily lives: the right to live in the community, to be educated along nondisabled peers, to have access to employment, and to navigate the public sphere. Thus, when looking at disability activism we need to distinguish the type of disability rights a movement is organizing around, such as the right to integrated education, equal employment, equal access, or independent living. Each of these types of rights mandates elicits a different type of organizing strategy and has been invoked with different rates of success. In the Japanese case, the generational shift from welfare to rights organizing has meant a new focus on "barrier-free" equal access, independent living, antidiscrimination, and disability rights consciousness. The American experience with disability rights was a key inspiration for Japanese activists, many of whom traveled to the United States to learn about the disability rights model, to apprentice themselves to leaders in the American movement, and to organize "teaching tours" for American activists in Japan to inspire enthusiasm for the rights model. A clear testament to the importance of the American model has been the turn to "second generation" disability topics such as equal access, independent living, and rights consciousness.

"BARRIER-FREE" EQUAL ACCESS

Demands for "barrier-free" access to public buildings and public transportation systems constitute a cornerstone in modern disability activism, and Japan is no exception. A well-documented experience for foreign visitors to Japan has been the virtual absence of people with visible disabilities from the public sphere. A 2006 *Japan Times* series on disability begins with this very point. "Where are they?" the article asks. "Granted we see more station elevators, wheelchair accessible toilets and busses with passenger lifts nowadays. But many people hardly ever encounter those who use them. In fact . . . most Japanese quite likely live their whole lives without ever interacting with their disabled fellow citizens" (Otake 2006).[25] This invisibility is not exclusively due to an inaccessible public sphere, which is slowly adapting to the global movement toward barrier-free design. In fact, Koji Onoe, former president of the Japan branch of Disabled Peoples International, claims that the problem begins as early as elementary school, when students with disabilities are whisked into a segregated school system that does not allow for integrated education. "Japan is extremely behind other countries in the inclusion of the disabled in jobs and education," he says, echoing a commonly held notion (Otake 2006).

DPI Japan has been at the forefront of raising public awareness of the need to rethink the ways social structures made it impossible for people with mobility impairments to navigate the public sphere. Starting in 1989, DPI Japan organized yearly protests in large train stations all over the country to point out the inaccessibility of Japan's public transportation systems (Kawauchi 1996). The initial 1989 protest took place in Tokyo with approximately

100 disability activists gathering to use the subways and trains together, demonstrating to both station officials and the public the kind of commuting nightmare wheelchair users face every day because railway companies did not install elevators as a part of their policy. As described at the beginning of this chapter, in the absence of elevators station attendants are actively involved in carrying wheelchairs up and down many flights of stairs, and guiding wheelchair commuters into a specified compartment where they will then be met by the next station's attendant. The Tokyo protest was meant to overwhelm and, in many ways, shame the public transportation system for not providing equal access and treating commuters in an infantilizing manner. Not surprisingly, this deliberate refusal to show gratitude for hard-working station attendants and instead to demand equal rights to accessible stations elicited a strong response from the government. "They told us we had a bad attitude," Kawauchi recalls (1996).

The protest spread to over 30 other cities and has become one of the movement's most visible consciousness-raising techniques. The protests find a more sympathetic audience today, but in many ways the limited reforms of the nation's public transportation system is more a result of policies benefiting the elderly population than of an increased commitment to disability access rights by the Ministry of Transportation. The government's 1995 Normalization Plan was launched under the theme of a "barrier-free" campaign (using the Anglicized term, *bariafurii*) and promised to install escalators or elevators in 1,900 train stations for both elderly and disabled users. It also promised improved access to public buildings with the 1994 Law for Buildings Accessible to and Usable by the Elderly and Physically Disabled Persons. Commonly known as the Building with Heart Law (Hāto biruhō), this law became the official response to the UN mandate for social integration and barrier-free access. The law encourages, but does not require, owners of large public facilities (exceeding 2,000 square meters), such as hospitals, department stores, and hotels, to modify entrance designs and to submit barrier-free plans before construction or renovation. There are no penalties for those who ignore it, only financial incentives to those who comply.[26] In May 2000, the Diet passed the Barrier-Free Transportation Law, which mandates operators of all public transportation systems, including buses, trains, and airplanes, to make both their vehicles and the surrounding facilities user-friendly for elderly and disabled passengers. All newly constructed facilities that have 5,000 or more users must be made accessible to disabled and elderly users. The law established a system of fines for noncompliance, aided by the Health, Labor and Welfare Ministry's Project for Building Barrier-Free Cities (Bariafurii no Machizukuri no Katsudōjigyō) to fund such projects. The term *bariafurii* became popular with a television drama airing at the time, *Beautiful Life*, which featured a romance between an able-bodied man and a woman using a wheelchair. Television viewers followed the happy couple navigating endless stairways, steps, or curbs, and, most crucially, trying to find an accessible restaurant for their first date (Stevens 2007, 266).

Accessibility issues in Japan frequently arise not only as a response to disability policy but also—perhaps more urgently—as a response to the pressures facing one of the world's most rapidly aging societies. There is a vast Japanese literature on disability as it refers to aging, and many of the reforms made to improve barrier-free access have been made with Japan's elderly in mind. The most common examples of barrier-free accessibility in Japan are curb cuts, ramps, chirping pedestrian crossing signals, accessible public toilets, no-step buses, and subway elevators. Japan's frequent earthquakes present a major problem, even the frequent minor shocks, because they prompt closure of all elevators. Even on nonearthquake days, many station elevators, installed at the farthest corners of stations, are locked shut, forcing commuters to ask a stationmaster to unlock them each time. Frequently wheelchair users are told that they should be accompanied by somebody to assist them when taking public transportation, which flies in the face of barrier-free access and strikes activists as a form of paternalism that undermines the movement's goal of "independent living" in the community.[27]

INDEPENDENT LIVING

The notion of independent living lies at the heart of current disability activism. It represents the shift from the medical model, which places decisions about care and welfare provisions in the hands of rehabilitation specialists, to what Gerben DeJong (1979) first identified as an "independent living model," which places control back in the hands of the people on the receiving end of welfare services, now renamed "consumers." The term "consumers" evolved to indicate a desired position of control within the service economy: welfare and rehabilitation services should be marketed to the disabled consumers directly, rather than being marketed to the nursing home managers who then tell the disabled clients on a daily basis what to eat, what to wear, and how to spend their time. Wrestling public funds from what they consider the "nursing home mafia" has become a central concern for the independent living movement. People with disabilities should be able to live in the community and receive the assistance they may need in daily living from personal attendants, who can be hired, trained, and fired as necessary by the disabled consumer. As one of the pioneers of the IL philosophy, Adolf Ratzka, explains:

> Independent Living does not mean that we want to do everything by ourselves, do not need anybody or like to live in isolation. Independent Living means that we demand the same choices and control in our every-day lives that our non-disabled brothers and sisters, neighbors and friends take for granted. We want to grow up in our families, go to the neighborhood school, use the same bus as our neighbors, work in jobs that are in line with our education and interests, and raise families of our own. We are profoundly ordinary people sharing the same need to feel included, recognized and loved.[28]

The independent living philosophy came to Japan as a direct import from the United States, prompted by the international emphasis of the UN's International Year of Disabled Persons in 1981. Prominent disability activists such as Ed Roberts and Judy Heumann were invited to Japan and impressed activists with their descriptions of independent living centers in Berkeley and other U.S. cities. Japanese activists, especially those of the post–Aoi Shiba generation, seized the moment and, after establishing corporate sponsorship, traveled to the United States to learn about the independent living philosophy.[29] One of these activists was Nakanishi Shōji, who founded Human Care, Japan's first independent living center, in Hachiōji, a suburb of Tokyo, in 1986. The American influence, or rather that of the Berkeley movement, is palpable: immediately upon entering the center the visitor is confronted with a life-sized portrait of Ed Roberts. There are currently 125 ILCs nationwide, which united in 1991 under the Japan Council on Independent Living Centers (Zenkoku Jiritsu Seikatsu Centā Kyōkai). The council's first executive director was Higuchi Keiko, another American-trained activist and close friend of Judy Heumann's (Higuchi 1998, 103).

Japanese ILCs assist people with disabilities to make the transition from institutions or group homes to independent lives in their own apartments. This includes organizing peer counseling services and training sessions for independent living skills, arranging for attendant care, and counseling consumers on how to communicate better with attendants and family members. Activists believe that it is especially important in promoting notions of self-determination for people with disabilities in Japan because they have been taught from an early age to accept and acknowledge their dependence on the care they receive from parents and the state. Japanese society expects people with disabilities to be conscious of the "burden" (*meiwaku*) they impose on others and to express gratitude for the help they receive from others. According to Japanese disability scholar Miho Iwakuma, this burden stems from "a Japanese group-oriented, collective tendency which harshly criticizes disturbing the group harmony and not following cultural scripts" (Iwakuma 2005). Disability difference disrupts the cultural norms of a homogeneous society and traditionally merits isolation and shame for the entire family. The Aoi Shiba protests of the 1960s provided a vivid example of deliberate attempts to disrupt these Japanese norms. The group's provocative refusal to adhere to cultural disability scripts—meek, humble, and grateful for the benevolence of others—became a central part of their politics. The American import of self-determination and independent living thus poses a formidable challenge for Japanese disability activists who seek to transplant the IL philosophy into a setting that traditionally does not value independence and assertiveness.

Junko Asaka was one of the activists trained in the IL philosophy at Berkeley during the 1990s. She had worked tirelessly in the Japanese disability movement—which she considered a lifelong calling—and was elated to be one of the "pioneers" who would bring IL to Japan (Asaka 1997). From the beginning, cultural differences abounded. American staffers at the Berkeley Center for Independent Living shared her passion for disability rights, but they also considered themselves professionals doing their job, which they got to leave at the end of the business day at five o'clock. This clear distinction between personal and professional lives was an eye-opening experience for Asaka, who had lived her activism 24/7 and didn't feel that she could claim a life away from the cause (Asaka 1997, 46). Like her fellow German "rights tourists" learning about disability rights in Berkeley, Asaka was dismayed by the levels of poverty she witnessed in the U.S. disability community, especially the high rates of homelessness that resulted from the deinstitutionalization movement. The Japanese welfare model might be paternalistic and segregating, but it would not leave people destitute.

Another central difference she experienced had to do with American notions of independence. The American IL movement champions notions of independence that automatically assume independence from the family.

This independence is likened to that of a child reaching maturity by being able to live away from the parents' home. Japanese culture does not place the same positive value on independence and separation from families of origin as a form of maturity. The dependence on a mother's care is especially viewed as positive and desirable. The expectation of young women to remain living at home until marriage is heightened for Japanese women with disabilities, who are not expected to get married at all. Asserting independence from "spoiling" parents is a particularly difficult task for Japanese people with disabilities (Nakanishi 1992).

Thus, when Asaka returned home to Japan, she initially faced tremendous resistance to the Western IL import as being too assertive and threatening to the existing Japanese social structure. The pioneers of the Japanese IL movement, including Asaka, thus faced the unique task of integrating foreign concepts into a Japanese setting by simultaneously promoting and negating their foreign-ness. On the one hand, the American IL principle was enticing in its difference—it allowed activists to inject themselves with the kind of courage and determination they learned from their American mentors and challenge Japanese assumptions about disability as a source of stigma and shame. At the same time, activists sought to temper the American import to allow for more culturally appropriate modifications. For example, self-determination might not automatically have to mean living apart from one's family or selfishly asserting your will without regard for others. It does, however, place the consumer at the center of analysis and starts a process of determining life choices based on an awareness of rights and equal opportunities. A central aspect for making the independent living philosophy work in Japan is to challenge traditional notions of caregiving and place more control in the hands of those receiving the care.

During a 1998 symposium honoring Beignt Nirje's work on the normalization principle and its implications in Japan, *Asahi Shinbun* journalist Okuma Yukiko summarized the meaning of the normalization principle for Japanese society. She suggested that "the normalization principle is deeply embedded in notions of rights, equality, and government responsibility. But in Japan, we tend to translate it into a mere wish of 'let's all be friends and get along well.'"[30] It will be the profound challenge for the new generation of Japanese disability activists to find creative translations and interpretations of Western imports such as normalization, equal rights, and self-determination to allow them to fully take hold in the Japanese cultural and political imagination.

2005 WELFARE REFORM

In this quest for a new understanding of disability rights, Japanese IL activists received an unexpected boost from reforms to the welfare services for the elderly. Similar to the reforms enacted in barrier-free public accommodations, progress in the IL movement is intricately linked with larger Japanese concerns over their aging society. For example, notions of user autonomy first surfaced in 1995 when the Ministry of Health, Labor and Welfare issued a report on social insurance reform that called for more efficiency and quality improvement through the introduction of "market forces." Japan was considered "extremely behind" about the ways social welfare was managed for the elderly and people with disabilities. In order to develop a "mature" social welfare system, Japan would have to introduce notions of consumer control over services received.[31] There was a strong sense that the Japanese welfare system needed to be made more efficient and modern by introducing market forces into the provision and quality of services. The freedom of users to select their own service providers was seen as a hallmark of such a modern system. This modernization attempt was also part of the larger movement to lessen reliance on government services.

The social insurance system (*kaigo hoken*) for people aged 64 or older received a significant overhaul in 2000, instituting such end-user control. A similar reform was instituted for the welfare system of people with disabilities in April 2003 with the introduction of a support payment system (*shienpi seido*) that made people with severe disabilities eligible, for the first time, for part-time or full-time personal assistance coverage if they wished to leave the nursing homes or their families' homes and live independently. The *shienpi* system was a tax-based entitlement system for disability services that was meant to complement the *kaigo hoken* system.[32] This was a big change from the previous "mandated" (*sochi*) system, which placed local disability officers in charge of approving and arranging for services. The previous system had people with disabilities apply for services in their local city hall's disability services section, where office workers would not only approve the kinds of services they were entitled to but also arrange for service providers. This had resulted in a system where services providers tended not to take consumer needs into account since they were being paid by the local government, not the consumer—precisely the situation independent living activists had been criticizing for so long.

Not surprisingly, the *shienpi* system was incredibly popular in the disabil-

ity community—for very low user fees and no premium payments, people
with disabilities could finally leave nursing homes and make independent
living a reality—all facilitated by the network of ILCs that coordinated attendant services. The system, however, soon faced large budget overruns, so
in January 2004, after just eight months, the ministry announced that it
would unify both systems into a single system (called the Grand Design) to
cover all disabled residents regardless of age and finance it through premiums and co-payments like the *kaigo hoken* system. This switch from tax-based
entitlements to social insurance meant that the ministry could start recover-
ing the drain on tax revenues incurred by the *shienpi* system, but, predict-
ably, it caused an outrage in the disability community, which saw entitlements taken away after just eight months. Disability organizations
universally accused the Japanese government of a deliberate attempt to save
the *kaigo hoken* system at the expense of the *shienpi,* which has a much higher
maximum user service usage limit and therefore is more expensive. In many
ways the often converging interests of the elderly population and people
with disabilities came to a head as disability organizations essentially accused the government of privileging the interests of the elderly.[33] DPI Japan
was at the head of an unprecedented cross-disability protest alliance that
united more than 600 organizations. Under the slogan "Nothing About Us
Without Us," protests were held on the grounds of the Diet and the Health,
Labor and Welfare Ministry in Tokyo and soon spread throughout the nation. The July 5, 2005, protest was reported to have more than 11,000 participants.[34] As a result, the Japanese Diet initially delayed proceedings surrounding the bill, although it was eventually passed after general elections
later that year. The 2006 Disabled Persons Independence Support Law
(Shōgaisha jiritsu shenhō) added a 10 percent co-payment to disability welfare services and included mental disability services in the *shienpi* system.

LEGAL REFORMS, ANTIDISCRIMINATION, AND THE "JAPANESE WITH DISABILITIES ACT"

The unprecedented and broad mobilization of disability rights consciousness in response to the government's welfare reform is indicative of a new
direction in Japanese disability activism. A new generation of activists, inspired by the American example and encouraged by the spread of the disability rights model in international human rights instruments, is looking

for new ways to incorporate notions of disability equality and antidiscrimination into Japanese law, using the language of rights in framing their interpretations of disability discrimination. One source of their oppression, they
argue, is the law itself. Specifically, activists point to the presence of disqualifying clauses (*kekkaku jōkō*) in Japanese law. These clauses restrict, or even
prohibit, people with disabilities from obtaining licenses or certifications,
from being engaged in certain professions, and from using certain facilities
and receiving services.[35] For example, when a ministry issues a particular license or certification, the applicant is required to submit to a medical exam
certifying that the applicant's condition does not contradict *kekkaku jōkō*
limitations. If the doctor performing the routine exam writes that the applicant's disability falls under the restrictive clause, the government will not
issue the license and the applicant has no recourse. Applicants who prove
their intellectual or physical capabilities by passing the licensing exam will
still be denied certification if their medical exam gives evidence of certain
disabilities. As a result, people with certain disabilities can be prohibited
from, among other activities, serving on juries,[36] using public transportation unaccompanied, boarding commercial ships, living in public housing,
owning a horse, or becoming a politician. Similarly, people who are deaf cannot obtain driver's licenses, and those with psychiatric disabilities are barred
from receiving licensing in all medical fields.

Here again, foreign pressure provided a powerful tool for reform. Activists
collected examples from other countries regarding the presence or absence of
such restrictive clauses, which they see as human rights violations and barriers to employment. They argued that qualification for licenses or certifications should be based on a person's ability to perform the tasks rather than on
assumptions regarding limitations imposed by their physical or mental disability. The foreign examples were meant to lobby and shame the government into completely abolishing *kekkaku jōkō,* rather than just revising them,
by exposing their official justification as backward and discriminatory.

The lobbying has been partially successful. A 1999 revision of *kekkaku
jōkō* resulted in the abolishment of six of the 63 laws officially recognized by
the Japanese government as discriminatory. The rest were changed to "relative condition," which allows consideration to the state of the impairment,
from "absolute condition," which denies eligibility automatically. However,
the Citizen's Committee to Eliminate Disqualifying Clauses still counts
around 300 clauses still in existence.[37] In December 1999 an advisory panel
to the Health, Labor and Welfare Ministry began suggesting reforms for the

Medical Practitioners Law that would allow people with disabilities to obtain licenses in the medical field. They acknowledged that some disabilities do not necessarily inhibit performance, and recommended that only those be barred from licenses whose disabilities prevented them from performing the necessary tasks. This has led to a proliferation of popular news stories of people with impairments seeking medical careers.[38]

Once Japanese law has been purged from these discriminatory clauses, activists argue, it will be ready for more comprehensive reforms, culminating in Japan's own disability antidiscrimination law. Networks of academics and activists have formed around the country looking for ways to include antidiscrimination legislation in existing disability laws during the regular five-year legislative revisions.[39] They are also discussing the path toward Japan's own disability antidiscrimination law: a "Japanese with Disabilities Act" (JDA), closely modeled after the American example. Second-generation activists—with DPI at the lead—argue that only such a law would truly fulfill the government's promise to incorporate the normalization principle and move toward equal rights (Sekigawa 1998).

THE PROMISE OF ANTIDISCRIMINATION LAW

In fact, a DPI-generated draft for an antidiscrimination clause made its way into the governing coalition's amendment bill in July 2003.[40] In 2004, the Japanese Diet amended the Fundamental Law for Persons with Disabilities to include an antidiscrimination provision, stating that "nobody shall discriminate [against] persons with disabilities or perform other discriminating acts to violate their rights and benefits, because of their disabilities" (Section 3). The amendment also increased the responsibility of local governments to create and monitor the action plans, mandated that barrier-free buildings and information be promoted, and increased the participation of persons with disabilities in government policy decisions. The clause does not apply to discrimination by third-party private entities, and, as is the case with much of Japanese disability law, it does not provide administrative or judicial penalties. Thus, its legal effectiveness and binding force are quite weak.

Despite these weaknesses, the Fundamental Law's antidiscrimination clause represents a first step toward the Japanese government's official recognition of the antidiscrimination principle since its embrace of the normalization principle during the 1980s. When the United Nations ratified the

Convention on the Rights of Persons with Disabilities (the subject of the book's next chapter) in 2006, Japan was an enthusiastic supporter. The CRPD embraces a disability rights model by mandating reasonable accommodations and forbidding all forms of disability discrimination. By signing the Convention in September 2006, the Japanese government signaled that it would pass some form of antidiscrimination law in preparation for ratification.[41] The Japanese Cabinet Office has convened a task force and charged it with developing legislative and policy proposals for Japanese disability antidiscrimination law. The task force not only considers the ADA as an example but has broadened its gaze to Germany, France, New Zealand, and Great Britain. The Ministry of Health, Labor and Welfare convened a separate study group to examine disability employment policy in other countries and ponder the implications for reasonable accommodations in Japanese disability employment policy. The ADA remains a powerful example, however: task force members are considering how Japan's future antidiscrimination laws can address some of the challenges that the ADA's reasonable accommodations mandate has faced in the courts (Nakagawa and Blanck 2010). Japanese disability scholars are well versed in the American legal literature that has debated the question of legitimacy facing the ADA's reasonable accommodations mandate: How can reasonable accommodations be reconciled as a form of equal treatment under a civil rights doctrine? The specific nature of disability accommodations frequently collides with traditional understandings of formal equality. In the same vein, Japanese scholars debating the future of Japan's own "JDA" are mindful of the unique challenges resulting from discriminatory practices that are unintentional, meaning that they are not the result of open prejudice and bias, but rather are forms of "rational discrimination" (differential treatment based on cost-saving measures) and "disparate impact" (seemingly neutral rules that negatively impact people with disabilities).[42] Moreover, Japanese scholars are calling for an expanded legal definition of disability that reflects the complex relationship between disability and environment. They are inspired by the ADA's three-prong definition that defines disability as a relationship between impairment and environment ("a physical or mental impairment that substantially limits one or more major life activities"), and that also protects individuals with past disabilities (having a "record of" a disability), and those that are "regarded as" having a disability. Finally, Japanese scholars are examining the question of enforcement and dispute resolution. Here they look toward the Japanese experience with equal employment opportunity law that was passed by a reluctant Diet in response to Japan's ratification of the UN Convention on the Elimination of All Forms of Discrimination against Women. Japanese antidiscrimination law is notoriously "soft" in that it provides no legal remedies for noncompliance but rather seeks to change social norms slowly by merely requiring businesses to "endeavor" to treat women workers equally. Similarly, Japanese labor law provides powerful protections against dismissal, but these emerge from the employer's paternalistic duty to "protect" and "care" for workers, rather than from a rights-based paradigm. Both of these traditions give Japanese reformers reason to renew their engagement with the American rights model and place their faith in legal mechanisms that protect against disability discrimination.

MOBILIZING JAPANESE DISABILITY RIGHTS

A future "Japanese with Disabilities Act" or any form of antidiscrimination law that the Diet will pass in preparation for ratifying the UN Convention has long been anticipated in Japan. Before the CRPD was even a reality beyond activists' wildest dreams, the question of disability rights in Japan was discussed broadly. How can rights work in a country that traditionally eschews legal consciousness and the use of the law as a tool for social change? How will disability rights become active in the lives of their intended beneficiaries? The JDA will be liberating for the movement only if people with disabilities truly understand that they have certain rights and are willing to act upon them, argue a group of lawyers specializing in disability law who formed the Legal Advocacy on Disability Development Committee (LADD). This group formed in 1996 during a consciousness-raising trip to what is considered the Mecca of disability rights and activism—Berkeley, California. They hold monthly meetings to draft what they call a "Japanese declaration of disability rights" (*kenri shōten*) and generally outline the ways the ADA might serve as a model for Japanese antidiscrimination legislation. The group's goal is to politicize the Japanese disability movement by increasing the role of rights and rights consciousness. People with disabilities should not only be aware of the rights they currently have but also feel empowered by using them, making rights the main tool toward leading self-determined lives. Group members often hold talks at community centers stressing this point, which inevitably becomes the focus of heated discussion centering on the question of "how do we assert our rights without being seen as selfish?"

This question is likely to become a central issue in the Japanese disability movement's quest to emphasize rights consciousness and orient itself along a rights model. How can rights become instruments for personal empowerment without the risk of alienation and separation from the community? How can rights be set to work in a historical and cultural setting that has emphasized difference and separate worlds, rather than equality and integration? Moreover, there are cultural norms surrounding caregiving and gratitude that, in the eyes of the audience at LADD presentations, pose a fundamental conflict between notions of rights and selfishness. It is considered inappropriate, for example, for a person using a wheelchair to criticize the lack of accessible train stations and complain when stationmasters must carry them down long flights of stairs. Similarly, a person living in a nursing home commented that he would feel selfish exercising his right to self-determination when, for example, getting dressed in the morning. "If my nurse decides on the blue sweater for me, I would never choose the red one," he summarized. "I have no right to treat somebody caring for me that way."[43]

It is these assumptions that LADD is trying to change, advocating for a "new, livable society" (*seikatsu shiyasui shakai*) where rights advocacy benefits not only people with disabilities but the society at large. Framing arguments for disability rights in terms of general social benefits—everybody will benefit from curb cuts, elevators at train stations, flexible work hours, and informed consent laws—will allow the movement to appear less self-centered and separate from the community. It also echoes calls for disability policy based on universal design principles outlined in the second chapter of this book. Thus, while disability law and activism in the United States continue to provide powerful inspiration to Japanese legal scholars, they also look to Japan's constitutional guarantees, which provide a path toward more substantive legal equality. Frequently invoked are the Japanese Constitution's guarantee of individual dignity (Article 13); equality of race, religion, social status, and gender (Article 14); the right to a healthy and cultured life, including the state's duty to ensure a minimum standard of living (Article 25); and the right (and duty) to work (Article 27). The Japanese promise of protecting disability difference through positive welfare rights arose from a history of segregation and stigma and represents the basic assumptions of the medical model of disability, which have been universally criticized by disability rights movements across the globe. And yet, Japanese activists will not completely abandon this history in favor of a U.S.-style rights model, but instead work toward a blending of the two models.

The disability rights model continues to provide powerful inspiration to activists in their efforts to expand disability independence, autonomy, and pride. Western notions of equal rights, individual self-assertion, and nondiscrimination allow Japanese activists to imagine both political and legal reforms toward full participation and inclusion. The U.S. rights model allows them to point to the damage caused by segregation and invisibility, and to challenge the paternalism and discrimination inherent in traditional attitudes toward disability. Thus, the rights model has been most successful in the generation of disability law and policy regarding independent living, accessible housing, and public access. However, when it comes to the foundations of the Japanese welfare model—segregated education and employment quotas—the Western import becomes more problematic. Japanese disability law activism remains deeply committed to aspects of disability policy that protect positive rights, especially the employment quota. For Japanese disability activists, a move away from the welfare and rehabilitation model becomes problematic when the right to equal treatment does not include a guarantee to protect difference and where tremendous resources have been devoted to the maintenance of separate facilities. For example, Japanese disability scholars and activists remain firmly committed to the disability employment quota, something that confounds their American counterparts. Embracing disability employment rights does not mean abandoning the quota system in favor of equal employment opportunity and antidiscrimination law: in fact, the two are not considered binary opposites. In an American setting, quotas often connote reverse discrimination or tokenism, and they are commonly seen as the antithesis of equal opportunities. In Japan, however, the quota system is not automatically viewed as incompatible with antidiscrimination law (Sakuraba 2008).

Rights advocacy in the Japanese disability movement stands at a new crossroads. On the one hand, the movement is energized by the global spread of the disability rights model, and by the powerful influence that global human rights norms have on Japanese domestic politics—something I will discuss in more detail in chapter 5. On the other hand, American notions of rights, self-determination, and independence continue to clash with Japanese cultural norms that value social harmony, interdependence, and reliance on family care. Peer advocates in the Japanese IL movement have to recognize these fundamental contrasts and struggle to translate the Western import of independent living in a way that does not offend family cohesion. At the same time, the very foreign-ness of the notion of independent living can offer a welcome liberation from "spoiling parents" because it offers a Western and thus progressive approach to disability rights that feeds into Japan's self-consciousness as lagging behind the West in disability rights consciousness. A new generation of disability activists is translating the U.S.-inspired and now global disability rights model to take on culturally relevant meanings, which, in the Japanese setting, maintain the role of the welfare state for protecting both disability equality and disability difference.

Japan's preparation to ratify the UN CRPD is now shifting the very basis of disability policy. The Japanese disability rights movement faces the difficult challenge of translating rights-based principles into difference-based social policy and legislation so that they are both culturally appropriate and politically useful. Notions of equality and rights consciousness are still considered to be concepts foreign to Japanese civic culture. As a strategizing tool, the difference-based welfare model used by traditional disability organizations has clearly been more successful than calls for equal rights and antidiscrimination legislation. And yet, Japan's formal embrace of international disability rights instruments has opened the door to a new engagement with the disability rights model.

CHAPTER FIVE

Disability Rights as Human Rights

After decades as a global leader in the civil and human rights of persons
with disabilities, the United States is reconnecting with the
international community by affirming the basic human rights of all
people with disabilities and positioning us to better contribute our
expertise on the global level.[1]

Marca Bristo, the longtime disability activist and current president of the
U.S. International Council on Disabilities,[2] issued this statement com-
mending President Barack Obama's signature of the UN Convention on the
Rights of Persons with Disabilities on July 24, 2009. This signature fulfilled
Obama's 2008 campaign promise to reverse the Bush administration's refusal to become a state party to the Convention. This refusal had not come
as a surprise to disability activists, who were well aware of the United State's
long-standing resistance to being subject to international human rights instruments. In this case, however, the previous administration's refusal was
not only based on issues of national sovereignty but also on the assertion
that American disability law is "among the most comprehensive civil rights
law protecting the rights of people with disabilities in the world," and thus
precludes the need to adopt the Convention.[3] In this way, the United States'
initial refusal to be part of CRPD was marked by a sense of accomplishment,
if not superiority, regarding the American commitment to disability rights.
Bristo's statement makes a similar claim—the United States should, indeed,
be considered a "global leader" in the articulation and protection of disability rights—but follows with a very different conclusion. Bristo is suggesting
that both signature and ratification (as the important next step) of the UN
Convention are necessary for the United States to remain engaged with the
developing discourse on disability equality and thus maintain its global
leadership position.

Bristo's comment represents the U.S. disability community's self-awareness of its leadership position in the international disability community. There is a broad consensus, both within the United States and abroad, that the United States provided the model for the international shift in disability policy toward equality, inclusion, antidiscrimination, and rights-based advocacy. The United States should therefore be considered a global leader in the spread of the disability rights model, of which the 2006 United Nations Convention on the Rights of Persons with Disabilities is the most recent manifestation. Indeed, as this book has argued, the 1990 Americans with Disabilities Act was the first international disability rights law that broadly defined and outlawed disability discrimination. As a result, both the ADA and the U.S. disability rights movement became international models for a "paradigm shift" in global thinking about disability, away from a medical model of disability, which views people with disabilities as needing charity and welfare, and toward a rights model of disability, which views people with disabilities as rights holders and equal participants in their respective societies. The CRPD reflects central aspects of this disability rights model by emphasizing equal participation, equal opportunities, and the right to be free from disability-based discrimination. It echoes the disability rights movement's emphasis on autonomy, self-determination, and social inclusion that grew out of their opposition to the paternalism and disenfranchisement reflected in disability law and policy of the past.

The CRPD is the first international human rights treaty that explicitly addresses the human rights of people with disabilities. It is considered the most rapidly negotiated human rights treaty: eighty-one states and the European Union signed the CRPD at its opening ceremony on March 30, 2007, the highest number of opening signatures recorded for any human rights treaty.[4] The negotiations leading to the Convention also broke human rights treaty-making records by having the largest number of representatives from civil society—specifically, disabled peoples organizations (DPOs)—involved in the deliberations. In that sense the Convention represents a "historic break from a state-centric model of treaty negotiation, in which instruments are negotiated behind closed doors, away from the very people they are intended to benefit" (Melish 2007). Embodying the international motto of "nothing about us without us" (Charlton 1998), the CRPD took a participatory approach centered on the views and lived experience of the Convention's intended beneficiaries. DPOs were present and involved in the Convention from the start, especially in the working group that drafted a foundational text. This unprecedented access is reflected in both the language and principles spelled out in the Convention. For example, the CRPD preamble mandates the inclusion of disabled persons and DPOs in the process of determining the direction of their lives.[5] Article 4 requires government parties to closely consult and actively engage with DPOs in developing and implementing laws and policies related to the CRPD.

Like the ADA, the CRPD was widely lauded as representing the "paradigm shift" from welfare to rights in the human rights arena, which, in the words of the UN High Commissioner for Human Rights, rejects the "view of persons with disabilities as objects of charity, medical treatments and social protection" in favor of a view of people with disability as "subjects of rights, able to claim those rights as active members of society."[6] In that sense the UN Convention was internationally heralded as "the dawn of a new era" that would finally empower the world's largest minority—the UN estimates that about 10 percent of the world population, or about 650 million people, have a disability. This chapter considers the influence of the UN Convention on the Rights of Persons with Disabilities on the development of disability rights in my two case studies of Germany and Japan.

How does the new thinking about disability rights as inclusive and comprehensive affect German and Japanese disability law? Previous chapters have traced the initial contact with the rights model in Germany and Japan as activists in these countries looked toward the Americans with Disabilities Act as a model for reform. This chapter considers the second wave of influence provided by the CRPD. The UN Convention offers a comprehensive approach to disability rights that goes beyond the initial promise of the American-inspired rights model. German and Japanese disability activists and legal reformers are inspired by this new promise as they prepare for a second wave of reforms prompted by international law. In the German case, the chapter examines the Convention's promise of "inclusive education" (Article 24) and uses it as a case study to mark the development of the rights model in a country that remains deeply invested in segregated education. Germany presents an ideal case to uncover the workings of international norms because of the continued legitimacy of segregated education nationally, while the rest of the world is slowly converging toward inclusive education. In the Japanese case, the chapter examines the impact of the right to reasonable accommodations in employment policies (Article 27). Japan provides a useful example here because it remains committed to the national employment quota and believes that it can combine what traditionally are considered contradictory policies: the guarantee of equal opportunities in the form of antidiscrimination law, and the promise of equality of result in the form of the disability employment quota. Before examining the impact of the CRPD, however, it will be useful to consider the process of recognizing disability as an important and legitimate addition to human rights instruments. How did disability rights become human rights?

DISABILITY RIGHTS AS HUMAN RIGHTS

Even though people with disabilities constitute the largest minority in the world, the international community has been slow in recognizing disability as a human rights issue. International human rights texts have adopted two basic approaches toward disability: universal instruments in which disability is not listed as a separate category but falls under the general rights guarantees, and specialized instruments that target people with disabilities directly. The 1948 Universal Declaration of Human Rights does not mention disability at all, despite its long list of protected categories, which include race, sex, color, language, religion, political opinion, national origin, property, birth, or other social statuses. Neither of the equality clauses of the two United Nations' international covenants, the Covenant of Civil and Political Rights (1966) or the Covenant on Economic, Social and Cultural Rights (1966), mentions disability as a protected category. In theory, each of the seven core UN human rights treaties[7] implicitly protects people with disabilities, as I explain below. In practice, however, to invoke protection under international human rights law, people with disabilities would have to either fall under a universal provision or posses a separately protected characteristic—such as race or gender—in addition to their disability. Australian law professor Philip Alston explains that "[t]here was often an unstated assumption that in the case of persons with disabilities a significant range of otherwise applicable human rights was for some reason mysteriously suspended or rendered inapplicable" (Alston 1995, 98).

There were three unsuccessful attempts during the 1980s to persuade the international community to adopt a disability convention.[8] The UN General Assembly rejected these because of the widely held assumption that existing human rights documents sufficiently protected the rights of people with disabilities under the same rights as other persons. Commonly cited examples were that the right of equal treatment for women with disabilities was already covered in the 1979 Convention on the Elimination of All Forms of Discrimination against Women,[9] and that children's disability rights were addressed in the 1989 Convention on the Rights of the Child. Article 23 of the children's rights convention, for example, specifically guarantees the rights of children with disabilities to enjoy "full and decent" lives and the right to participate in their communities. Furthermore, the 1984 Convention against Torture and Other Cruel, Inhuman, or Degrading Treatment or Punishment is also considered a potentially powerful human rights tool for the disability community, especially for its broad definition of the term "torture," which could be interpreted to include involuntary institutionalization of persons with mental illness.

The general invisibility of people with disabilities in the core human rights treaties was paralleled by a tendency to enact separate instruments targeting just for disability. These were "soft laws," meaning that they were not legally binding and did not include enforcement measures. As early as 1955, the International Labor Organization passed its Recommendations on the Vocational Rehabilitation of the Disabled, which for the first time established a preference for integrated employment and training, but solidly reflects the basic assumptions of the medical model of disability that dominated thinking about disability at the time. The ILO Recommendations emphasized the individual "suffering" from a disability and the ways this suffering can be reduced via individualized rehabilitation (Waddington and Diller 2000, 11). By 1971, the United Nations had recognized the "inherent rights and dignity of disabled persons" in the preamble of the Declaration of the Rights of Mentally Retarded Persons, asserting that "the mentally retarded person has, to the maximum degree of feasibility, the same rights as other human beings." The General Assembly followed this with a more far-reaching Declaration on the Rights of Disabled Persons in 1975, providing a general indication of how the rights of persons with disabilities should be protected. Both of these early instruments remain grounded in the medicalized views of disability by focusing on protections, welfare, and the need for disability-specific facilities. In 1982, the UN General Assembly passed the World Programme of Action Concerning Disabled Persons, which became the guiding framework for the UN Decade of Disabled Persons (1982–93), and promoted, for the first time, the equalization of opportunities as a goal for disability human rights law. The UN Decade's emphasis on "full participation and equality," as well as the ADA's antidiscrimination mandate, became milestones in the shift toward equality in international thinking on disability rights. In fact, the 1990s are considered a "banner decade" in the generation of disability rights law: more than twenty nations enacted some form of disability equality or antidiscrimination law during this period (Degener 2000).

Most significant among the soft laws targeting disability is the 1993 Standard Rules on the Equalization of Opportunities for Persons with Disabilities. This was the first international human rights instrument that expressly recognized that persons with disabilities are entitled to enjoy all human rights in the same way as other members of the community. "Equalization of opportunities" was defined as the process through which "the various systems of society, environment such as services, activities, information and documentation, are made available to all, and particularly to persons with disabilities."[10] Until the adoption of the 2006 Convention on the Rights of Persons with Disabilities, the 1993 Standard Rules were widely hailed as one of the more far-reaching and progressive international instruments, setting a new standard for the development of equality-based disability law around the world. Their emphasis on environmental, rather than on individual, factors that contribute to the experience of a disability clearly place them within the social model of disability, which had emerged as a political critique of the traditional disability policy in activist and academic circles a decade earlier. The Standard Rules openly criticize the ways terms such as "disability" and "handicap" have been used to reflect a medical approach, rather than "the imperfections and deficiencies of the surrounding society." Moreover, they reflect a more comprehensive and substantive notion of equality by using "rights" and "needs" interchangeably, claiming that "the principle of equal rights implies that the needs of each and every individual are of equal importance, and that those needs must be made the basis for planning" (Waddington and Diller 2000, 11).

The Standard Rules' emphasis on reporting, monitoring, transparency, and the active involvement of disability NGOs all contributed to a growing sense in the international community that disability rights were, indeed, a legitimate and important addition to the existing pantheon of human rights. Disability activists were emboldened to continue their push for a disability-specific convention. In 2001, the government of Mexico initiated another attempt to convince the UN General Assembly, but this time the argument for a disability convention was framed in light of the recently released Millennium Development Goals. The Millennium Development Goals had a stated goal to halve global poverty by 2015 but had not identified people with disabilities as a target group for action, despite the fact that this group is significantly overrepresented among the world's poorest populations. The argument was that, in light of this omission, only a disability-specific convention would ensure that people with disabilities would not be left behind in the fight against global poverty. Other developing economies enthusiastically supported this effort, and in December 2001 the UN General Assembly adopted—by consensus—a resolution to develop a disability convention. The negotiation process leading to the adoption of the Convention on the Rights of Persons with Disabilities in 2006 was one of the fastest ever.

THE CRPD: DAWN OF A "NEW ERA" AND "TOWARD A DUAL APPROACH"

When the UN General Assembly adopted the Convention on the Rights of Persons with Disabilities on December 13, 2006, outgoing Secretary General Kofi Annan lauded it as the "dawn of a new era" for the international recognition of disability rights as human rights, "an era in which disabled people will no longer have to endure the discriminatory practices and attitudes that have been permitted to prevail for all too long."[11] The CRPD is indeed considered as the dawn of a new era for the 650 million people with disabilities who make up approximately 10 percent of the world's population. Eighty percent of these live in developing countries where they encounter material deprivation, "barriers in their participation as equal members of society" and "violations of their human rights in all parts of the world."[12]

The CRPD's central purpose is to "promote, protect and ensure the full and equal enjoyment of all human rights and fundamental freedoms by all persons with disabilities and to promote respect for their inherent dignity" (Article 1). The equality principle holds a central place in the CRPD, but it is a substantive form of equality that goes beyond the traditional limitations of the formal equality principle. Formal equality posits equality as sameness, and demands that similarly situated persons be treated the same. The guarantee of equal treatment is limited, however, to the extent that signs of difference can be used to deny the application of the equality doctrine. This is especially true for the ways disability difference has been applied in law and policy. As I explored in chapter 1, the formal equality doctrine ignores—or posits as neutral—the environmental and attitudinal barriers that inhibit the full inclusion and participation of people with disabilities.

In contrast, substantive equality is less concerned with equal treatment and more focused on outcomes: How can marginalized groups truly enjoy equal opportunities and benefit equally from the promises of citizenship? Substantive forms of equality cannot rest on negative rights alone: it is not enough to promise the right to be free from discriminatory treatment. Rather, what is required for substantive equality is the recognition and facilitation of positive rights—the right to education, work, or housing, for example—that will require the state to take positive action, most commonly in the allocation of resources. The Ad Hoc Committee, charged by the UN General Assembly with beginning the process of formulating the CRPD, recognized the importance of substantive equality early on in the process when it stated that "equality does not simply mean treating everybody the same way. Indeed, accommodating peoples' differences is the essence of a substantive equality, and this understanding is especially key to eliminating discrimination against persons with disabilities."[13]

The CRPD thus embraces the principles of substantive equality as applied to the disability experience. For example, Article 3 refers to respect for the "inherent dignity," "autonomy," and "independence" of people with disabilities (Article 3 (a)) while also calling for "equality of opportunity," "nondiscrimination," "accessibility," and, perhaps most significant, "full and effective participation and inclusion in society" (Article 3 (b) (c) (e) (f)). Thus, people with disabilities must not only be guaranteed the right to be free from discriminatory treatment but they also have the right to be included in every aspect of social, political, and economic life. To accomplish this, state parties to the Convention are under the "general obligation" to "introduce legislative, administrative and other measures to secure relevant rights for disabled people" (Article 4 (a) (b)) and for "taking positive steps to promote the development of universal design, of assistive technology, and of mobility aids" (Article 4 (f) (g)). Most significant here is the duty to provide for "reasonable accommodations." As I argued in chapter 1, equality guarantees for people with disabilities are only as effective as the reasonable accommodations guarantees that accompany them. Reasonable accommodations policies require select employers and providers of public goods and services to take reasonable steps to adjust policies or physical environments in ways that remove the barriers facing individuals with disabilities. The CRPD's Article 2 defines reasonable accommodations as "necessary and appropriate modification and adjustments not imposing a disproportionate or undue burden, where needed in a particular case, to ensure to persons with disabilities the enjoyment or exercise on an equal basis with others of all human rights and fundamental freedoms." State parties to the Convention must "take appropriate steps" to ensure the provision of reasonable accommodations (Article 5 (3)), which can be interpreted as a requirement to raise awareness of the existence and nature of reasonable accommodations, and perhaps more substantively as a call for state parties to provide subsidies or incentives for the provision of accommodations (Lawson 2007, 599).

Reasonable accommodations are explicitly mentioned in the articles dealing with education (Article 24), employment (Article 27), access to justice (Article 13), and liberty and security of persons (Article 14). For disabled people to be able to compete on an equal basis in the labor force, or enjoy equal access to education or the justice system, they have the right to demand disability-specific adjustments to policies or practices, or the purchase of additional equipment or support, unless these impose an "undue burden." The Convention—like its intellectual predecessor, the 1990 Americans with Disabilities Act—defines failure to provide reasonable accommodations as a form of discrimination. It requires state parties to prohibit such failures (Article 5 (2)) and to do so *immediately* as the right to be free from discrimination is a civil and political right to which the principle of "progressive realization" does not apply.

Human rights law typically makes distinctions between civil and political rights being "immediately applicable" upon ratification, whereas economic, social, and cultural rights will take significantly more time to become realized, given the difficulties most states face in fully realizing such rights. Thus, the principle of "progressive" or gradual realization becomes attached to treaties outlining economic, social, and cultural rights, such as the right to food, health, housing, education, and work. In contrast, civil and political rights, including the right to nondiscrimination, impose an immediate duty on the state. Since nondiscrimination is a procedural right and immediately applicable, and the right to reasonable accommodations is inherent in the disability nondiscrimination mandate, the reasonable accommodations principle thus transforms a political right into a substantive right to have access to education and employment. As a positive right—and due to the fact that reasonable accommodations are often associated with expenditures— the reasonable accommodations mandate was not free from controversy during CRPD negotiations. However, as Anna Lawson reminds us, the concepts of reasonableness and, by extension, undue burden by themselves bring with them an aspect of progressive realization, since they are very dependent on the particular situation of the disabled individual in need of accommodations and of the circumstances of the bearer of this duty. What is considered reasonable may change just as much as what is considered unduly costly (Lawson 2009, 104).

What is significant here, however, is the "bridging" function that the concept of reasonable accommodations plays in the realization of disability human rights law. Reasonable accommodations are a form of nondiscrimination and as such fall under the category of political and civil rights, which long formed the basis of our thinking about rights. By including reasonable accommodations in the nondiscrimination guarantee, the CRPD effectively challenges the traditional division between first-generation civil and political rights and second-generation social and economic rights. This is because reasonable accommodations are necessary to ensure that the enjoyment of *all* rights—political, social, economic, and cultural—are meaningful for people with disabilities. In that sense they serve as an important reminder that human rights by their very nature impose both positive and negative duties on states. Human rights scholarship has long criticized the artificial distinction between these two types of rights, and pointed to the notion that *all* human rights, in the words of the 2003 Vienna Declaration, are "indivisible, interrelated and interconnected."[14] Yet the theoretical equality of human rights goes largely unrecognized in practice. Socioeconomic rights pose a significant challenge to the traditional thinking about rights that posits rights as individual entitlements that supersede the public good and maintain a limited-government paradigm. In that sense, socioeconomic rights have traditionally ranked below civil and political rights in human rights doctrine. The CRPD, on the other hand, presents a notable exception to this trend by bridging the gap between political and economic rights, and by reflecting the interconnectedness between first- and second-generation human rights.

The CRPD's reasonable accommodations mandate requires state parties to address the disability-specific needs of people with disabilities as they exercise their right to education (Article 24) and to work (Article 27). In both cases, the CRPD guarantees a general right to work and education, combined with the right to reasonable accommodations to make these rights a reality. In the section that follows I will outline the consequences of this right to education in Germany, specifically, the right to an *inclusive* education, which poses a significant challenge to a country with a highly segregated education system. The Japanese case study examines the right to reasonable accommodations at work and the future of the Japanese employment quota as Japan prepares for ratification of the Convention.

CRPD ARTICLE 24: THE RIGHT TO INCLUSIVE EDUCATION

The CRPD's Article 24 obliges states to provide an "inclusive system of education and of life-long learning." This means that state parties must ensure that people with disabilities are able to access an inclusive and good quality primary and secondary education, in their own communities, on an equal basis with others, and be given the appropriate support to do so.[15] Article 24 also posits that the inclusive education of children with disabilities must reflect the CRPD's fundamental goals of dignity and self-worth, the development of human personality and potential, respect for human rights, human diversity, and effective participation in a free society. To make education fully inclusive, state parties must ensure that reasonable accommodations for disability-related needs are provided at all levels of the education system, including individualized modes of instruction, individualized education plans, and the provision of auxiliary aids and services for students with sensory impairments. Thus, students with sensory impairments must have the opportunity to learn Braille, sign language, or alternative modes of communication from teachers who are appropriately qualified. Instruction must be delivered in the most appropriate language or mode of communication for a student's specific disability. Children must be given mentoring and peer support to develop a positive self-image and social networks. State parties must promote the "linguistic identity" of students who are deaf (Article 24 (3-c)). The fact that Article 24 purposefully does not mention special education or separate facilities signals the fact that the CRPD intends for the entire education system to cover every student's specific need. The framers of the CRPD saw the continued existence of parallel tracks for students with disabilities as a central barrier to the educational rights for students with disabilities (particularly students with disabilities other than visual or hearing disabilities). Article 24 offers a highly contextualized and disability-specific articulation of education rights. It is one of the more detailed articulations of rights in the Convention. The concept of full inclusion in the education system is further articulated in Article 20, which outlines the right to participation in cultural life, recreation, leisure, and sport.

THE CRPD IN GERMANY: IMPLEMENTING INCLUSIVE EDUCATION

Germany was an early supporter of the UN CRPD and signed both the Convention and the Optional Protocol on March 30, 2007. The Bundestag ratified the Convention and Optional Protocol in February 2009, and in March 2009 the CPRD officially came into force in Germany. The ratification make the right to an inclusive education available to all German students with disabilities—regardless of the type or severity of their disability—which means that they no longer can be forced to attend a segregated school against their will. For German disability activists, Article 24 was one of the more highly anticipated aspects of the UN Convention. Germany has one of the most highly segregated education systems in the world, educating the vast majority (85 percent) of children with special education needs in segregated special schools (called *Sonderschule* or *Förderschule,* depending on the federal state). In fact, Germany's entire education system, for students with and without disabilities, is among the most highly differentiated in the world. Tracking students into separate schools by ability level and based on grades and test scores is a long-standing historical practice in Germany. Children with no identifiable disabilities (traditionally called *Regelschüler,* "regular students") get tracked into a system with four separate and hierarchically ordered secondary school types (*Hauptschule, Realschule, Gesamtschule, Gymnasium*) at a very early age—mostly around the age of ten as they transition from primary to secondary school. The system divides students into three levels—the highest level, geared at attending university after 13 years of schooling; the middle level, which ends at 10 years, prepares students for middle-level, nonprofessional careers; and the lowest level, ending at nine years, funnels students into vocational training.

There is a separate school system for students who have been determined to have "special education needs." It operates as an entirely separate track within the public school system, consisting of eight or nine grades depending on the state and the "category of educational support" (*Förderschwerpunkt*) they serve. These categories are equivalent to the special education classifications in the United States.[16] In Germany, there are nine categories: language, social and emotional development, intellectual development, learning disability, illness, and seeing, hearing, physical, and motor skills.[17] Once a child is placed in a separate school it becomes very difficult, if not impossible, to integrate back into the regular school system: the schools for the disabled are considered a "one-way street" (Heyl 1998, 687). Even for students without disabilities, school segregation at an early age is widely considered to be a major source of social inequality that permeates their life course. For example, the 2001 Program for International Student Assessment study of the reading and math performance of fifteen year olds certified that among the 34 OECD countries, Germany earned the dubious honor of leading the list of countries whose educational systems consistently reproduced social status.[18] For students with disabilities, the results of segregation are even more severe: four-fifths of students leaving Germany's segregated special schools do not attain the lowest qualified certificate (*Hauptschulabschluss*), without which vocational training opportunities and hence labor market opportunities are seriously limited (Powell 2009, 165).

There is broad support for Germany's segregated education system—both politically, in the federal states ruled by the conservative party (Christian Democrats), and from the powerful professional association of special education teachers, the German Special Education Association (Verband deutscher Sonderpädagogik), which has "provided a strong voice and professional legitimacy for the special school system" (Powell 2009, 176). The Association provided the impetus for the construction of the postwar segregated education system when it circulated a 1954 white paper to the states' education ministries, leading to a "profession-inspired, not empirically validated, differentiation of separate school types" (Powell 2009). Since then, special educators have established, controlled, and defended a dozen discrete school types based on disability categories. Teachers at the segregated schools receive specialized training and receive higher pay than their peers teaching at regular schools. Class sizes are considerably smaller as well. Thus, rather than educating students with disabilities in integrated settings (as is, in contrast, the norm in the United States, where children attend the same school but get tracked into different classes), Germany continues to educate children with disabilities in separate institutions. Other European countries, such as Italy and a host of Scandinavian countries, have abolished the segregated special education system. In Germany, however, despite ratification of the UN Convention, school segregation continues to be understood as necessary and legitimate (Pfahl and Powell 2011).

TRANSLATING THE UN CONVENTION: INTEGRATION VS. INCLUSION

Article 24 is based on a broad understanding of human rights law and the law of children's rights: all children have the right to learn and play together.

Children belong together and should not be devalued or segregated because of a disability. Human rights instruments make the point that there is no legitimate reason to separate children for the duration of their schooling—they do not need to be protected from one another. While there is a general agreement on basic rights, there is quite a lot of diversity when it comes to the implementation of these rights. Article 24 became a source of contention from the start. When the German government ratified the Convention, it had to translate the English language document into German. In its official translation, the German government used the term "integration" (*Integration*) to translate Article 24's mandate for "inclusion." While these terms might sound similar, they signify very different approaches to special education, and posit very different outcomes for education politics.

The special education literature makes an important distinction between *integration* (a term that first surfaced in the 1960s and 1970s) and its more contemporary counterpart, *inclusion*. Integration tends to focus on an individual (or a small group of students) for whom the curriculum is adapted, different work is devised, or support assistants are provided once that student joins a mainstream classroom. The emphasis was on how best to assimilate individual students with identified special educational needs into existing forms of schooling. The task of integration thus became all about the process of joining the mainstream—to become like the others—and its success depended on the ability to best approximate the nondisabled norm. In contrast, inclusion was developed as a process that would go beyond simple integration. Rather than focusing on an individual student's "deficits" and attempting to mitigate them, inclusion was conceptualized as a process by which a school attempts to respond to all students as individuals. This process necessarily would lead to a reconstruction of the curriculum in order to reach out to all students as individuals, not just students with special education needs. Thus, the locus of the problem to be addressed is not the individual's difference, but rather the social structures that create consequences for that difference. It is not the student who needs to change or adapt, it is the school that needs to rethink structural and pedagogical arrangements that segregate students in the first place. The UN Convention's theme of "full participation and inclusion" reflects this larger concern with inclusive education.

When the Bundestag ratified the Convention in 2009, German activists paid close attention to the language used to translate these important concepts. Already there had been broad criticism regarding the lack of involvement of German NGOs, but when activists saw the choice of the term "integration" to translate the broader reach of the "inclusion" mandate (as well as some other language), they felt betrayed and that the transformative potential of the CRPD had been thwarted. To counter this in good NGO fashion, German disability activists, under the leadership of Netzwerk Artikel 3, published a "shadow report."[19] Shadow reports are a common and very effective method for NGOs to supplement or present alternative information to the periodic government reports that state parties are required to submit under human rights treaties. NGOs play an essential role in providing both reliable and independent information to UN committees on sensitive issues (such as violence against women), which are often overlooked or misrepresented in official reports by state parties. Shadow reports are usually filed right after, and in direct contrast to, the official government reports.

The German NGO shadow report used a translation of English terminology that they claim is more aligned with the transformative potential of the Convention. For example, the choice of the German government to translate Article 24 with the term "integration" was indicative of a state structure that would not be willing to abolish its segregated education system. The shadow report "corrected" this term and used the anglicized term *"inklusiv"* to signal the important difference in the approach to education rights. German activists saw this turn to the English terminology as a political choice to orient themselves to international norms and to indicate that Germany's days of mandatory segregation were numbered:

> The English term "inclusion" has become part of the international language. That's why we are using the English term. It signals to us that children [with disabilities] should be part [of education] from the very beginning, not just added on as an afterthought. They have a right to be educated along with their peers. This is the new state of things. And that's why we consider this a political term.[20]

The concept of inclusive education fundamentally threatens the future of the segregated school system. It would require "regular schools" (*Regelschulen*) to adapt both curriculum and teaching methods to address the diversity of the entire student body. For example, group work would replace the traditional reliance on student-and-teacher-focused teaching. Here is an elementary school principal of one of the few experimental "inclusion" schools in Berlin explaining the concept in action:

Both parents and teachers will have to rethink the notion of teaching and learning. There is a strong urge to use the traditional grading system to categorize and compare students. Thus, Max might have a "B" in Math, but this will be a different "B" from that of a student who is on a completely different learning trajectory. We have to look at individualized intellectual growth, and not just ask which level of math a student is able to master.[21]

INCLUSIVE EDUCATION RIGHTS ACTIVISM IN GERMANY

Such visions of inclusive education are motivating parents' groups to push for reforms. Beginning in the 1980s, parents began to criticize the "one-way street" of the *Sonderschule* system. First, they founded and then lobbied successfully for the establishment of a number of experimental projects (*Schul-Versuche*) beginning in the primary grades that integrated children with disabilities in the general schools. Working closely with university researchers, parents worked hard to bring children with disabilities into contact with their nondisabled peers and to initiate a shifts toward flexibility in a rigid system (Heyl 1998, 687).[22] They also managed to disrupt the one-way street in limited ways, making it at least technically possible for children attending special schools to transfer to the lowest level regular school (*Hauptschule*). This transfer is still extremely rare, however, and most students attending a segregated school will tend to stay there for the remainder of their schooling (Pfahl and Powell 2011, 10).

The primary criticism of the segregated system is the notion of stigma. The legacy of the *Hilfschule* ("support schools"), which assumed central functions in the Nazi eugenic program, remains strong. Activists contend that the only way to address the stigma is to normalize relationships between the disabled and the rest of society, and that a central first step in this normalization is children going to school together. Thus, while the *Sonderschule* may provide special protection for disability-appropriate needs—something that many parents remain fearful of giving up—the general criticism is of the lack of interaction between children of different abilities. The segregated school system has made classrooms in Germany extremely homogeneous—only children with similar disabilities (in the case of the *Sonderschule*) or academic abilities (in the general schools) share a classroom. Parents of students with disabilities felt that the costs of stigmatization and isolation were too great and began lobbying for inclusive education. Increasingly, Germany's segregated special education system is being criticized nationally and internationally by the UN Special Rapporteur on Disability Rights (Muñoz 2007) for failing to provide educational opportunities or to sufficiently reduce the disadvantages faced by students with disabilities.

The contemporary movement for inclusive education is represented by the country's only nationwide advocacy organization, Eine Schule für Alle (One School for All). This group advances a rich discourse of inclusion and accountability for the failure of the special school system to adequately prepare students with disabilities to enter the workforce. Moreover, their education rights activism transcends the interests of students with disabilities and launches a comprehensive critique of Germany's elitist education system. For example, the organization advances a "manifesto of inclusion" that stresses the importance of social inclusion of all people marked "different," not only people with disabilities.[23] The focus here is on children from low socioeconomic backgrounds and children who are labeled as "foreign" (from non-German backgrounds, primarily from Turkey and other non-Western countries that have increased immigration to Germany). Germany's homogeneous classrooms typically prevent contact with students from different backgrounds so that each new generation grows up with limited experience of the variety of human abilities. Another part of the manifesto is a comprehensive critique of Germany's belief in innate academic talent, which results in the placement of students into hierarchically differentiated secondary schools after just four years of elementary school. School administrators place students into the "appropriate" school for the ascribed intellectual level and assumed academic ability, and in the process rigidly predetermine students' future educational opportunities. This system has long been critiqued for reifying and reproducing existing class boundaries. For example, Gunther Opp (2001) explains that "historically, the [three-tiered] German education system reflected a three class model of society (working class, middle class, and upper class) and the schools had to prepare their student population for their future functions within these social classes." The segregation of students with disabilities into a "fourth" class of the school system underscores this critique.

RESISTANCE TO INCLUSION: PROTECTING DIFFERENCE

What, then, stands in the way of inclusive education? Studies of professional attitudes toward integration show mainstream teachers generally agreeing with the theoretical principles of inclusive education, but then demonstrating remarkable uncertainty when they are asked about their readiness to teach children with disabilities in their own classrooms. Teachers largely accept and support the achievement orientation of German elementary schools, and thus tend to view school failure as an individual problem of the student rather than as a collective failure of the school (Heyl 1998). The provision of a separate education system for students with disabilities is commonly viewed as providing a "protective space" or "safe territory" (*Schonraum*) in which disabled students are shielded from societal expectations. This hails back to the beginnings of special education ideology in Germany during the early 1900s, which sought to support students viewed as feebleminded or "idiotic" as a result of the social conditions produced by poverty and illness. The "support schools" (*Hilfschule*) provided specific measures as part of the larger state responsibility for all children, such as a breakfast (which continues today), a weekly bath, and sex education, to strengthen children in body and spirit. Pfahl and Powell (2011, 12) explain the construction of special education as a "scientific articulation of the nineteenth century idea of a particular societal distribution of innate talent that demands the 'protection' of the most disadvantaged pupils not only from the insults and dangers of capitalist society but also from themselves." By compensating for the disadvantages brought on by poverty, special educators sought to create conditions conducive to learning, and thus to protect and support their students. At the same time, however, school segregation—and the resulting divergent life chances—also became a way of protecting "society" from dangerous underprivileged individuals as its class and dis/ability boundaries are reproduced (Pfahl and Powell 2011, 12). Special education's protective function thus sheltered vulnerable students from the ravages of early capitalism, but it simultaneously sheltered them from the expectation and the right to participate in the market. This history of benevolent paternalism is a powerful legacy facing educational reformers today.

USING THE CRPD TO CHALLENGE
GERMANY'S SEGREGATED EDUCATION SYSTEM

Germany's ratification of the CPRD opened new spaces for legal mobilization against the segregated education system. Parents' groups today share an uneasy endorsement of the paternalism in German special education. On the one hand, they point to the twenty-some years of evidence provided by the experimental inclusive schools demonstrating how much better all students learn when they are in diverse classrooms and receive individualized attention. The education literature has long documented the ways in which inclusive education benefits all students, and not only those marked as having special education needs. On the other hand, parents of students with disabilities are wary of depriving their children of the protection provided by segregated schools. They recognize that regular schools simply are not equipped to accommodate students with diverse disabilities and fear that their children will not get the disability-specific educational accommodations they need. The transition to an inclusive education system will not only bring logistical challenges but a fundamental reevaluation of German thinking regarding education, which includes challenging the assumptions about children's "innate intelligence" (*Begabung*) and the necessity of homogeneous classrooms to promote learning. "For most Germans, the full inclusion of students who are Deaf, or those with severe disabilities, or those with autism is simply unimaginable," explains special education professor Anne-Dore Stein.[24]

And yet, beginning in 2010, local and national parents' associations such as Gemeinsam Leben, Gemeinsam Lernen (Living and Learning Together) or Eine Schule für Alle (One School for All) began bringing legal challenges to school administrators' decisions to transfer children to segregated schools. Once a school makes this decision, parents lose the right to keep their child in the regular school (usually elementary school), meaning that the child is legally barred from attending that school and must report to a segregated school instead. With the UN Convention becoming active in Germany, parents feel they finally have the law on their side in challenging these decisions. One School for All has published a detailed manual for parents, reminding them to "prepare to fight" for their children's right to be educated alongside their nondisabled peers. This manual (Eine Schule für Alle 2010) outlines procedures and arguments, explains how to take notes during meetings with school administrators (since these would be subpoenaed during hearings), reminds parents to remain nonargumentative but firm in the face of opposition, and generally coaches them on how to become advocates for their children. This turn toward legal advocacy—long taken for granted by U.S. parents' groups that provided much of the impetus for special education reform in the United States—is a new development for German parents' groups.

A host of cases brought beginning in 2009 all used Article 24 of the UN Convention as a means to protest the mandatory matriculation into a segregated school. As an example, consider the first case in the federal state of Hessen in November 2009, which set an important precedent.[25] Here the administrative court ruled that the state was not obligated to uphold the right to an integrated education as mandated by the UN Convention until this right was established by the education law of the respective federal state.[26] In other words, the UN Convention isn't active until each state has made the appropriate legal reform.

This decision is based on the fact that education policy is set exclusively at the state level in Germany. Each federal state in Germany is particularly protective of its individual cultural heritage and considers maintaining control over its educational systems as essential (Heyl 1998, 684). State governments consistently resist efforts from the national level to dictate education policy and practice. Thus, because integration opportunities must be won state by state, parents' groups in Germany have had to work from the local level up, building community and state-level support to accomplish their goal. As a result, there is tremendous variance among the different states' support for inclusive education.[27] Germany's ratification of the CRPD has now become a question of the reach of international law to the state level: To what degree does the federal ratification of the Convention trump state sovereignty over education policy? Is the right to inclusive education an individual right that is immediately executable, or is it a right that can only be realized "progressively," giving federal states ample time to reform their education systems?

The Hessen court denied the Convention's reach to the state level, claiming that federal states are not yet bound by the inclusive education mandate. State education ministries maintain the right to enforce the segregated education system by mandating students' matriculation to segregated schools if the regular schools are incapable of meeting a specific student's special education needs. The court concluded with a call to the legislature to implement the necessary reforms to implement the CRPD, but it affirmed the right of school districts to enforce current education law, which legalizes segregated schooling.

The ruling signified a tremendous blow to disability rights activists. The Kassel Ruling, as it became known in activist circles, became a de facto precedent in other lawsuits and was widely cited in the court opinions of other states (beginning just a month later in the state of Niedersachsen's Supreme Administrative Court). The German Institute for Human Rights (Deutsches Institut für Menschenrechte)—the agency in charge of monitoring Germany's compliance with the Convention—published a lengthy report in the wake of the Kassel case, chiding the court for its misinterpretation of human rights law.[28] Article 24 is, in fact, active immediately, the Institute claimed, and not just when the legislatures have enacted reforms. This is because the denial of Article 24 inclusive education rights is considered a form of discrimination, and freedom from discrimination is a civil and political right that is immediately realized under international human rights law. As for education policy, the UN Convention trumps the federal system, which gives states sole jurisdiction over educational policy. Once the federal government has ratified the Convention, the law is immediately applicable to all of the states. This has been the case for previous human rights conventions, and it is the case for the disability convention as well. The Institute's report was especially critical of the court's claim that "current conditions make integration impossible," which clearly goes against the immediate applicability of the Convention's nondiscrimination mandate.

The courts are not the only social force resisting the transformative potential of the UN Convention. The federation of state education ministries (Kultusminister Konferenz) has also registered its intent to view the reach of Article 24 in limited ways. In a November 2010 statement the federation outlined Germany's responsibility toward the CRPD by reasserting education policy as an exclusive state issue. They also affirmed their view of education rights as a matter of "progressive realization," meaning that "the realization [of inclusive education] would not be able to be realized in a short period of time" and that it would have to "compete with equally pressing state responsibilities."[29] The idea that inclusive education would threaten the future of Germany's segregated schools has mobilized not only the professional association of special education administrators and teachers (Verband Deutscher Sonderpädagogik) but also the Christian Democrats (CDU), the conservative party. For example, in the state of Baden-Württemberg, the conservative party posted slogans in direct opposition to the CRPD that called for "support[ing] students [in special schools] instead of including them" (*Fördern, statt Inklusion!*) (Spiewak 2011). Saxony's education minister called the state's education system "inclusive"—despite the fact that over 80 percent of disabled students are segregated—by claiming that "we educate our special needs students in the first place!"[30]

German disability activists remain undeterred. They view the CRPD as an important tool in their struggle against such attitudes, not only regarding inclusive education but also in the larger paradigm change the Convention engenders. The promise of inclusion begins with education, teaching children that disability is a normal part of the human experience, but it reaches into all aspects of public life if Germany is going to truly follow the spirit of the Convention. A German independent living organization, ForseA (Bundesverbands Forum selbstbestimmter Assistenz behinderter Menschen), which focuses on the right to paid personal assistance services, produced a wildly popular video series on the impact of the CRPD in Germany, entitled *The CRPD—Why It Will Become a Successful Model*. The message is clear: disability activists must use the court system to force Germany to enact the Convention, and the courts must be given the opportunity to do the right thing and rule in their favor. The video stresses the point that litigation is an unusual political choice, but that Germany's disability movement must adapt with the times and use the law as a tool for social change.

> I'm afraid we will need to use the courts to truly enact the Convention. But, optimistically speaking, every time we choose this path we give the courts the opportunity to interpret the Convention from our points of view and in our favor. We need to give the justice system the opportunity to rule on the ways the Convention acts in specific instances in peoples' lives.[31]

THE CRPD IN JAPAN: THE RIGHT TO WORK (ARTICLE 27)

The right to work for people with disabilities has long been debated in the disability literature. The International Labor Organization specifies the right to "decent" work in order to distinguish employment rights from the tradition of sheltered workshops, which often exploited and underpaid disabled workers and contributed to their social and economic marginalization (O'Reilly 2003). The right to work is as fundamental to people with disabilities as it is to everybody else, not only as a means to support one's livelihood but also as an opportunity for social interaction, individual development, and self-worth. The CRPD anchors this right in Article 27, defining it as "the right of persons with disabilities to work, on an equal basis with others; this includes the right to the opportunity to gain a living by work freely chosen or accepted in a labour market and work environment that is open, inclusive and accessible to persons with disabilities" (Article 27.1). State parties must "safeguard and promote the realization of the right to work" through a list of eleven possible actions listed in Article 27, such as prohibiting employment discrimination (Article 27-a), guaranteeing equal pay (Article 27-b), providing vocational rehabilitation and training (Article 27-k), and providing equal employment opportunities (Article 27-f). Most prominently, Article 27 links the right to reasonable accommodations with their provision (Article 27-i), and as such exemplifies the Convention's commitment to provide a substantive form of equality to people with disabilities.

Another substantive form of equality in the employment context is the disability employment quota, which is a prominent feature in both Germany's and Japan's disability employment laws. While not specifically mentioned in Article 27, the CRPD still calls for the promotion of private sector employment "through appropriate policies and measures, which may include affirmative action programs, incentives and other measures" (Article 27-h). The CRPD does not endorse employment quotas, but it allows them as a form of "positive action" necessary to "accelerate or achieve the de facto equality of persons with disabilities (Article 5.4). In that sense, disability employment quotas and "other measures designed to increase the labor force participation of disabled peoples" are not prohibited (Article 5.4). International instruments have long recognized disability employment quotas as a part of employment policy. The 1983 ILO Convention on Rehabilitation and Vocational Training of Persons with Disabilities, which was the only internationally binding multilateral treaty solely devoted to persons with disabilities until the CRPD came into force, specifically posits that "special positive measures aimed at effective equality of opportunity and treatment between disabled workers and other workers shall not be regarded as discriminating against other workers" (Article 4). The 1993 Standard Rules mention "incentive-oriented quota schemes" as just one of many employment promotion policies, along with more conventional free market measures such as tax incentives, technical and financial assistance, training, and "reasonable adjustments" for workers with disabilities (Rule 7).

The question of employment quotas as a legitimate policy response becomes important in light of the CRPD's emphasis on equal employment opportunities, a concept considered as fundamentally incompatible with the quota system. Despite the convergence toward right-based disability law and policy in countries across the globe, the employment quota remains a central part of disability policy in fourteen countries around the world.[32] Efforts to implement the CRPD's Article 27 in Japan, a country deeply committed to employment quotas, will challenge the assumed incompatibility between rights and quotas.

ACTIVATING THE CRPD IN JAPAN

The Japanese government signed the CRPD on September 28, 2006, and simultaneously promised to ratify it by 2013. Signing the Convention does not legally obligate Japan to ratify it, but the signature signals general agreement with the CRPD's principles. In the meantime, however, Japan is not legally bound by the convention. The CPRD itself does not provide guidelines for ratification, but instead leaves it to individual nations to decide how to best fulfill its treaty obligations. In most cases, however, the ratifying body—the Japanese Diet in this case—will review its existing disability laws and enact the necessary reforms to bring its laws into line with the equality and inclusion mandate of the convention. The Japanese delegation to the treaty promised the UN General Assembly that "Japan will do its utmost to ratify the Convention" (Japan Times 2007). And yet, when the Japanese government attempted to send the CRPD to the Diet for ratification in March 2009, the disability community revolted and effectively blocked ratification. The CRPD had been met with enthusiasm by the Japanese disability rights community and reflected the movement's increasingly international outlook. In fact, the Japan Disability Forum[33] emerged as a collection of twelve DPOs at the culmination of the 2002 DPI World Conference in Sapporo, and formally united in 2004 to send observers to the Ad Hoc Committee to the UN CRPD. The resistance to early ratification thus came from a movement deeply invested in international disability law, but wary of a government that had proposed only "cosmetic" reforms of domestic law to prepare for ratification.

The struggle surrounding ratification emerged from the Japanese practice of enacting major "harmonization" with international law before ratification. In direct contrast, Germany ratified the Convention before substantially harmonizing its domestic laws with the principles spelled out in the CRPD, and is now facing tremendous domestic struggles over the inclusive education mandate. Thus, Japan took almost five years to ratify the Convention on the Elimination of All Forms of Discrimination against Women because it had to pass an equal employment opportunities law first, and waited for close to four years to ratify the Convention on the Rights of the Child. The Japan Disability Forum's successful campaign against what they considered "cosmetic ratification" by the conservative Liberal Democratic Party (Jimintō) was aided by parliamentary elections later that year, which ushered in a new government led by the Democratic Party of Japan (Minshutō) in September 2009. The Democrats had made campaign promises to work on serious harmonization and soon formed a "disability policy reform" platform. This platform has stalled somewhat since the reelection of the conservative party in 2012, but the reforms initiated under the CPRD will have a major impact on Japanese disability law and signal new ways for the disability rights model to take hold in Japan.

TOWARD HARMONIZATION: DISABILITY POLICY REFORMS

Under the leadership of the prime minister, the Committee for Disability Policy Reform started meeting in 2010 to spell out three major policy reforms that would accomplish harmonization with the CRPD. This committee is headed by Higashi Toshihiro of DPI Japan, and consists of 24 members, the majority of whom are people with disabilities or family members of people with disabilities. This was a deliberate choice to reflect the CRPD's emphasis on self-advocacy and the important role the DPOs played in the passage of the Convention. In that spirit, the Committee meetings were open to the public and broadcast live on the Web with subtitles and sign language interpretation. Committee members also adopted a color-card system for self-advocates that they had learned from European activists: members with intellectual disabilities would raise green cards to indicate understanding of the discussion, yellow cards to slow down the discussion, and red cards to indicate that they fail to understand what is being discussed (Y. Nakanishi 2010).

The Committee adopted a three-point reform map that would bring Japan into line with the CRPD. The first was a revision of the legal definition of disability to reflect the social model's emphasis on social barriers, which I will discuss in more detail below. The second was the enactment of social services legislation to reform the highly unpopular 2005 Services and Supports for Persons with Disabilities Act (Shōgaisha Jiritsu Shien Hō), which was under intense criticism by the disability community for increasing individual contributions from disability service users. The new 2012 Comprehensive Support Act expanded the coverage of disability services to include persons with chronic illness, and included home care services for persons with intellectual disabilities that would incorporate the concept of "supported decision making," reflecting the CRPD's emphasis on self-determination and self-advocacy. The third reform was going to be the most difficult: the passage of a disability antidiscrimination law that includes a definition of discrimination and the concept of reasonable accommodations. This will be especially important as Japan considers the future of the disability employment quota as it harmonizes with Article 27.

HARMONIZING DEFINITIONS OF DISABILITY

The question of how or whether disability law should include definitions of disability has motivated important scholarship in disability legal studies (Hahn 1993; Stein and Stein 2006; Kaplan 1999). International law is no exception: in 2004, the question of whether the Convention should include definitions of "disability" and "persons with disabilities" ended up generating intense discussion in the working group of the ad hoc committee while it was preparing the draft of the CRPD language. Most disabled people's organizations as well as some countries were determined to ensure that the Convention applied to *all* people with disabilities and successfully lobbied against the use of definitions to avoid excluding present or future disabilities. Other states were concerned that this would "open the floodgates" and force them to recognize types of impairments they traditionally did not view as legitimately belonging in the disability category (Kayess and French 2008). Persons with HIV/AIDS and persons with psychosocial or developmental disabilities tend to fall into this group—as early as 1989 resistance to HIV/AIDS coverage was at the forefront of the congressional debates surrounding the ADA's disability definition (Colker 2005).

A more central criticism of the tendency to define—and consequently limit—disability was waged by the International Disability Caucus, which claimed the right to "self-determine" a disability identity and rejected "externally imposed definitions" that would inevitably derive from a medical model of disability (Kayess and French 2008, 23). There was a general concern that a society's understanding of disability would emerge over time, and that a definition of disability would run the risk of time-locking the CRPD, as well as potentially imposing Western disability norms on non-Western countries. As a result, Article 2 of the final text providing definitions for CRPD includes neither the term "disability" nor "persons with disabilities." It defines other central terms of the Convention, such as "communication" and "language" to include Braille, sign, plain language, or other forms of augmented and accessible communications. Article 2 also defines "discrimination on the basis of disability" to mean "any distinction, exclusion or restriction on the basis of disability which has the purpose or effect of impairing or nullifying the recognition, enjoyment or exercise, on an equal basis with others, of all human rights and fundamental freedoms. It includes all forms of discrimination, including denial of reasonable accommodation" (Article 2-c). Finally, the terms "reasonable accommodation" and "universal design" find their way into the article on definitions, but not the term "disability." The Convention's preamble refers to "disability," but again without giving a definition, claiming instead that it is "an evolving concept." The preamble also makes it clear that disability is to be understood in accordance with the social model of disability, claiming that "disability results from the interaction between persons with impairments and attitudinal and environmental barriers that hinders their full and effective participation in society on an equal basis with others" (CRPD Preamble, Section E).

It is this call to integrate the social model that initiated the first level of Japanese harmonization reforms of the Disability Policy Committee. In 2011 the Japanese Diet amended the Fundamental Law for Disabled Persons, which is the basic law covering all people with disabilities (separate laws specify disability definitions for the three disability categories used in Japanese law: physical disability, intellectual disability, and mental disability). Article 3 (1) defines persons with disabilities as "individuals who have physical, intellectual or mental impairments [including developmental disability] and whose daily life or social life is substantially and continuously limited due to their impairments and various social barriers." This definition recognizes the affect of social norms and barriers on the production of disability, rather than focusing on individual impairments, and as such firmly anchors the social model in Japanese disability law. The 2011 revision also establishes three fundamental principles to guide Japanese disability law and policy: the promotion of independent living in the community, the prohibition of disability-based discrimination, and the promotion of international partnerships.

While these reforms align Japanese disability law with the social model called for in the CRPD's preamble, Japanese disability law does not protect from bias regarding past or future disability, or bias resulting from assumptions about disability. Japanese reformers remain inspired by the three-prong definition of disability of the Americans with Disabilities Act, which covers actual disability, a record of disability, and being regarded as having a disability (ADA Section 12102). The ADA definition is a source of inspiration because it recognizes that much of disability discrimination is not actually intentional, but comes as a result of ignorance, fear, stigma, and general lack of awareness of disability issues (Nakagawa and Blanck 2010, 208).

Japanese reformers also look toward the American experience with the ADA's workplace discrimination cases in thinking about how the new Japanese law should define concepts such as "reasonable accommodations" and "undue hardship." They are keenly aware of the complex and often contentious process of determining when workplace accommodations are deemed "reasonable" and to what degree employers may claim an "undue hardship" as a defense against workers' accommodation claims. American employers reacted to the passage of ADA with unease, if not hostility. They assumed that the law would force them to hire unqualified workers, that accommodations would impose excessive costs, and that, generally, the ADA would provide a "windfall for plaintiffs" making illegitimate claims (Colker 1999). Twenty-some years of empirical research on the impact of the ADA has refuted these claims, but in many ways the ADA is still viewed as an encroachment on employers' freedom to determine their business practices. Japanese reformers are cautioned to learn from these experiences and embrace a view of disability employment law that is more cooperative and constructive. "If Japanese employers initially understood the limitations of undue hardship on the duty to accommodate, negative fear may be lessened and corporate attitudes may be more supportive, flexible, cooperative, and constructive for new relationships with persons with disabilities" (Nakagawa and Blanck 2010, 211).

Japanese employers are well acquainted with legal requirements to hire employees with disabilities via the quota-levy system, as well as the unique features of Japanese contract law that limit employers' rights of dismissal. These two features of Japanese employment law may ease the initial resistance to workplace accommodation claims. However, the practice of negotiating reasonable accommodations, which American law stipulates as an individualized and interactive negotiation between employee and employer, might prove more difficult for Japanese employees. Empirical studies of Japanese corporate culture show that formal dispute resolution mechanisms, such as grievance committees, are underused and do not function well.[34] These findings are consistent with larger studies regarding the Japanese tendency to eschew formalized dispute resolution and to prefer private and informal mediation.[35] Thus, Japanese reformers are calling for a clear and "culturally acceptable" negotiation process regarding the provision of reasonable accommodations in Japan's future disability antidiscrimination law (Nakagawa and Blanck 2010, 214).

HARMONIZING REASONABLE ACCOMMODATIONS
IN JAPANESE EMPLOYMENT LAW

A central issue is the question of disability-based employment discrimination. How should Japanese law address the issue of reasonable accommodations: What is considered reasonable, and what would count as an undue hardship for employers? As mentioned earlier in this chapter, the issue of reasonable accommodations is a key component of the way that the CRPD guarantees a substantive form of equality by ensuring that people with disabilities have the opportunity to exercise their rights in the first place. When it comes to employment discrimination issues, Japanese labor law does not explicitly provide for reasonable accommodations. However, unique features of Japanese contract law offer limited protections for workers with full-time employment contracts. Japanese employment law thus provides a legal basis for the duty of employers to provide reasonable accommodations to their employees; however, these have little to do with civil rights or antidiscrimination law. These features have to do with the traditional protection from dismissal that is inherent in Japan's postwar protection of workers' rights, as well as more paternalistic protections of workers' health and safety. Generally, Japanese labor law imposes strong procedural safeguards against dismissal, affirmed by the courts' reluctance to grant a broad exercise of the right of dismissal (Nakagawa and Blanck 2010, 182). Employers may dismiss an employee who cannot perform the essential functions of the job, or if there are long-term issues of incompetence. In general, however, Japanese law requires employers to avoid dismissal of employees with disabilities and to rely on transfers or reassignments instead. In 1998 the Japanese Supreme Court affirmed the right of contracted employees to fulfill their employment contracts by being reassigned to different or lighter duties, rather than being forced to take unpaid leave.[36] And yet these protections remain limited to transfers, limited assignments, sick leave, and reduction of workloads, rather than encompassing the larger duty to accommodate difference.

An example of this shortcoming is the well-cited 2005 Yokohama case, which outlines the limitations of disability-related dismissals. Here the Tokyo Court of Appeals affirmed the dismissal of a dental hygienist who had been conducting dental exams on elementary school children. She was using a wheelchair, which made it difficult to conduct exams, and had requested a series of relatively modest accommodations—a separate chair for herself, or having children lie down during exams—all of which were refused. The court agreed with the refusal to accommodate, ruling that employers are not required to provide accommodations if these make the employee less efficient in performing the job. In the hygienist's case, the accommodation presented a burden on the employer (or the students) that was beyond the employer's duty to accommodate.[37] Thus, Japanese law provides only the minimal protection that is based on the paternalistic tradition of employer-employee relationship. The UN Convention's concept of reasonable accommodations is much broader in its understanding of reasonable accommodations and offers more comprehensive coverage of disabled workers' rights to disability-related accommodations.

Thus, if Japanese disability law is to incorporate the broader understanding of reasonable accommodations mandated by the UN Convention, it is clear that Japan will need to implement significant reforms. The first question for the legal task force commissioned by the Health, Labor and Welfare Ministry, then, was to consider where the duty of reasonable accommodations should be located. The preferred option was to follow the U.S. example and connect the duty to provide reasonable accommodations with an anti-discrimination guarantee, such as the 2004 antidiscrimination measure embedded in the Fundamental Law, as described in chapter 4 (Nakagawa and Blanck 2010, 198). Japanese experts also followed the U.S. experience with disability discrimination being considered a form of "rational discrimination" where cost considerations are concerned (as I outlined in chapter 2). Here, the concern was that reasonable accommodations are often delegitimized for violating the norms of simple equality inherent in U.S. antidiscrimination law—in which disability-based accommodations are seen as a form of preferential treatment. Thus, any new disability discrimination law that Japan passes in the process of ratifying the Convention must establish a broad understanding of reasonable accommodations that prohibits rational discrimination and firmly lodges reasonable accommodations in the non-discrimination paradigm as a form of equal treatment. Moreover, Japanese reformers argue that such laws cannot be based in paternalistic labor law traditions, but must reflect a civil rights tradition that views disability discrimination as analogous to other forms of illegitimate discrimination.

COMBINING RIGHTS AND QUOTAS

Once the Japanese government embraces the reasonable accommodations mandate, will it still be able to maintain its employment quota system? Under this system, described in detail in chapter 4, private employers of more than 56 employees are legally obligated to maintain a disability employment quota of 2.0 percent. Employers of over 200 employees that fall short of this quota must pay a levy of ¥50,000 (approximately $625) per month for each employee they fall short. The income generated from the levy system is then used to fund employment promotion programs for workers with disabilities. The question of the future of the quota system looms large. In legal terms, antidiscrimination laws and quotas are generally viewed as embracing mutually exclusive principles: we either offer equal opportunities for disabled workers to compete in an open labor market, or we obligate employers to hire workers specifically on the basis of their disability. The common assumption is that once a country moves to embrace the disability nondiscrimination paradigm, as Great Britain did in 1995, it will abolish the employment quota in favor of equal opportunities laws. In an interesting move, the Japanese government believes it can combine the two. Both panels of legal experts convened by the Ministry of Health, Labor and Welfare after Japan signed the CRPD concluded that quotas and antidiscrimination systems are not mutually exclusive and that Japan should not prepare to abolish the employment quota in preparation for ratifying the UN Convention (Kawashima and Matsui 2011).

Japan now finds itself in the position of balancing opposing principles. Legal experts acknowledge that "we know little about how to appropriately balance these two approaches" (Kawashima and Matsui 2011). There is an understanding that the quota system continues to fulfill an important function of increasing the number of workers with disabilities in open employment. At the same time, the reasonable accommodations mandate is an important new addition to the legal paradigm designed to increase the quality of employment opportunities for workers with disabilities. Traditional thinking on disability employment places the two concepts in an opposing binary: while the quota system is designed to contribute to the *quantity* of employment, antidiscrimination measures are said to contribute to the *quality* of employment (Kawashima and Matsui 2011). Japanese labor economists had already begun to rethink the role of the employment quota more broadly: they argued that although the quota certainly contributes quantity by increasing workforce participation, at the same time the levy/grant system also contributes to the quality of employment by contributing funds to innovative employment promotion grants.[38] With the development of the disability antidiscrimination concept during the 1990s, however, a synergy between the two concepts is becoming more feasible. When employers refuse to employ workers with disabilities, antidiscrimination law creates an individual enforceable right. However, these rights apply only to the individual and are after the fact. The quota system, in contrast, does not rely on employee initiative and instead forces employers to do the right thing. A synergy between these two initiatives combines their different strengths (employer responsibility and individual initiative) to improve disability employment in the long run.

The Japanese task force is now investigating ways that Japan can incorporate the reasonable accommodations principle into its present quota scheme. Specifically the question is the limit of the expense employers should be asked to incur when providing reasonable accommodations (known as the "undue burden" defense in the American case), and, in direct contrast to the American experience, how much financial assistance the Japanese government should offer employers that provide accommodations. Japanese researchers are eager to learn about the costs of reasonable accommodations from the American experience, which, as I discuss in detail in chapter 1, has shown that average accommodations costs tend to be very moderate, ranging from about $500 to completely cost-free.[39] Given the existing quota system in Japan, then, Kawashima and Matsui (2011, 24) propose setting the monthly levy payment of ¥50,000/$625 (for employers to whom the quota applies) as a minimum threshold cost for reasonable accommodations, which would add up to ¥600,000/$7,500 for the fiscal year. This way, the cost of improving the quality of disability employment would be seen as the equivalent of the cost of improving the quantity.

When it comes to questions of state support for employers providing reasonable accommodations, Japan is looking toward Germany rather than toward the United States. State financial support of reasonable accommodations can be seen as a fusion of the antidiscrimination and quota systems. Japan already has a grant system generated by the levies collected by employers who fall short of the quota, so it is not a far stretch to apply these grants to the provision of reasonable accommodations and have it administered by the Japan Organization for the Elderly and Persons with Disabilities, which is in charge of implementing the quota-levy system. Thus, in the Japanese evolution toward antidiscrimination law, the present quota system is not an impediment, as traditionally assumed, but rather an advantage, as it allows for the combination of positive (quotas) and negative (antidiscrimination) rights envisioned by the CRPD.

THE IMPACT OF INTERNATIONAL NORMS
ON JAPANESE DISABILITY LAW

The Japanese response to the CRPD—and to the UN's International Decade of Disabled Persons earlier—shows the positive impact of international legal norms on Japanese disability law. This is significant in comparison to the profound levels of resistance toward inclusive education as part of Germany's ratification of the Convention. International instruments that are not binding under international law, such as declarations on human rights, are non-self-executing, and in the past the Japanese government has shown great reluctance to sign them. Nevertheless, they have become an important symbol for Japan's participation in the international human rights community and its role in the international political arena. Japan has ratified some of the most important human rights conventions in the last twenty years, including those on economic, social, cultural, and political rights (1979), refugees (1982), women (1985), children (1994), and racial discrimination (1995). Ratification of these treaties in most cases forced Japan to revise its laws to bring them into conformity with the requirements of the treaties. The Japanese Constitution (Article 98.2) establishes that treaties and customary international law have the domestic legal force of law in Japan and thus prevail over Diet statutes.

This was the case with Japan's 1985 ratification of the 1979 UN Convention on the Elimination of All Forms of Discrimination against Women mentioned earlier in this chapter. Japan initially opposed the Women's Rights Convention for conflicting with many aspects of Japanese law regarding women and work. Thus, the Japanese delegation rejected clauses regarding equal rights for women in respect to their children's nationality, paid maternity leave, and prevention of dismissal from employment due to marriage and childbirth. In fact, Japan probably would not have signed the Convention had it not been for the pressure of women's groups and female Diet members, who portrayed the Japanese government as out of touch with international norms regarding gender equality (Gelb 2003). Once the Japanese government ratified the Convention it was forced to reform its employment law to reflect the new emphasis on equal opportunities. The resulting 1985 Equal Employment Opportunity Law recognizes discriminatory treatment against women workers but does not impose enforceable remedies for discriminatory treatment.

International influence has played a large role in the development and reform of Japanese disability law. In 1955, the International Labor Organization passed its Recommendation on Vocational Rehabilitation, which became the internationally recognized guideline for vocational rehabilitation and spurred appropriate legislation in most member nations. Based on this example, a coalition of disability groups led by the Japanese Society of Disabled People for Rehabilitation, one of the first-generation disability groups formed by disabled war veterans, demanded that the Japanese government take concrete action. The result was the 1960 Physically Disabled Persons Employment Promotion Law, which established an employment quota. In 1987, under the influence of the International Year of Disabled Persons and the ILO Convention Concerning Vocational Rehabilitation and Employment of Disabled Persons, which was geared primarily to expand employment opportunities, the Japanese government renamed the law and expanded the quota and the levy systems to include people with mental disabilities. The 1990 ADA prompted a shift in Japanese disability activism that began to work toward notions of disability rights consciousness, equal treatment, and antidiscrimination. The culmination of this movement will be the legal reforms implemented as a result of Japan's eventual ratification of the CRPD, and the introduction of Japan's first comprehensive disability antidiscrimination law.

Why has the international example—be it from the United States or the United Nations—provided such a powerful impetus for reform in Japanese disability law? In assessing the impact of international human rights law on Japanese domestic law and policy, legal scholar Yuji Iwasawa (1998, 292) claims that Japanese courts are remarkably reluctant to deal with international human rights law mainly due to their unfamiliarity with this relatively new branch of law. As a result, courts tend to ignore arguments based on international human rights law, preferring to interpret the Japanese Constitution instead. The courts' reluctance to deal with international human rights law is not restricted to human rights cases, Iwasawa argues, but reflects their general practice of judicial restraint. The most powerful affect of international law, then, is in the ratification of treaties. Once the Japanese government decides to enter into a treaty, it makes great efforts to bring Japanese law into conformity. As a result, Japanese social movements tend to welcome international pressure on the Japanese government to generate a public commitment to human rights principles. In the last few decades, international human rights law has enjoyed unprecedented interest in Japan, generating a growing body of literature. Direct invocation of international law tends to be unsuccessful in the courts, but the laws that were challenged were often amended in the political process (Iwasawa 1998, 308). International law has become a powerful tool for generating public awareness and mobilizing support for social change, leading some to claim that the effect of international covenants on Japanese legal norms serves as a powerful example of the profound influence of international laws on domestic policy regardless of the lack of enforcement powers (Port 1991, 140–41).

The impact of global norms on Japanese domestic law is especially strong because Japan is tightly linked to international society and carefully considers its role as both a political and economic leader in Asia. Integrated countries are more vulnerable to international pressure to comply with global standards, which have greater legitimacy and tend to be accompanied by stronger political institutions and nongovernmental activist networks (Tsutsui and Shin 2008). To what degree Japan's scheduled ratification of the CRPD exemplifies this process remains to be seen. Japanese reformers are inspired by the broad promise the CRPD holds for the future of Japanese disability law, which may successfully combine traditional guarantees of positive rights (in the form of employment quotas) with the new commitment to antidiscrimination.

CONCLUSION: MOBILIZING GLOBAL DISABILITY RIGHTS

As the first binding human rights instruments of the 21st century, the CRPD is also the first document that effectively disrupts the conventional separation of first- and second-generation human rights documents. The CRPD acknowledges that in the provision of disability rights, guarantees of formal equality and guarantees of substantive equality—positive and negative rights—must be addressed as interrelated and connected. The Convention officially recognizes what disability scholars and activists have been claiming all along: the promise of equal treatment for people with disabilities will be meaningful only if we go beyond simple notions of equality and provide the means necessary to act on the equal rights provided in the first place. The American experience with disability rights initiated the global transformation of thinking about disability as a rights issue. The ADA's inclusion of reasonable accommodations into the disability rights paradigm was an important first step gesturing toward more complex interpretations of what disability equality might entail. When applied in the American context of antidiscrimination law, however, the promise of disability equality often fell short. The American origins of the rights model still limited rights as being antithetical to welfare. It was the disability rights model's journey to other countries that began its transformation: German and Japanese reformers applied the disability rights model in a social and political context that did not automatically assume a binary opposition between antidiscrimination law and positive equality guarantees such as employment quotas. By the time the rights model reached the international level, it had evolved from a civil rights model based on the U.S. experience with antidiscrimination law to a broad and comprehensive mandate toward full inclusion and equality. This chapter has examined the journey of the rights model to the international arena by following the impact of the CRPD's promise of substantive equality in two case studies: inclusive education in Germany and employment law in Japan.

German and Japanese activists have mobilized the CRPD's equality mandates to challenge their governments to enact legal reforms. In both cases activists have used aspects of the "shaming" process to expose what they consider their government's backward attitudes toward disability rights and to push for domestic reforms. The traditional understanding of "shaming" in human rights discourse reserves this strategy for the United Nations itself, which adds it to its arsenal of informal and nonlegal sanctions to motivate compliance with human rights standards (Drinan 2002). Mobilizing shame has become an alternative to political and economic sanctions—which have been criticized for their tendency to turn countries into international pariahs—for moving the locus of change away from national governments and toward individual bureaucrats to cooperate with the corresponding agencies of the "offending" country to help bring it into compliance.

While shaming is becoming a well-used tool for United Nations human rights discourse, the German and Japanese examples described in this chapter demonstrate activists taking on this function themselves. German and Japanese activists seek to redefine disability rights based on the American model while also learning from the mistakes of their American mentors. With the UN Convention the rights model has come full circle as it seeks to expand traditional notions of disability equality. A new generation of disability activists can now build on the political promise of rights—to frame demands and to bestow autonomy and humanity—in order to create a new approach to disability that is equally rooted in a political commitment to social welfare and substantive notions of equality.

Conclusion: Tools for Going Global

Never before has the disability community had such tools for
communication and joint action on the national and international
level. Never before have we had such means of rapid dissemination of
facts and figures, arguments and examples of good practice. Never
before have we had such fast and inexpensive ways of consulting with
each other, pooling our resources and winning allies for our cause
across the globe. (Institute for Independent Living, "Seven Tools for
Going Global")

DISABILITY GOING GLOBAL

Disability rights have gone global. As the above statement attests, disability
rights movements now have the tools and means of communication that
transcend national networks and traditional forms of activism. The passage
of the 2006 UN Convention on the Rights of Persons with Disabilities was a
truly global affair and emerged from a level of transnational networking that
even the authors of this article (published in 1999 by the Swedish Institute
on Independent Living) could hardly anticipate.[1] Asking "are you and your
organization prepared for globalization?" the article outlines the need for
global cooperation among disability NGOs. The tools it offers include an online database of 150 disability organizations that lists their activities, special-
ization, resources, and interest in participating in joint projects with groups
or organizations in other parts of the world. The Institute also maintains a
virtual library for these organizations to publish their materials, a database
on disability-related e-mail discussion groups, a media tool kit, and an event
notification service; in short, everything a "global activist" needs to be
plugged into the international disability rights network.

The globalization tools outlined by the Swedish newsletter fifteen years ago have become staples in the toolboxes of most disability activists today. Even before the UN Convention on the Rights of Persons with Disabilities raised the bar on international cooperation among disability NGOs and policy makers, disability activism was an international effort from the get-go. The passage of the first round of disability equality laws, particularly Section 504 and the ADA in the United States, generated international attention and inspired the wave of "rights tourism" described in this book. The gradual adoption of disability rights at the regional and international level offered a new arena for activists to draw attention to those rights and to put pressure on their governments to enact reforms. The fact that disability rights are considered a second-generation civil rights movement has also contributed to the movement's international character: disability rights movements could witness the power of international cooperation of other social movements—particularly the women's movement—and adapt their strategies accordingly. In that sense, the international aspect of current disability activism is both a product of what is generally considered the globalization of law and a conscious political effort by activists to connect their struggles to international human rights principles.

A growing number of disability organizations reflect this focus on international activism. Besides the International Federation of the Blind and the World Federation of the Deaf, two disability-specific organizations that preceded the founding of Disabled Peoples International, there is Inclusion International, a grassroots advocacy organization for people with mental disabilities, and Mental Disability Rights International, a U.S.-based advocacy organization that promotes international oversight of mental disability rights. Mental Disability Rights International has conducted fact-finding missions and assisted activists in a growing number of countries,[2] helping with reform efforts in the psychiatric hospitals they visit. Other examples include the World Institute on Disability, the United Cerebral Palsy Association, Gallaudet University's Center for Global Education, Mobility International USA, the European Disability Forum, the European Network on Independent Living, and the Inter-American Institute on Disability. The research community is starting to pay attention to the global context as witnessed by the growing number of publications comparing disability law and policy and research centers focusing on international developments.[3] An Internet-based disability news service, Disability World, features regular news briefs on disability related developments around the globe. This final chapter will outline more contemporary "tools for going global" that have emerged from the UN Convention: an unprecedented degree of transnational activism that is placing pressure on national governments is using notions of shame, submitting shadow reports, and deploying the CRPD's awareness-raising mandate to contribute to global norm transformation.

THE CRPD AND GLOBAL ACTIVISM

As the first binding human rights instruments of the 21st century, the Convention on the Rights of People with Disabilities is also the first document that effectively disrupts the conventional separation of first- and second-generation human rights documents. The CRPD acknowledges that in the provision of disability rights, guarantees of formal equality and guarantees of substantive equality—positive and negative rights—must be addressed as interrelated and connected. In that sense the Convention officially recognizes what disability scholars and activists have been claiming all along: the promise of equal treatment for people with disabilities will only be meaningful if we go beyond simple notions of equality and provide the means necessary to act on the equal rights provided in the first place. The American experience with disability rights initiated the global transformation of thinking about disability as a rights issue. The ADA's inclusion of reasonable accommodations in the disability rights paradigm was an important first step that gestured toward more complex interpretations of what disability equality might entail. It theorized the refusal to accommodate disability difference as a form of discrimination, and in the process it revolutionized legal and political responses to disability difference. When applied in the American context of antidiscrimination law, however, the promise of disability equality often fell short. It was the disability rights model's journey to other countries that began its transformation. German and Japanese disability activists expanded the reach of disability rights by refusing to hold equal rights and differential treatment as mutually exclusive. The disability rights model is most effective in combating disability discrimination in a setting where the binary opposition between negative rights (such as antidiscrimination measures) and positive rights (employment quotas) is disrupted.

By the time the rights model reached the international level, it had evolved into a more comprehensive model that encompassed broader guarantees of disability equality rights. This is most evident in the CRPD's emphasis on full inclusion and reasonable accommodations, which has had a significant impact on the ways disability laws and policy conceptualize the right to equal education and equal employment opportunities for people with disabilities. *Rights Enabled* has followed the journey of the rights model from the United States to Germany and Japan, beginning with the impact of the ADA and concluding with the CRPD's promise of substantive equality in employment rights and inclusive education. In both Germany and Japan, international norms that posit disability as a human rights issue have become a powerful source of activism and legal reform. In two important points of contact that this book has described, German and Japanese disability activists have used the CRPD to challenge the traditional understanding of disability in their home countries. The first was the impact of the Americans with Disabilities Act during the 1990s, which had German and Japanese norm entrepreneurs challenge traditional thinking about disability as an issue of medical care and social welfare. The second point of contact occurred with the adoption of the UN Convention on the Rights of Persons with Disabilities in 2006, which has integrated the original promise of disability equality into a human rights framework.

MOBILIZING GLOBAL NORMS

Both points of contact with the rights model have afforded disability activists unique opportunities to engage global norms in their struggle to contest local norms regarding disability, difference, and the state's role in combating discrimination. Engaging disability as a civil rights question allowed activists to challenge traditional assumptions about disability as the absence of ability, to make visible everyday forms of discrimination and stigma, and to point to collective responsibilities to address environmental and attitudinal barriers. The German, Japanese, and U.S. activists featured in this book have formed advocacy networks that transcend national boundaries and engage disability rights on a global level. Such transnational advocacy networks have become the source of much scholarly attention in the social movement and globalization literature for acting as the main engine of transformation and norm diffusion at the global level. These advocacy networks work internationally to build links among activists, states, and international organizations to bring about a transformation of global norms. Activists can initiate a "boomerang effect" that initially allows them to bypass their (recalcitrant) state and directly search out international allies to bring pressure on their state from the outside, either through intergovernmental organizations or through direct pressure from other governments (Keck and Sikkink 1998, 13).

What binds these networks is a strong sense of "shared values, a common discourse, and dense exchanges of information and services" (Keck and Sikkink 1998, 2) *Rights Enabled* has followed the "shared value" as the spread of the disability rights model into national disability policy and ultimately into international human rights law. These networks often emerge when isolated or marginalized domestic social actors are initially denied access to the political process to change their situation. These transnational networks then "shame" the human rights violator and mobilize further support from national or international institutions. As part of the transnational disability rights advocacy network, German and Japanese activists have become "norm entrepreneurs" (Finnemore and Sikkink 1998) that work to spread the promise of disability equality, inclusion, and nondiscrimination as first outlined by the American disability rights model. As norm entrepreneurs German and Japanese disability activists have come to challenge the traditional understanding of disability in their home countries and use international pressure to shame their governments into reforms.

In both Germany and Japan, then, international norms have become a powerful source of activism and legal reform. Especially in the Japanese case, activists have used shaming processes to expose what they consider their government's backward attitudes toward disability rights. The two case studies in this book suggest that the possibility of shaming rests on notions of national identity: activists compare their national standards of disability law to those of other countries and to those set by regional and international instruments to raise national awareness about how their own countries are lacking, and then simultaneously shame their governments into initiating reforms. Activists thus work within a discourse of national identity as tied to standards of disability policy. For example, it was Japan's international reputation as an advanced and Western nation that was at stake when activists exposed human rights violations in psychiatric hospitals. In Germany, its national standing as a member of the European Union and the German embrace of the jurisdiction of European sovereignty underscores the power of international norms. Thus, Japan's orientation toward the West and embrace of "internationalization" and Germany's identity as a European power played an important role in each country's adoption of international disability rights discourse.

The awareness of international standards and comparisons between countries had a curious effect on my fieldwork as well. During my site visits to Japan, for example, it became clear that I (born and raised in Germany but also an academic living in the United States) had become an unwitting representative of the progressive German welfare system—the one that invented the disability quota. The directors of the numerous welfare institutions I visited spent considerable time with me on what might be considered a public relations effort showing the West that Japan did not lag far behind in its treatment of the disabled population. Similarly, when I talked to activists they were eager to hear about current developments in Germany and the United States and wanted to measure how far behind their country was considered. In Japan, then, the power of the international comparison was considerable. In Germany, in contrast, welfare and rehabilitation officials were more confident in their policies. Activists criticized the state of German disability politics but primarily in regard to the development of disability rights and the unfulfilled promise of the equalizing law. They knew very well that the U.S. model didn't always suit them (and in this case I became a representative of the United States, rather than Germany). My argument about the power of international norms thus repeated itself in the microcosm of my fieldwork: I came to represent an international observer with the power to judge and shame.

In both Germany and Japan, international norms that posit disability as a human rights issue have become a powerful tool for disability advocacy networks. And yet, disability activists that seek to redefine disability rights based on the American model simultaneously challenge some of the basic assumptions of the American disability model as antithetical to welfare and positive rights. German and Japanese activists remain enamored with disability rights, yet they are determined to learn from the mistakes of their American mentors. Once the rights model arrived at the international level it expanded to bridge the gap between antidiscrimination guarantees and positive entitlements. A new generation of disability activists can now build on the political promise of rights—to frame demands and to bestow autonomy and humanity—in order to create a new approach to disability that is equally rooted in a political commitment to social welfare and substantive notions of equality.

RAISING AWARENESS AND MONITORING RIGHTS

Besides providing concrete norms regarding the ways that national disability law should reflect the growing understanding of disability discrimination, the CRPD also provides a powerful awareness-raising tool for activists. Article 8 requires state parties "to adopt immediate, effective and appropriate measures . . . [t]o raise awareness throughout society, including at the family level, regarding persons with disabilities, and to foster respect for the rights and dignity of persons with disabilities." This means, initially, that state parties must either develop or significantly reform their domestic disability law and policy to reflect the Convention's emphasis on equal opportunities and social integration. Equally important, however, Article 8 provides a tremendous opportunity for activists to raise awareness and confront national governments that are reluctant to reform disability law. In that sense, Janet Lord and Michael Stein have argued persuasively that the CRPD has "expressive value" because it signals the global community's recognition that persons with disabilities have equal dignity, autonomy, and worth. An expressive value analysis of the CRPD suggests that the Convention actually has the capability of legislating a "belief change" about people with disabilities by better informing societies about the meaning and lived experience of disability (Lord and Stein 2008).

The Convention is the first human rights document that promotes a disability rights view and reflects a social model of disability. Stein and Lord suggest that these notions create a point of departure for understanding the Convention itself as a "process through which actor identities and interests may be shaped and reconstituted" (2008, 32). It obligates state parties to designate "focal points" within their governments for implementation (Article 33.1) and monitoring (Article 33.2) the CRPD, and requires the involvement of nonstate disability organizations (DPOs) in the monitoring process (Article 33.4). The CRPD's 18-member oversight committee (Article 34) evaluates the efforts made by state parties to implement the Convention, which they submit as periodic reports (Article 35), and they can make suggestions and general recommendations (Article 36). Shadow reports submitted by DPOs are not mentioned in the Convention, but they are becoming increasingly important resources for United Nations monitoring committees, as they offer alternative (and often critical) evaluations of their respective country's implementation efforts. The DPO involvement requirement in Article 33 has opened important new avenues for political impact by disability organizations that force governments to listen to the voices of people with disabilities and consider the ways disability law impacts its intended beneficiaries.

By recognizing the political importance of DPOs and by mandating state parties to become active in awareness-raising, the CRPD provides an important tool in the growing arsenal of disability NGOs to transform global norms on disability rights. It promotes disability rights as "rights of inclusion," as powerfully theorized by David Engel and Frank Munger (2003), and recognizes the substantial benefits of this inclusion not only for persons with disabilities but in the ways that it allows them to contribute to their respective societies. The CRPD's preamble acknowledges that "full participation by persons with disabilities will result in their enhanced sense of belonging and in significant advances in the human, social and economic development of society and the eradication of poverty" (CRPD Preamble, Section M). German and Japanese disability activists, who first traveled to the United States as "rights tourists" to learn about the initial manifestation of disability rights, now have a broader and more powerful *global* instrument to shape the future of their own countries' disability law and policy. They are no longer bound by the political and legal limitations of the initial rights model but can advocate for a more robust understanding of disability equality.

As an example, consider Germany's implementation of Article 8's awareness-raising mandate. In 2011 the federal government launched a 10-year "action plan" for the implementation of the CRPD's inclusion mandate that budgeted 100 million euros[4] for disability employment promotion measures alone. For Article 8 the action plan budgets 1.8 million euros (approximately $2.5 million) each year for the next 10 years for awareness-raising campaigns.[5] The campaign's central theme—*Behindern ist heilbar:* "disabling is curable"—is a pun on common assumptions that we need to cure disability, and suggests instead that what needs curing are disabling assumptions and attitudes. Similar to the 1997 campaign to promote public awareness of the disability equality clause in the German Constitution (see chapter 3), this campaign features billboards, posters, and other materials that activists can disseminate in strategic areas, featuring, at the bottom of each image, the unifying message that "Together we will implement the Disability Rights Convention."[6]

As I discussed in chapter 5, the German government's 2011 action plan and state party report to the United Nations was broadly criticized by the German disability community, particularly regarding their assessment of the government's failure to properly address the question of inclusive education. As a response, activists formed the CRPD Alliance (BRK-Allianz) and composed a detailed shadow report to accompany the federal government's official accountability report to the United Nations.[7] The awareness-raising mandate of the CRPD's Article 8 played an important role in this effort as well: the organization responsible for the wildly successful 1997 campaign, Aktion Mensch, has developed its own awareness campaign beginning in 2011 to parallel that of the federal government. Now in its third year, the campaign theorizes "inclusion" as different from "integration" to distinctly promote the CRPD's inclusion mandate as broader than the more limited forms of integration that the government's national plan had embraced. Inclusion mandates a society that promotes the equal participation of embodied difference—be it on the basis of race, sex, disability, or immigration status—from the beginning, rather than retrofitting established structures and social arrangements that had excluded people on that basis. In that sense, the campaign offered a familiar array of materials (posters, billboards, and TV clips) that gave everyday examples of inclusive arrangements at work, in school, and at play as taken for granted aspects of a society that respects disability rights.[8] The CRPD has generated disability awareness campaigns from both the public and private sectors that push for new understandings of notions of disability and difference and an inclusive society.

DISABILITY RIGHTS ON THE ROAD: IMPLICATIONS FOR THE UNITED STATES

The United States' refusal to ratify the Convention on the Rights of Persons with Disabilities has been broadly criticized by the disability rights community as a missed opportunity by a "global leader" to share its experience with the world (Thornburgh 2008). It was this very leadership position that prompted the initial refusal of the Bush administration to even sign the Convention in the first place, claiming that Americans did not need the protections of an international treaty because of the ADA's comprehensive civil rights guarantees.[9] This book has outlined both the strengths and weaknesses of the ADA and the disability rights model more generally. It is now time to ask to what degree an expanded rights model, built on the experience of other countries and broadened into a human rights guarantee, may influence U.S. disability rights law and activism. As the rights model returns to its country of origin, how can it inspire U.S. advocates to strengthen international ties and continue to work toward equal opportunities and justice for people with disabilities? This question is especially pressing as the United States is facing unprecedented waves of veterans with disabilities returning from Iraq and Afghanistan who challenge a comprehensive response to disability unemployment and support policies (Waterstone 2009). U.S. disability rights scholars have paid close attention to the ways the UN Convention both supports and exceeds the protections provided by the ADA (Palmer 2013; Perlin 2011; National Council on Disability 2008).

Rights Enabled has followed the journey of disability rights from the United States to Germany and Japan and eventually to the United Nations. As such it raises important issues not only for comparative rights scholarship or globalization studies, but also for our understanding of the uses and limitations of rights-based activism in the United States. The globalization of disability rights offers a new perspective on the limitations of equality discourse and the politics of rights, and thus provides a critical mirror for American rights culture. American political culture tends to see itself as either insulated from global pressure or as the global model for democratization and legal reform. This book challenges this view by showing the American rights model evolving once it gets reinterpreted in domestic and international disability law.

As disability rights set foot in Germany and Japan they become reinterpreted in ways that may offer more comprehensive interpretations of the equality guarantee. In Germany the individualized rights model collides with labor and welfare traditions that offer more comprehensive or positive rights against the state. In Japan it encounters communitarian critiques of rights that challenge the individualizing effect of rights talk and focus on the importance of community integration. This encounter is not a one-time affair but continues throughout the cycles of a movement.

For the comparativist and legal scholar, the injection of an American-inspired disability rights model poses important questions about the nature of American legal and political hegemony. As rights go global they lose their institutional anchors and get reinterpreted in culturally appropriate ways. Will this reinterpretation include a grappling with the limitations of the American original? The German and Japanese engagement with disability rights might give American rights activists reason to pause and consider mobilization strategies that are less tied to the equality frame and to legal remedies. As the rights model gets incorporated in new settings, it should hold as much interest for the original American pioneers as it continues to hold for those on the current and future frontiers of disability rights.

Notes

Introduction

1. This book follows the convention of capitalizing the term *Deaf* when referring to members of the Deaf Community who consider themselves as "culturally Deaf" by using sign language as their first language, identifying as members of a community and Deaf culture, and not considering themselves as impaired or in need of a remedy.

Chapter One

1. WID speeches by Ed Roberts, http://wid.org/about-wid/highlights-from-speeches-by-ed-roberts.

2. www.edrobertscampus.org.

3. The United States has yet to accept the ICESCR despite the fact that it has been approved by 149 countries. Similarly, the United States is the only country other than Somalia that has not ratified the Convention on the Rights of the Child, the most widely and rapidly ratified human rights treaty in history.

4. During the signing ceremony, President George H. W. Bush famously referenced the recent fall of the Berlin Wall and intoned, "Let the shameful wall of exclusion finally come tumbling down."

5. ADA Findings Section 42 U.S.C. § 12101 (a) (8).

6. Kemp had experienced disability discrimination first hand: an honors law school graduate, he received rejections from 39 law schools and later was denied a promotion with the Securities and Exchange Commission for using a wheelchair. He became a vocal critic of disabling stereotypes presented in the Muscular Dystrophy telethons and joined a variety of disability organizations. In 1990 President Bush named Kemp as Chair of the U.S. Equal Employment Opportunity Commission.

7. NCD 1986, "Toward Independence" (http://www.ncd.gov/newsroom/publications/1986/toward.htm).

8. Attorney General Richard Thornburgh quoted in "ADA: A Special Issue," 24.

9. Congressman Steny H. Hoyer, statement, *Congressional Record,* v. 136 (May 17, 1990), 2426–27.

10. Representative Steve Bartlett, quoted in "The Americans with Disabilities Act: Ensuring Equal Access to the American Dream," National Council on Disability, 1995. http://www.ncd.gov/publications/1995/01262005.

11. Congressman Tony Coelho, statement, Senate Hearings (May 9, 1989, 7), introducing a version of the ADA (H.R. 2273). That same day, Senators Harkin and Kennedy introduced the identical bill (S. 933) in the Senate.

12. See, most prominently, Richard Epstein, *Forbidden Grounds: The Case against Employment Discrimination Laws* (Cambridge: Harvard University Press, 1995).

13. The most prominent representative of empirical studies demonstrating the productive and efficient use of disability accommodations is the 1994 study (and its 1996 follow-up study) of pre- and post-ADA employment practices of the Sears Company. See Peter Blanck, "Communicating the Americans with Disabilities Act, Transcending Compliance: 1996 Follow-Up Report on Sears, Roebuck and Co." (Iowa City, Iowa, 1996).

14. The regulations for Section 504 of the Rehabilitation Act state that "[a] small daycare center might not be required to expend more than a nominal sum, such as that necessary to equip a telephone for use by a secretary with impaired hearing, but a larger school district might be required to make available a teacher's aide to a blind applicant for a teacher's job" (42 Fed. Reg. 22672, May 4, 1977).

15. 135 Congressional Record S10, 733 (September 8, 1989).

16. EEOC Compliance Manual (BNA), n. 11, March 1, 1999.

17. *Vande Zande v. State of Wisconsin Dept. of Administration,* 44 F.3rd 538 (7th Circuit 1995) and *Borkowski v. Valley Central School District,* 63 F.3rd 131 (2nd Circuit 1995).

18. *Jackson v. City of Joliet,* 715 F.2d 1200, 1203 (7th Cir. 1989) (Posner).

19. Shawn Fremstad, "Half in Ten: Why Taking Disability into Account Is Essential to Reducing Income Poverty and Expanding Economic Inclusion," Center for Economic and Policy Research, September 2009 (cited in Mark C. Weber, "Disability Rights, Welfare Law," 32 *Cardozo Law Review* [2011], 2486), available at www.cepr.net/documents/publications/poverty-disability-2009-09.pdf.

Chapter 2

1. As cited in Charles Wilson, "The Other Movement That Rosa Parks Inspired," *Washington Post,* October 30, 2005.

2. Email communication with ADAPT activists on a disability research discussion list (www.jiscmail.ac.uk/lists/disability-research.html), April 6, 2010.

3. The 1974 Rehabilitation Act Amendment defines a handicapped individual as "any person who (i) has a physical or mental impairment which substantially limits one or more of such person's major life activities, (ii) has a record of such an impairment, or (iii) is regarded as having such an impairment." *29 U.S.C. § 706 (8).* The ADA copied this definition verbatim, except for replacing the term

"handicapped" with "individual with a disability" to reflect a new preference for people-first language.

4. See *Griggs v. Duke Power Co.*, 402 U.S. 424 (1971), for the court's recognition of the disparate impact theory of discrimination.

5. *Frontiero v. Richardson*, 411 U.S. 677 (1973).

6. *Frontiero v. Richardson*, 411 U.S. at 684.

7. When the U.S. Supreme Court encounters laws based on "real differences" between the sexes, it will use the lowest level of judicial scrutiny, the rational basis test. For example, in *Geduldig v. Aiello*, 417 U.S. (1974) the court held that a government rule to exclude pregnancy from publicly funded medical benefits was not a form of sex discrimination, as it merely discriminated between "the pregnant and the non-pregnant" rather than between women and men. Similarly, statutory rape laws protected underage girls more than boys because of a "natural differences" that gave girls an automatic disincentive from underage sex (unwanted pregnancy), whereas boys would need the added disincentive of a criminal law. *Michael M. v. Super. Ct. of Sonoma County*, 450 U.S. (1981).

8. *Loving v. Virginia*, 388 U.S. 1 (1967).

9. *Sutton v. United Airlines, Inc.*, 527 U.S. 471 (1999); *Murphy v. United Parcel Service, Inc.*, 527 U.S. 516 (1999); *Albertsons, Inc. v. Kirkingburg*, 527 U.S. 555 (1999).

10. "Whether a person has a disability should be assessed without regard to the availability of mitigating measures, such as reasonable accommodations or auxiliary aids." Senate Report No. 101–116 at 121 (1989).

11. *Toyota Motor Manufacturing, Kentucky, Inc. v. Williams*, 534 U.S. 184 (2002) at 201–202.

12. In all federal courts, disability plaintiffs would lose at astounding rates— over 90 percent of employment discrimination cases were resolved in favor of the employer (Colker 1999).

13. Pub. L. No. 110-325 Sec. 2(b)(5), 122 Stat. 3553, 3554.

14. Ibid.

15. *Manhart* (*City of Los Angeles v. Manhart*, 435 U.S. 702 [1978]) demonstrates that even where an employer has a well-grounded, bottom-line focused justification for its discrimination (in this case, that women live longer than men and will collect retirement benefits longer, and so should be required to contribute more to cover their larger expected benefits), Title VII will not grant it a business justification defense.

16. *Johnson Controls* (*Automobile Workers v. Johnson Controls, Inc.*, 499 U.S. 187 [1991]) had instituted a sex-specific fetal protection policy that excluded potentially fertile women workers from jobs entailing large exposure to lead. Here the court, too, rejected the benign fetus-protection policy as a form of disparate treatment in violation of Title VII.

17. 536 U.S. 73 (2002).

18. "Americans with Disabilities Act: Hearing Before the House Committee on Small Business," 101st Congress 126 (1990) (testimony of Arlene Mayerson).

19. This is not to say that there should not be legitimate concerns about main-

taining OSHA standards, which after all force employers to provide a "workplace free from recognized hazards." The question becomes to what degree employers can cite a concern with OSHA standards as a way of avoiding discrimination charges. *Automobile Workers v. Johnson Controls, Inc.*, 499 U.S. 187 (1991); *Dothard v. Rawlinson*, 433 U.S. 321 (1977).

20. 527 U.S. 555 (1999).

Chapter 3

1. Unpublished poem by Tanja Muster, English translation is mine. This poem uses a pun on the German term *Urteil* (judgment) and *Vorurteil* (prejudice).

2. Bundesverfassungsgericht, Karlsruhe, October 29, 1997.

3. "Constitutional Court Decision on Educational Integration Met with Widespread Indignation" (*Breite Empörung gegen das Verfassungsgerichtsurteil zur schulischen Integration Behinderter*), October 29, 1997, press release by the Independent Living Organization (Behindertenverband Interessenvertretung 'Selbstbestimmt Leben' Deutschland e.V.), www.behinderte.de/bvg/bvg-isl.htm.

4. The most prominent English language representations of this literature are Gallagher 1995; Friedlander 1997; Lifton 2000; and, more generally, Poore 2007.

5. The proper translation of the term *Schwerbschädigter* is "severely damaged" instead of disabled; something that was changed when the law was reformed in the mid-1970s. The new law replaced the term "damaged" with the term "disabled."

6. A more detailed discussion of the German education system and parents activism is described in chapter 5.

7. After legislative reforms in 2001 the office is now called the Integrationsamt (Integration Office).

8. The disability ID card does not contain medical data but a description of the specific disability: "walking disability," "extreme walking disability," "blind," "helpless," "entitled to accompaniment in public transportation" (*ständige Begleitung*).

9. The title of Seifert's book is *Versorgt bis zur Unmündigkeit*.

10. Gusti Steiner, Wie Alles Anfing: Konsequenzen Politischer Behindertenselbsthilfe, 2003; http://www.forsea.de/projekte/20_jahre_assistenz/steiner.shtml.

11. The official title of the government liaison is "the representative of the needs of the disabled before the federal government." Activists, however, like to call him the "representative of the needs of the government before the disabled." So far the disability liaison office has been held by career politicians, none of them disabled (www.behindertenbeauftragter.de).

12. For a more extensive account of his one-year visit to Berkeley see Ottmar Miles-Paul, *Wir Sind Nicht Mehr Aufzuhalten* (We Are Unstoppable) (Munich: AG Spak Bücher, 1992).

13. The PDS (Partei des Demokratischen Sozialismus) became the Left Party (Die Linke) in 2005.

14. *Der Dritte Rehabilitationsbericht der Bundesregierung* (1994), document no. 14.7, p. 306.

15. M. Höck, *Die Hilfsschule im Dritten Reich* (1977). See, generally, Martin Rudnick, *Behinderte im Nationalsozialismus: von der Ausgrenzung und Zwangssterilisation zur "Euthenasie"* (Weinheim: Beltz, 1985), and Klara Nowak, "Verweigerte Anerkennung als NS-Verfolgte: Zwangssterelisierte und Euthanasie-Geschädigte." in *Medizin und Gewissen: 50 Jahre nach dem Nürnberger Aezteprozeß,* ed. Stephan Kolb and Horst Seithe (Frankfurt: Mabuse, 1998).

16. Until reunification in 1990 the West German Constitution was called a "Basic Law" to recognize its provisional nature in a divided country. The framers in 1949 did not want to prejudice the possibility of future unification under a permanent constitution.

17. The U.S. equivalent to this is was the ongoing protest against Jerry Lewis's telethon, covered brilliantly in the pages of the movement magazine *Disability Rag* (see Barett Shaw, ed., *The Ragged Edge: The Disability Experience from the Pages of the First Fifteen Years of the* Disability Rag (Louisville, KY: Advocado Press, 1994). See also Harriet Johnson, *Too Late To Die Young* (New York: Picador, 2005).

18. www.aktion-grundgesetz.de.

19. The German phrase is *"Ich sehe was, was Du nicht siehst."*

20. Comment by Johann Kraiter (Active Disabled in Stuttgart). All testimony regarding the Operation cited here was published on their website (www.aktion-sorgenkind.de), which was taken down once the organization changed its name. The content is now no longer available online.

21. http://www.aktion-mensch.de/wirueberuns/print/namensaenderung. html (link no longer active; last accessed in 2003).

22. Comment by Octavio Paz of the Disability Counseling Institute from the now-defunct website www.aktion-sorgenkind.de.

23. Comment by Gisela Hermes of bivos e. V., see ibid.

24. Comment by Stefan Dose of the Federal Association for Supported Employment, at www.aktion-sorgenkind.de (see note 22).

25. E. Klee, *Behinderte im Urlaub? Das Frankfurter Urteil: Eine Dokumentation* (Frankfurt am Main: Fischer Taschenbuch Verlag, 1980).

26. Flensburg, decision of August 27, 1992 (63C 264/92).

27. I am translating the term *Gleichstellungsgesetz* as "equalizing law" rather than just "equality law" because the term *Gleichstellung* ("equalization of status") goes beyond the more limited notion of equality (*Gleichheit*) as captured by an antidiscrimination mandate.

28. *Aktuelle Informationen zum Sachstand eines Bundesgleichstellungsgesetzes* (Latest Information on the Status of the Equalizing Law) from the office of the government's disability liaison, www.behindertenbeauftragte.de/bundesgleich.stm.

29. Available at www.nw3.de/dbr/lobbytips.htm.

30. www.aktionmensch.de.

31. The Bundestag (lower house) passed the law on February 28, 2002, and the Bundesrat (upper house) passed it on March 22, 2002, with a large majority vote in both houses.

32. The draft was entitled *Forum behinderter Juristinnen und Juristen. Entwurf eines Gleichstellungsgesetzes für Menschen mit Behinderungen in der Bundesrepublic Deutschland.* The draft by the Forum was altered substantially before introduced to the Bundestag for passage (www.behindertenbeauftragter.de/pdfs/111641 8775_pdf.pdf).

33. The revised WHO Classifications from 2001 have become the International Classification of Function, Disability and Health (ICF). They focus on interdependency instead of a chain of causation, and seek to implement participation into the definition of disability.

34. § 2 SGB IX. The German text reads in § 2 (1) SGB IX: "Menschen sind behindert, wenn ihre körperliche Funktion, geistige Fähigkeit oder seelische Gesundheit mit hoher Wahrscheinlichkeit länger als sechs Monate von dem für das Lebensalter typischen Zustand abweichen und daher ihre Teilhabe am Leben in der Gesellschaft beeinträchtigt ist."

35. Section 77(2) spells out a tiered levy system: employers must pay 105 euros per month for each unfilled post if they employ 3 percent up to the legal quota on annual average. If they employ between 2 percent and 3 percent the payment goes up to 180 euros. If they employ less than 2 percent the levy raises again to 260 euros.

36. The relevant law covering inns and restaurants was amended as a result of the BGG requiring newly constructed buildings to be accessible (*Gaststättengesetz* of 1998, Section 4).

37. The original Forum draft had stipulated that half of all jobs achieved through the employment quota be reserved for women with disabilities, and that local state governments offer publicly funded self-defense courses. *Entwurf eines Gleichstellungsgesetzes für Behinderte* (draft of a disability equalizing law) of January 8, 2000. Unpublished.

38. As an example, consider an essay in the Aktion Sorgenkind magazine's anniversary issue entitled "We Want Laws Like This in Germany" gives a science fiction account of the American feminist disability movement in the year 2015, demanding their rights as women with disabilities based on the model their German sisters provided in the year 2000 (www.aktionsorgenkind.de, no longer available online).

Chapter 4

1. "Wheelchair Pioneer Out to Change Public Perceptions," *Japan Times*, January 1, 2011, http://search.japantimes.co.jp/print/fl20110101a1.html.

2. "Japan is 20 years behind the Europeans in disability politics, and 30 years behind the United States" is a statement I heard repeatedly during my fieldwork in Japan, from both disability activists and bureaucrats.

3. Author's e-mail conversation with Nagase Osamu, January 16, 2001.

4. "Overcoming Blind Discrimination," *Japan Times*, January 27, 2000. The article did not state where Yamamoto got her statistics on blind U.S. lawyers.

5. Due to the change in government the Japanese Diet did not vote to ratify the Treaty in 2013, and had not done so by the time this book went to press in the fall of 2014.

6. For the full Japanese text of all disability laws cited here, see http://www.dinf.ne.jp/doc/law/jsrd/z00002/z00002.htm.

7. The term "intellectual disability" is slowly replacing the official term "mental weakness" (*seishin hakujakusha*), which is considered derogatory and discriminatory by most activists.

8. See http://www.dinf.ne.jp/doc/law/jsrd/z00002/z00002.htm.

9. During my visits to Japan on several occasions I have heard a woman scolding her child not to use the accessible toilet because "it's dirty in there."

10. Author's interview with Kawauchi, November 1998, Tokyo.

11. Japan's International Cooperation Agency, part of the Office for Development Assistance, has trained foreign rehabilitation professionals and disability activists since 1986 in policy issues, leadership seminars, and international cooperation, and has provided resources and experts to various South Asian countries (JICA Research Institute: http://jica-ri.jica.go.jp/index.html).

12. JEED Research Report #1 2010 (Overview of Persons with Disabilities and Employment), http://www.jeed.or.jp/english/supporting.html.

13. A 1998 *Nikkeiren* survey counted 65 *tokurei kogaisha* with a total of 4, 000 employees. Of these 3,400 were people with disabilities, including 2,000 with severe disabilities, which count double for the quota (*Tokurei Kogaisha no Keiei ni kan suru Ankeeto Chôsa*, March 1998, 10). As of June 2008 that number had almost quadrupled: there were 242 special subsidiary companies, employing around 7,700 persons with disabilities with more than 40 percent being persons with intellectual disabilities (Matsui 2010, 10).

14. Author's interview with the director of Seibi Shokugyō Jisshūsho, the nation's first private workshop established in 1969 in Tokyo.

15. See Nagae 2008, 3, which cites the study by T. Nakajima, S. Nakano, and S. Imai, "Waga kuni no shōgaisha kōyō nōhukinnseido no keizai bunseki—shōgaisha kōyō no sokushin ni mukete" [The economic analysis of the quota-levy system in Japan—toward the promotion of disability employment], PRI Discussion Paper Series No. 05A-23 (2006).

16. Since the U.S. education system is not segregated in this way, there is no equivalent terminology for "regular schools" (*tsuujougakkou* in Japanese and *Regelschule* in German) in English.

17. This trend is strengthened with the increasingly common policy of firms of only hiring workers with a high school diploma.

18. Mothers are considered "natural" caregivers and automatically assumed to provide for their children's needs in school. There is little reflection on the gendered nature of women's caregiving work within the disability education literature.

19. The book is entitled *Nobody's Perfect* in the English translation (Tokyo: Kodansha, 2000).

20. Personal communication with Nagase Osamu, September 1998.

21. The event has become known in disability circles as the 1977 Kawasaki Basu Toso.

22. Nirje has acknowledged the criticism he has received for his choice of the term "normal," which many say engenders a sanctioning of a nondisabled norm. He maintains, however, that this term does not imply forcing this norm on people with mental retardation ("25 Years of the Normalization Principle," a presentation by Beignt Nirje at a symposium in Yokohama, October 15, 1998, honoring his work and activism).

23. Ministry of Health and Welfare, Annual Report on Health and Welfare (Tokyo, 1992), p. 2.

24. On October 1, 1997, the Osaka prefectural government withdrew the license for Yamatogawa Hospital, three years after mental health and human rights activists started their movement to force an official response to the human rights abuses occurring there. Miyuki Yamamoto, "Seishin Iriyou Jinken Centaa" [Osaka Human Rights Center for the Mentally Ill], unpublished Address before the Zenkaren Conference, Tokyo, 1998.

25. Tomoko Otake, "Disability in Japan: Is 'Disability' Still a Dirty Word in Japan?" *Japan Times,* August 27, 2006 (http://search.japantimes.co.jp/cgi-bin/fl20060827x1.html).

26. For examples, those complying with the law may receive a 10-year corporate tax reduction, low-interest loans, and an exemption from paying property taxes on the buildings being reconstructed.

27. Mary Lou Breslin interviewing Yoshihiko Kawauchi, December 16, 2002, on file with the "Disability Rights and Independent Living Movement Oral History Project," University of California, Berkeley.

28. Adolf Ratzka, www.independentliving.org.

29. The Mr. Donuts restaurant chain established a travel scholarship for people with disabilities.

30. This seminar was entitled 21-seiki no Normalization and took place on October 15, 1998.

31. MHLW 1999 White Paper, 1999 *Hakusho,* www.mhlw.go.jp.

32. Both systems emerged from the same ministry, but from different departments. The *shienpi* system was developed by the Health and Welfare Department for Persons with Disabilities (*shougai koken fukushibu*), whereas the *kaigo hoken* system emerged from the Health and Welfare Bureau of the Elderly (*ryouken kyoku*). Both systems share many similarities, in terms of philosophy (user autonomy) and types of services (home-helpers, day care, and so forth). The central difference lies in the way the systems are financed: tax revenues finance the *shienpi* system, whereas premiums and co-payments finance the *kaigo hoken* system.

33. Japan Council on Disabilities, 2004 Report (www.normanet.ne.jp), and DPI Japan, 2004 Report (www.dpi-japan.org).

34. Japan National Assembly of Disabled Peoples International, *Annual Report* (April 2005–March 2006), http://www.dpi-japan.org/index.html.

35. The Citizens' Committee on Abolishing Disqualifying Clauses counts 274 clauses, in contrast to 79 clauses acknowledged by the government. For a full list of restrictions, see the online database *Shōgaisha wo Shokugyō nado kara jogai suru kekkaku jōkō wo motsu hōritsu no dētashū* (Database of Restrictive Clauses Eliminating People with Disabilities from Occupations) at http://www.humind.or.jp/welfare/disablep/restrict/index.html.

36. The ban on juries is mainly symbolic. Japan introduced the jury system for criminal cases in 1923, but juries were suspended during World War II and never officially reinstated. Thus, the jury system has never been repealed, but juries are no longer used. In 2001, however, the Judicial Reform Council report recommended a modified jury/civilian participation scheme for Japan (http://www.kantei.go.jp/foreign/judiciary/2001/0612report.html). See Richard Lempert, "A Jury for Japan?," *American Journal of Comparative Law* 40 (1992): 37.

37. Citizens Committee to Eliminate Disqualifying Clauses: "From No to Yes" (http://www.dpi-japan.org/friend/restrict/).

38. Kumi Goto, "I Want to Be a Pharmacist Who Can Treat Patients, Whether They Can Hear or Not," *Asahi Shinbun,* January 28, 2000. See also "Let Disabled Pursue Medicine Career: Panel," *Japan Times,* December 8, 2000.

39. Such as the Disability Policy Research Group (Shōgaisha Seisaku Kenkyūkai, or SSK).

40. DPI Japan 2003 Report, www.dpi-japan.org/english/e-report.html.

41. Once a state party signs the CRPD it promises to uphold its central mandates. In most cases this means that passage of comprehensive antidiscrimination law is required before the state party can ratify the Convention. The CRPD does not give detailed instructions on how to ratify the Convention, but leaves it to individual state parties.

42. Chapter 2 discusses these challenges facing the ADA in more detail.

43. At a lecture given by Ikehara Yoshikazu of LADD, July 29, 1998, at the Shinjuku Fukushi Community Center, Tokyo.

Chapter 5

1. "Americans with Disabilities Applaud President Obama's Intention to Sign the Convention on the Rights of Persons with Disabilities," USICD, July 21, 2009 (http://www.usicd.org/index.cfm/news_obama-media1-release).

2. The USICD is a federation of U.S. nongovernmental disability organizations focused on the promotion of international disability rights.

3. Letter from Kim Holmes, assistant secretary of state for international organization affairs, to the National Council on Disabilities, June 3, 2004 (http://www.usicd.org/StateDept_Letter_to_NCD.gov).

4. On March 30, 2007, the CRPD officially opened for signature and ratification. An unprecedented 82 countries signed the convention and 44 countries signed the Optional Protocol. The Convention came into force 30 days past the date of ratification by its 20th signatory. Once ratified, state parties to the Convention are expected to adopt domestic laws prohibiting discrimination on the

basis of disability and eliminate existing discriminatory laws. By the end of 2013, 158 countries had signed the Convention, and 138 have ratified it (http://www. un.org/disabilities/index.asp).

5. The CRPD Preamble states that "persons with disabilities should have the opportunity to be actively involved in decision-making processes about policies and programmes."

6. Office of the High Commissioner for Human Rights, Statement by Louise Arbor, December 5, 2006, to the UN General Assembly (www.ohchr.org).

7. The seven core human rights treaties (before the passage of the CRPD) consist of the International Convention on the Elimination of All Forms of Racial Discrimination (1965), the International Covenant on Civil and Political Rights (1966), the International Covenant on Economic, Social and Cultural Rights (1966), the Convention on the Elimination of All Forms of Discrimination Against Women (1979), The Convention against Torture (1984), the Convention on the Rights of the Child (1989), the International Convention on the Protection of the Rights of Migrant Workers (1990), and the International Convention for the Protection of All Persons from Enforced Disappearance (2006).

8. The UN General Assembly rejected the proposals for a Convention on the Elimination of All Forms of Discrimination Against Disabled Persons in 1982, 1987, and 1989.

9. Disabled women were not specifically mentioned in the Convention, so the treaty committee passed a recommendation reminding state parties that CEDAW does indeed protect the human rights of women with disabilities. It wasn't until the Nairobi World Conference on Women, which took place during the UN Women's Decade in 1985, that women with disabilities were recognized as a group. (Degener 1995, 19).

10. UN Enable, Standard Rules on the Equalization of Opportunities for Persons with Disabilities, 2010, http://www.un.org/esa/socdev/enable/dissreOO. htm.

11. www.un.org/News/Press/docs/2006/sgsm10797.doc.htm.

12. CRPD Preamble, (y) and (h).

13. Statement by Ambassador Henri-Paul Normandin, deputy permanent representative of Canada to the United Nations to the 61st Session of the United Nations General Assembly on the Convention on the Rights of Persons with Disabilities, New York, December 13, 2006, http://www.un.org/esa/socdev/enable/convstatementgov#ca. The General Assembly established the Ad Hoc Committee with resolution 56/168 of December 19, 2001, and charged it to "consider proposals for a comprehensive and integral international convention to promote and protect the rights and dignity of persons with disabilities, based on the holistic approach in the work done in the fields of social development, human rights and non-discrimination." http://legal.un.org/avl/ha/crpd/crpd.html.

14. Vienna Declaration and Programme of Action of 2003: http://www.un-hchr.ch/huridocda/huridoca.nsf/(Symbol)/A.CONF.157.23.En.

15. CRPD, Article 24 (2) (a) (b) (d).

16. In the United States, the special education classifications are speech/language impairments, emotionally disturbed, gifted and talented, specific learning disabilities, mental retardation, developmental delay, autism, visual impairments, deaf-blindness, hearing impairments, orthopedic impairments, other health impairments, multiple disabilities, and traumatic brain injury.

17. Notably absent in Germany is the category of "gifted and talented" as well as "deaf-blind" as special education classifications.

18. Deutsches PISA Konsortium 2001, as cited in Powell 2009, 176.

19. Shadow report of Netzwerk Artikel 3 e.V., *Korrigierte Fassung der zwischen Deutschland, Liechtenstein, Österreich und der Schweiz abgestimmten Übersetzung.*

20. Ulf Preuss-Lausitz, cited in Wibke Bergemann and Isabel Fannrich, "Eine Schule für alle Neue Wege zur Inklusion" (www.dradio.de/dlf/sendungen/hinter grundpolitik/1206538/).

21. Ulf Preuss-Lausitz, ibid.

22. Their activism also benefited from demographic shifts in the 1980s (a low birth rate), which prompted administrators to slow down the stream of special education students referred out to special schools because losing students in times of a low birth rate would have threatened the closure of many primary schools (Heyl 1998, 701).

23. www.eine-schule-fuer-alle.

24. Von Martina Schwager, "Inclusion: Jessica will nicht auf eine Förderschule" (Inclusion: Jessica does not want to attend special school), February 22, 2011, http://www2.evangelisch.de/themen/gesellschaft/inklusion-jessica-will-nicht-auf-eine-f%C3%B6rderschule34709.

25. In a 2008 administrative court case in Freiburg the court ruled in favor of a private school's quest to officially be labeled as an inclusive school, but the court did not use the UN Convention in its reasoning, presumably to avoid setting a legal precedent. Instead, the court used Article 7 (4) in the German Constitution, which outlines the right to establish private schools (www.freitag.de/datenbank/freitag/2009/27/bildungspolitik).

26. Case 7 B 2763/09 (Verwaltungsgericht 7 L 948/09.DA), Verwaltungsgericht Hessen, November 12, 2009.

27. For example, in 2010 Bremen became the first state to mandate inclusive education. Starting in 2011, regular schools would have to integrate students with disabilities. Parents may still chose to send their children to special schools, but even these would be phased out by 2017.

28. *Stellungnahme der Monitoring Stelle zur UN Behindertenrechtskonvention: Stellung der UN-Behindertenrechtskonvention innerhalb der deutschen Rechtsordnung und ihre Bedeutung für behördliche Verfahren und deren gerichtliche Überprüfung, insbesondere ihre Anforderungen im Bereich des Rechts auf inklusive Bildung nach Artikel 24 UN- Behindertenrechtskonvention. Gleichzeitig eine Kritik an dem Beschluss des Hessischen Verwaltungsgerichtshofs vom 12. November 2009* (http://www.institut-fuer menschenrechte.de/de/presse/stellungnahmen.html).

29. www.kmk.org, as quoted in Demke 2011.

30. *March 31, 2011: Stellungnahme der Monitoring Stelle: Eckpunkte zur Verwirklichung eines inklusiven Bildungssytems und Empfehlung an die Länder, die Kultusministerkonferenz, und den Bund* (http://www.institut-fuer-menschenrechte.de/de/presse/stellungnahmen.html).

31. Dr. Corina Zolle interviewt Dr. Klaus Mück, beide Vorstandsmitglieder des Bundesverbands Forum selbstbestimmter Assistenz behinderter Menschen ForseA e.V. zum Thema "Die Behindertenrechtskonvention der Vereinten Nationen—Warum sie ein Erfolgsmodell wird," http://www.zslschweiz.ch/news/detail.php?iid=238&aid=4.

32. Countries with a disability employment quota system are France, Germany, Poland, Italy, Spain, Austria, Hungary, the Czech Republic, Romania, Japan, Korea, Vietnam, Venezuela, and China.

33. Their website is http://www.normanet.ne.jp/~jdf/.

34. Akio Kihara, *"Kigyo-nai Funso No Yobou To Syori"* [An Empirical Study of the Dispute Resolution Systems Inside Companies in Japan], *Business Labor Trend* 7 (2008): 2, as cited in Nakagawa and Blanck 2010, 213.

35. See Frank Upham, *Law and Social Change in Postwar Japan* (Cambridge: Harvard University Press, 1987); Mark Ramseyer and Minoru Nakazata, *Japanese Law: An Economic Approach* (1999); Eric Feldman, *The Rituals of Rights in Japan* (Cambridge: Cambridge University Press, 2000); Mark West, *Law in Everyday Japan* (Chicago: University of Chicago Press, 2005).

36. The 1998 Katayama-gumi case is *Saiko Saibansho* 199, 736 *Rodo Hanrei* 15.

37. The Yokohama-shi Gakko Hokenkai case, Tokyo High Court (January 19, 2005) 890 Rohan 58.

38. Nemoto Yasutoshi, *Shōgaisha Koyō Gaido* (Disability Employment Guide) (1998), as cited in Kawashima and Matsui 2011, 24.

39. "Workplace Accommodations: Low Cost, High Impact," *Job Accommodations Network* 16 (January 2007), available at http://askjan.org/media/LowCostHighImpact.html.

Conclusion

1. "Seven Tools for Going Global," Institute for Independent Living newsletter, March 1999. www.independentliving.org.

2. Argentina, Mexico, Uruguay, Armenia, Azerbaijan, Romania, Russia, Hungary, Poland, the Czech Republic, Lithuania, Slovenia, and Slovakia (www.mdri.org).

3. Most prominent representatives in U.S. academia are the Project on Disability at Harvard Law School, the Burton Blatt Institute at Syracuse University, the Center for International Rehabilitation Research Information and Exchange at the State University of New York at Buffalo, and the Mental Disability Law Program at NYU Law School.

4. Approximately $137 million in U.S. dollars.

5. The government's action plan is available at the website of the Federal Min-

istry of Labor and Social Affairs (http://www.bmas.de/DE/Themen/Teilhabe-behinderter-Menschen/inhalt.html).

6. http://www.gemeinsam-einfach-machen.de/BRK/DE/StdS/Home/stds_node.html.

7. http://www.aktion-mensch.de/inklusion/parallelbericht/index.php.

8. The TV clips feature the friendship of a young girl and her basketball-loving best friend who uses a wheelchair; the experiences of a musician and his band who is hoping to move into his own apartment rather than moving into a home for developmentally disabled adults; and the internship of a young woman of short stature who went to an integrated school and now works as an accountant (http://www.aktion-mensch.de/inklusion/kampagne-2013.php).

9. President Obama signed the CRPD in 2009. See chapter 5 for a detailed discussion of the domestic debate surrounding the UN Convention.

References

Alston, Philip. 1995. "Disability and the International Covenant on Economic, Social and Cultural Rights." In *Human Rights and Disabled Persons: Essays and Relevant Human Rights Instruments,* edited by Theresia Degener and Yolan Koster-Dreese. Dordrecht: Martinus Nijhoff.

Arnade, Sigrid. 1998. *"Wer spinnt hier eigentlich? Amis, ADA und Alltagsfreuden"* [Who's nuts around here? Americans, the ADA, and the joys of everyday life]. In *Traumland USA: Zwischen Antidiskriminierung und Sozialer Armut* [Dreamland USA: Between antidiscrimination and social poverty], edited by Gisela Hermes. Kassel: bifos.

Asaka, Junko. 1997. "'Wahashi' E: 30 Nen Ni Tsuite" [To "me": About the 30 years]. In *Sei No Giho: Ie to Shisetsu Wo Dete Kurasu Shogaisha No Shakaigaku* [The method of life: A sociology of people with disabilities who live independent from family and institution], edited by Junko Asaka, Masayuki Okahara, Fumiya Okahara, and Shinya Tateiwa. Tokyo: Fujiwara Shoten.

Bagenstos, Samuel. 2003a. "The Americans with Disabilities Act as Welfare Reform." *William and Mary Law Review* 44:921–1028.

Bagenstos, Samuel. 2003b. "'Rational Discrimination,' Accommodation, and the Politics of (Disability) Civil Rights." *Virginia Law Review* 89:825–923.

Bagenstos, Samuel. 2009. *Law and the Contradictions of the Disability Rights Movement.* New Haven: Yale University Press.

Bandes, Susan. 1990. "The Negative Constitution: A Critique." *Michigan Law Review* 88:2271–2347.

Barnartt, Sharon, and Richard Scotch. 2001. *Disability Protests: Contentious Politics 1970–1999.* Washington, DC: Gallaudet University Press.

Baynton, Douglas. 2013. "Disability and the Justification of Inequality in American History." In *The Disability Studies Reader,* edited by Lennard Davis. New York: Routledge.

Bell, Derrick. 1979. "Brown v. Board of Education and the Interest-Convergence Dilemma." *Harvard Law Review* 93:518.

Benford, Robert, and David Snow. 1998. "Ideology, frame resonance, and participant mobilization." *International Social Movement Research* 1:197–217.

Bickenbach, Jerome. 2000. "The ADA v. the Canadian Charter of Rights: Disability Rights and the Social Model of Disability." In *Americans with Disabilities: Exploring Implications of the Law for Individuals and Institutions,* edited by Leslie Francis and Anita Silver. New York: Routledge.

Blanck, Peter. 2000. *Employment, Disability, and the Americans with Disabilities Act: Issues in Law, Public Policy, and Research.* Evanston, IL: Northwestern University Press.

Blanck, Peter, and Mollie Marti. 1997. "Attitudes, Behavior and the Employment Provisions of the Americans with Disabilities Act." *Villanova Law Review* 42:345–408.

Brückner, Dominik. 2000. "Behindertensorgen? Nicht in den USA" [Disability worries? Not in the USA]. *SoVD Zeitung,* August.

Burgdorf, Robert. 1983. "Accommodating the Spectrum of Individual Abilities." Washington, DC: U.S. Commission on Civil Rights.

Burkhauser, Richard, and Mary Daly. 1994. "The Economic Consequences of Disability: A Comparison of German and American People with Disabilities." *Journal of Disability Policy Studies* 5:25–52.

Charlton, James. 2000. *Nothing about Us without Us: Disability Oppression and Empowerment.* 1st ed. Berkeley: University of California Press.

Clark, Stephen. 2002. "Same-Sex but Equal: Reformulating the Miscegenation Analogy." *Rutgers Law Journal* 34:107–85.

Colker, Ruth. 1999. "The Americans with Disabilities Act: A Windfall for Defendants." *Harvard Civil Rights–Civil Liberties Review* 34:99.

Colker, Ruth. 2005. *The Disability Pendulum: The First Decade of the Americans with Disabilities Act.* New York: New York University Press.

Crossley, Mary 1999. "The Disability Kaleidoscope." *Notre Dame Law Review* 74:621–716.

Davis, Lennard. 2002. *Bending over Backwards: Disability, Dismodernism, and Other Difficult Positions.* New York: New York University Press.

Degener, Theresia. 1995. "Disabled Persons and Human Rights: The Legal Framework." In *Human Rights and Disabled Persons,* edited by Theresia Degener and Yolan Koster-Dreese, 9–39. Amsterdam: Martinus Nijhoff.

Degener, Theresia. 2000. "International Disability Law–A New Legal Subject on the Rise: The Interregional Experts' Meeting in Hong Kong, December 13–17, 1999." *Berkeley Journal of International Law* 18:180.

Degener, Theresia. 2006. "The Definition of Disability in German and Foreign Discrimination Law." *Disability Studies Quarterly* 26.

Degener, Theresia, and Gerard Quinn. 2002. "A Survey of International, Comparative, and Regional Disability Law Reform," In *Disability Rights Law and Policy: International and National Perspectives,* edited by Mary Lou Breslin and Sylvia Yee. Ardsley, NY: Transnational Publishers.

DeJong, Gerben. 1979. "Independent Living: From Social Movement to Analytic Paradigm." *Archives of Physical Medicine and Rehabilitation* 60:435–46.

Demke, Florian. 2011. *Das Übereinkommen der Vereinten Nationen über die Rechte von Menschen mit Behinderungen (UN-Behindertenrechtskonvention): Auswirkungen auf Sozialpolitik und Behindertenhilfe in Deutschland* [The United Nations Convention on the Rights of Persons with Disabilities: Impact on social policy and disability welfare in Germany]. Munich: GRIN Publishing.

Diller, Mathew. 2000. "Judicial Backlash, the ADA, and the Civil Rights Model." *Berkeley Journal of Employment and Labor Law* 21:19–52.

Driedger, Diane. 1989. *The Last Civil Rights Movement: Disabled Peoples' International.* New York: St. Martin's Press.

Drimmer, Jonathan. 1992. "Cripples, Overcomers, and Civil Rights: Tracing the Evolution of Federal Legislation and Social Policy for People with Disabilities." *UCLA Law Review* 40:1341.

Drinan, Robert. 2002. *The Mobilization of Shame: A World View of Human Rights.* New Haven: Yale University Press.

Dudziak, Mary. 2011. *Cold War Civil Rights: Race and the Image of American Democracy.* Princeton: Princeton University Press.

Edelman, Lauren, Gwendolyn Leachman, and Doug McAdam. 2010. "On Law, Organizations, and Social Movements." *Annual Review of Law and Social Science* 6:653–85.

Eine Schule für Alle. 2010. "Wegweiser: Wo Bitte Geht's Zur Integration?" [Signpost: How do I get to integration?]. Mittendrin Publishers, http://www.eine-schule-fuer-alle.info/shop-materialien/buecher/.

Ellison, Ralph. 1974. *The Invisible Man.* New York: Random House.

Engel, David, and Frank Munger. 2003. *Rights of Inclusion: Law and Identity in the Life Stories of Americans with Disabilities.* Chicago: University of Chicago Press.

Epstein, Richard A. 1995. *Forbidden Grounds: The Case against Employment Discrimination Laws.* Cambridge, MA: Harvard University Press.

Evans, Sara. 1997. *Personal Politics: The Roots of Women's Liberation in the Civil Rights Movement and the New Left.* New York: Random House.

Feldblum, Chai R. 2000. "Definition of Disability under Federal Anti-Discrimination Law: What Happened? Why? And What Can We Do about It?" *Berkeley Journal of Employment & Labor Law* 21:91–165.

Feldblum, Chai, Kevin Barry, and Emily Benfer. 2007. "The ADA Amendments Act of 2008." *Texas Journal on Civil Liberties & Civil Rights* 13:187.

Finnemore, Martha, and Kathryn Sikkink. 1998. "International Norm Dynamics and Political Change." *International Organizations* 52:887.

Fleischer, Doris Zames, and Frieda Zames. 2001. *The Disability Rights Movement: From Charity to Confrontation.* Philadelphia: Temple University Press.

French, Sally. 1993. "Disability, Impairment or Something in Between?" In *Disabling Barriers—Enabling Environments,* edited by John Swain, Vic Finkelstein, Sally French, and Mike Oliver. London: Sage.

Friedlander, Henry. 1997. *The Origins of Nazi Genocide: From Euthanasia to the Final Solution.* Chapel Hill: University of North Carolina Press.

Fritsch, Ingrid. 1996. *Japans Blinde Sänger* [Blind singers in Japan]. München: Iudicum.

Fujii, Katsunori. 1994. "Present Situation of Securing Work or Occupation for Disabled Persons in Japan." *Japanese Journal of Studies in Disability and Handicap* 22:140–58.

Gallagher, Hugh. 1995. *By Trust Betrayed: Patients, Physicians, and the License to Kill in the Third Reich*. St. Petersburg, FL: Vandamere Press.

Geist, Fiona, Bernd Petermann, and Volker Widhammer. 2002. "Disability Law in Germany." *Comparative Labor Law & Policy Journal* 24:563.

Gelb, Joyce. 2003. *Gender Policies in Japan and the United States: Comparing Women's Movements, Rights, and Politics*. New York: Palgrave Macmillan.

Gerber, Daniel. 2000. *Disabled Veterans in History. Corporealities: Discourses of Disability*. Ann Arbor: University of Michigan Press.

Goffman, Erving. 1963. *Stigma: Notes on the Management of Spoiled Identity*. London: Penguin.

Goto, Yoshihiko. 2008. "Cultural Commentary: Critical Understanding of the Special Support Education in Social Contexts." *Disability Studies Quarterly* 28 (3).

Gwin, Lucy. 1997. "True History." *Mouth* 7:26–27.

Hahn, Harlan. 1993. "The Political Implications of Disability Definitions and Data." *Journal of Disability Policy Studies* 4 (2): 41–52.

Halley, Janet. 1993. "Sexual Orientation and the Politics of Biology: A Critique of the Argument from Immutability." *Stanford Law Review* 46:503.

Harding, Thomas, J. Schneider, and H. Vistotsky. 1985. *Human Rights and Mental Patients in Japan*. Geneva: International Commission of Jurists.

Hayashi, Reiko, and Masako Okuhira. 2001. "The Disability Rights Movement in Japan: Past, Present, and Future." *Disability & Society* 16:855–69.

Hayashi, Reiko, and Masako Okuhira. 2008. "The Independent Living Movement in Asia: Solidarity from Japan." *Disability Society* 23:417–29.

Heiden, Hans-Günther, ed. 1996. *Niemand Darf Wegen Seiner Behinderung Benachteiligt Werden* [Nobody shall be disadvantaged because of disability]. Hamburg: rororo.

Hermes, Gisela. 1998. *Traumland USA: Zwischen Antidiskriminierung und Sozialer Armut*. Kassel: bifos Publishing.

Heyer, Katharina. 2000. "From Special Needs to Equal Rights: Japanese Disability Law." *Asia-Pacific Law & Policy Journal* 1:197–219.

Heyer, Katharina. 2002. "The ADA on the Road: Disability Rights in Germany." *Law & Social Inquiry* 27:723–62.

Heyer, Katharina. 2008. "No One's Perfect: Disability and Difference in Japan." In *Worlds Apart: Disability and Foreign Language Learning,* edited by Tammy Berberi, Elizabeth C. Hamilton, and Ian M. Sutherland. New Haven: Yale University Press.

Heyl, Barbara. 1998. "Parents, Politics, and the Public Purse: Activists in the Special Education Arena in Germany." *Disability & Society* 13:683.

Higuchi, Keiko. 1998. *Enjoy Jiritsu Seikatsu* [Enjoy independent living]. Tokyo: Kodansha.

Hirotada, Ototake. 1998. *Gotai Fumanzoku* [Nobody's perfect]. Tokyo: Kodansha.

Holmes, Stephen, and Cass R. Sunstein. 2000. *The Cost of Rights: Why Liberty Depends on Taxes.* New York: W. W. Norton.

Hoshika, Ryoji. 2012. "Appraisal of the Justifiability of the Japanese Quota System for Disabled People." In *Creating a Society for All: Disability and Economy,* edited by Akihiko Matsui, Osamu Nagase, Alison Sheldon, Dan Goodley, Yasuyuji Sawada, and Satoshi Kawashima. Leeds: Disability Press.

Illingworth, Patricia, and Wendy Parmet. 2000. "Positively Disabled: The Relationship between the Definition of Disability and Rights under the ADA." In *Americans with Disabilities: Exploring Implications of the Law for Individuals with Disabilities,* edited by Leslie Francis and Anita Silvers. New York: Routledge.

Ison, Terence. 1992. "Employment Quotas for Disabled People: The Japanese Experience." *Kobe University Law Review* 26:1–32.

Iwakuma, Miho. 2000. "Intercultural View of People with Disabilities in Asia and Africa." Unpublished conference paper, on file with author.

Iwakuma, Miho. 2005. "Culture, Disability, and Disability Community: Differences and Similarities in Japan and the United States." *Atenea* 25:131–43.

Iwasawa, Yuji. 1998. *International Law, Human Rights, and Japanese Law.* Oxford: Clarendon Press.

Jackson, Christopher. 1993. "Infirmative Action: The Law of the Severely Disabled in Germany." *Central European History* 26:417–55.

Japan Times. 2007. "Dignity for Disabled People." *Japan Times Online,* February 14. http://www.japantimes.co.jp/text/ed20070214a1.html.

Johnson, Harriet. 2006. *Too Late to Die Young: Nearly True Tales from a Life.* New York: Picador.

Johnson, Mary, Barrett Shaw, and Tom Olin. 2001. *To Ride the Public's Buses: The Fight That Built a Movement.* Louisville, KY: Advocado Press.

Kanter, Arlene. 2003. "The Globalization of Disability Rights Law." *Syracuse Journal of International Law and Commerce* 30:241.

Kaplan, Deborah. 1999. "The Definition of Disability: Perspective of the Disability Community." *Journal of Health Care Law & Policy* 3:352.

Karlan, Pamela, and George Rutherglen. 1996. "Disabilities, Discrimination, and Reasonable Accommodation." *Duke Law Journal* 46:1.

Kawashima, Satoshi, and Akihiko Matsui. 2011. "Anti-Discrimination and Disability Employment Quota in Japan." Paper presented at the International Conference on Disability Economics at Syracuse University, June 29.

Kawauchi, Yoshihiko. 1996. *Baria Furu Nippon* [Inaccessible Japan]. Tokyo: Gendai Shokan.

Kayess, Rosemary, and Phillip French. 2008. "Out of Darkness into Light? Introducing the Convention on the Rights of Persons with Disabilities." *Human Rights Law Review* 8:1.

Keck, Margaret, and Kathryn Sikkink. 1998. *Activists beyond Borders: Advocacy Networks in International Politics.* Cambridge: Cambridge University Press.

Kemp, Evan, Jr. 1981. "Stop 'Caring for' the Disabled." *Washington Post,* June 7.

Kommers, Donald. 1997. *The Constitutional Jurisprudence of the Federal Republic of Germany.* Durham, NC: Duke University Press.

Konnoth, Craig. 2011. "Created in Its Image: The Race Analogy, Gay Identity, and Gay Litigation in the 1950s-1970s." *Yale Law Journal* 119:316.

Koppelman, Andrew. 1988. "The Miscegenation Analogy: Sodomy Law as Sex Discrimination." *Yale Law Journal* 98:145.

Krieger, Linda, ed. 2003. *Backlash against the ADA: Reinterpreting Disability Rights.* Ann Arbor: University of Michigan Press.

Kuwana, Atsuko. 1997. "Korei: Satogaeri Sutoresu" [Homecoming stress]. *Fukushi Rōdō* 76:118.

Lawson, Anna. 2007. "The United Nations Convention on the Rights of Persons with Disabilities: New Era or False Dawn?" *Syracuse Journal of International Law & Commerce* 34:563–619.

Lawson, Anna. 2009. "The UN Convention on the Rights of Persons with Disabilities and European Disability Law: A Catalyst for Cohesion?" In *The United Nations Convention on the Rights of Persons with Disabilities: European and Scandinavian Perspectives,* edited by Oddný Mjöll Arnardóttir and Gerard Quinn, 81–109. Leiden: Martinus Nijhoff.

Lawson, Anna, and Caroline Gooding. 2005. *Disability Rights in Europe: From Theory to Practice.* Oxford: Hart.

Lifton, Robert. 2000. *The Nazi Doctors: Medical Killing and the Psychology of Genocide.* New York: Basic Books.

Linton, Simi. 1998. *Claiming Disability: Knowledge and Identity.* New York: New York University Press.

Longmore, Paul. 2001. *The New Disability History: American Perspectives.* New York: New York University Press.

Lord, Janet, and Michael Stein. 2008. "The Domestic Incorporation of Human Rights Law and the United Nations Convention on the Rights of Persons with Disabilities." *Washington Law Review* 83:449.

Mansbridge, Jane. 2001. *Oppositional Consciousness: The Subjective Roots of Social Protest.* Chicago: University of Chicago Press.

Marshall, T. H. 1950. *Citizenship and Social Class, and Other Essays.* Cambridge: Cambridge University Press.

Matsui, Ryosuke. 1994. "Employment Measures for People with Disabilities in Japan." *International Journal of Rehabilitation Research* 17:368–73.

Matsui, Ryosuke. 2008. "Employment Measures for Persons with Disabilities in Japan." *Focus: Asia Pacific Human Rights Information Center.* http://www.hurights.or.jp/archives/focus/section2/2008/12/employment-measures-for-persons-with-disabilities-in-japan.html.

Mayeri, Serena. 2001. "'A Common Fate of Discrimination': Race-Gender Analogies in Legal and Historical Perspective." *Yale Law Journal* 110:1045.

Mayeri, Serena. 2008. "Reconstructing the Race-Sex Analogy." *William and Mary Law Review* 49:1789.

Mayerson, Arlene. 1992. "The History of the ADA: A Movement Perspective." Disability Rights Education & Defense Fund. http://www.dredf.org/publications/ada_history.shtml.

McCann, Michael. 1994. *Rights at Work: Pay Equity Reform and the Politics of Legal Mobilization.* Chicago: University of Chicago Press.

Melish, Tara. 2007. "The UN Disability Convention: Historic Process, Strong Prospects, and Why the US Should Ratify." *Human Rights Brief* 14 (2).

Miles-Paul, Ottmar. 1992. *Wir sind nicht mehr Aufzuhalten* [Nobody can stop us]. Munich: AG SPAG.

Ministry of Health and Welfare. 1982. *Annual Report on Health and Welfare.* Tokyo.

Minow, Martha. 1990. *Making All the Difference: Inclusion, Exclusion, and American Law.* Ithaca: Cornell University Press.

Mittler, Karl-Josef, and Heike Zirden. 1997. *"Eine Kampagne? Eine Kampagne! Warum es die 'Aktion Grundgesetz' gibt."* [A campaign? A campaign! Why we have the "Operation Basic Law"]. In *Die Gesellschaft der Behinderer* [The society of dis-ablers], edited by Sigrid Arnade, Hans-Günter Heiden, Jutta vom Hofe, Karl-Josef Mittler, and Heike Zirden. Hamburg: Rohwolt.

Mogi, Toshihiko. 1992. "The Disabled in Society." *Japan Quarterly* 39:440–48.

Mostert, Mark. 2002. "Useless Eaters: Disability as Genocidal Marker in Nazi Germany." *Journal of Special Education* 36:157.

Muñoz, Vernor. 2007. "The Right to Education of Persons with Disabilities. Report of the Special Rapporteur." New York: United Nations General Assembly.

Nagae, Akira. 2008. "An Evaluation of the Disability Employment Policy with Respect to the Quota-Levy System in Japan: Evidence from a Natural Experiment on Stock Prices." *Waseda Institute for Advanced Study Discussion Paper* No. 2007-001. Tokyo: Waseda Institute for Advanced Study.

Nagase, Osamu. 1995. "Difference, Equality and Disabled People: Disability Rights and Disability Culture." MA thesis in Politics of Alternative Development Strategies at the Institute of Social Studies, the Hague, Netherlands.

Nakagawa, Jun, and Peter Blanck. 2010. "Future of Disability Law in Japan: Employment and Accommodation." *Loyola L.A. International & Comparative Law Review* 33:173–221.

Nakanishi, Shoji. 1997. "Historical Perspective and Development of Independent Living Movement in Japan." Disability Information Resources (DINF). http://www.dinf.ne.jp/doc/english/resource/z00009/z0000909.html.

Nakanishi, Yukiko. 1992. "Independence from Spoiling Parents: The Struggle of Women with Disabilities in Japan." In *Imprinting Our Image: An International Anthology by Women with Disabilities,* edited by Diane Driedger and Gray Swan, 25–30. Toronto: Gynergy Books.

Nakanishi, Yukiko. 2010. "Realization of CRPD in Japanese Way." Presentation given at the Disability Rights Tribunal for the Asia Pacific Conference, Australian Federation of Disability Organizations & Tokyo Advocacy Law Office, Melbourne, August 13.

National Council on Disability. 1997/2010. *Equality of Opportunity: The Making of*

the Americans with Disabilities Act. Available at http://www.ncd.gov/publica
tions/1997/equality_of_Opportunity_The_Making_of_the_Americans_
with_Disabilities_Act.

National Council on Disability. 2008. "Finding the Gaps: A Comparative Analysis of Disability Laws in the United States to the United Nations Convention
on the Rights of Persons with Disabilities." May 12. Washington, DC: National Council on Disability. Available at http://www.ncd.gov/publica-
tions/2008/May122008.

Nihon Shōgaisha Sokushin Kyōkai. 1998. *Shōgaisha no Koyō no Sokushin no tame ni*
[Employment promotion for people with disabilities]. Tokyo: Ministry of Labor.

Nirje, Bengt. 1969. "The Normalization Principle and Its Human Management
Implications." In *Changing Patterns in Residential Services for the Mentally Re-
tarded,* edited by Robert Kugel and Wolf Wolfensberger. Washington, DC:
President's Committee on Mental Retardation.

Oliver, Michael. 1990. *The Politics of Disablement.* London: Macmillan.

Oliver, Michael. 1996. *Understanding Disability: From Theory to Practice.* London:
Macmillan.

Opp, Gunther. 2001. "Learning Disabilities in Germany: A Retrospective Analysis, Current Status, and Future Trends." In *Research and Global Perspectives in
Learning Disabilities: Essay in Honor of William M. Cruickshank,* edited by Daniel Hallahan and Barbara Keogh, 217–38. Mahwah, NJ: Lawrence Erlbaum.

O'Reilly, Arthur. 2003. *The Right to Decent Work of Persons with Disabilities.* Geneva: International Labour Office.

Otake, Tomoko. 2006. "Is 'Disability' Still a Dirty Word in Japan?" *Japan Times,*
August 27.

Ototake, Hirotada. 1998. *Gotai Fumanzoku* [No one is perfect]. Tokyo: Kodansha.

Palmer, Jason. 2013. "The Convention on the Rights of Persons with Disabilities:
Will Ratification Lead to a Holistic Approach to Postsecondary Education for
Persons with Disabilities?" *Seton Hall Law Review* 43:551.

Pedriana, Nicholas. 2006. "From Protective to Equal Treatment: Legal Framing
Processes and Transformation of the Women's Movement in the 1960s."
American Journal of Sociology 111:1718.

Perlin, Michael. 2011. "Abandoned Love: The Impact of *Wyatt v. Stickney* on the
Intersection between International Human Rights and Domestic Mental Disability Law." *Law & Psychology Review* 35:122.

Pfahl, Lisa, and Justin Powell. 2011. "Legitimating School Segregation: The Special Education Profession and the Discourse of Learning Disability in Germany." *Disability & Society* 26:449–62.

Poore, Carol. 2007. *Disability in Twentieth-Century German Culture.* Ann Arbor:
University of Michigan Press.

Port, Kenneth. 1991. "The Japanese International Law 'Revolution': International
Human Rights Law and Its Impact in Japan." *Stanford Journal of International
Law* 28:139.

Powell, Justin. 2009. "To Segregate or to Separate? The Institutionalization of Special Education in the United States and Germany." *Comparative Education Review* 53:161.

Richards, David. 1999. *Identity and the Case for Gay Rights: Race, Gender, Religion as Analogies.* Chicago: University of Chicago Press.

Roberts, Edward. 1983. "When Others Speak for You, You Lose." *Edward V. Roberts Papers: Speech.* Berkeley: Bancroft Library, University of California.

Roeder, Maike. 2001. *Behinderte Menschen in Japan* [People with disabilities in Japan]. Bonn: Bier'sche Verlagsanstalt.

Sakuraba, Ryoko. 2008. "Employment Discrimination Law in Japan: Human Rights or Employment Policy." *Bulletin of Comparative Labor Relations: New Developments in Employment Discrimination Law* (68).

Salzberg, Stephen. 1991. "Japan's New Mental Health Law: More Light Shed on Dark Places?" *International Journal of Law and Psychiatry* 14:137.

Satz, Ani. 2008. "Disability, Vulnerability, and the Limits of Antidiscrimination." *Washington Law Review* 83:513.

Scheingold, Stuart A. 2004. *The Politics of Rights: Lawyers, Public Policy, and Political Change.* 2nd ed. Ann Arbor: University of Michigan Press.

Schimanski, Werner. 2008. Introduction to *Gemeinschaftskommentar Zum SGB IX.* Neuwied: Luchterhand Verlag.

Schweik, Susan. 2011. "Lomax's Matrix: Disability, Solidarity, and the Black Power of 504." *Disability Studies Quarterly* 31:1.

Scotch, Richard. 2001. *From Good Will to Civil Rights: Transforming Federal Disability Policy.* 2nd ed. Philadelphia: Temple University Press.

Scotch, Richard, and Kay Schriner. 1997. "Disability as Human Variation: Implications for Policy." *Annals of the American Academy of Political and Social Science* 148.

Seifert, Horst. 1991. *Versorgt bis zur Unmündigkeit* [Cared for but infantilized]. Berlin: Kolog Verlag.

Sekigawa, Hōkō. 1998. "*ADA, soshite JDA e*" [From the ADA to the JDA]. *Joyful Begin* 9:97–108.

Shapiro, Joseph. 1993. *No Pity: People with Disabilities Forging a New Civil Rights Movement.* 1st ed. New York: Times Books.

Shinya Tateiwa. 1998. "Shōgaisha undō kara miete kuru mono" [What we discover from the disability rights movement]. *Gendaishisō* [Journal of Contemporary Thought] 26.

Shōgaisha Hakusho. 2005. Annual Report on Government Measures for Persons with Disabilities. Available at http://www8.cao.go.jp/shougai/english/annualreport/2005/mokuji.html.

Sierck, Udo, and Nati Radtke. 1988. *Die Wohltäter-Mafia: Vom Erbgesundheitsgericht zur humangenetischen Beratung* [The welfare/do-gooder Mafia: From hereditary health law to genetic counseling]. Frankfurt: Mabuse-Verlag.

Silvers, Anita, ed. 1998a. *Disability, Difference, Discrimination: Perspectives on Justice in Bioethics and Public Policy.* Lanham, MD: Rowman & Littlefield.

Silvers, Anita. 1998b. "Formal Justice." In *Disability, Difference, Discrimination: Perspectives on Justice in Bioethics and Public Policy.* Lanham, MD: Rowman & Littlefield.

Skrentny, John. 2002. *The Minority Rights Revolution.* Cambridge, MA: Belknap Press of Harvard University Press.

Snow, David, and Robert Benford. 1988. "Ideology, Frame Resonance, and Participant Mobilization." *International Social Movement Research* 1:197.

Spiewak, Martin. 2011. "Förderschulen: Kein Sonderweg!" *Die Zeit,* 5 April. http://www.zeit.de/2011/14/Bildungspolitik-Foerderschule.

Stein, Michael. 2000. "Labor Markets, Rationality, and Workers with Disabilities." *Berkeley Journal of Employment and Labor Law* 21:314.

Stein, Michael. 2004. "Same Struggle, Different Difference: ADA Accommodations as Antidiscrimination." *University of Pennsylvania Law Review* 153:579–673.

Stein, Michael A., and Janet E. Lord. 2009. "Future Prospects for the United Nations Convention on the Rights of Persons with Disabilities." In *The UN Convention on the Rights of Persons with Disabilities: European and Scandinavian Perspectives,* edited by Oddný Mjöll Arnardóttir and Gerard Quinn. Leiden: Martinus Nijhoff.

Stein, Michael, and Penelope Stein. 2006. "Beyond Disability Civil Rights." *Hastings Law Journal* 58:1203.

Steiner, Gusti. 2003. *Wie Alles Anfing: Konsequenzen Politischer Behindertenselbsthilfe* [How it all began: The consequences of a politicized disability self-help movement]. http://www.forsea.de/projekte/20_jahre_assistenz/steiner.shtml.

Stevens, Carolyn. 2007. "Living with Disability in Urban Japan." *Japanese Studies* 27:263.

Stone, Deborah. 1984. *The Disabled State.* Philadelphia: Temple University Press.

Switzer, Jacqueline. 2003. *Disabled Rights: American Disability Policy and the Fight for Equality.* Washington, DC: Georgetown University Press.

Tarrow, Sidney. 2011. *Power in Movement: Social Movements and Contentious Politics.* Cambridge: Cambridge University Press.

Tateiwa, Shinya. 1990. "*Hayaku Yukkuri-Jiritsu Seikatsu undo no Seisei*" [Fast, slow: Rise and growth of independent living movement] in *Sei no giho: Ars Vivendi,* edited by Junko Asaka, M. Okahara, F. Onaka, and S. Tateiwa. Tokyo: Fujiwara shoten.

tenBroek, Jacobus. 1966. "The Right to Live in the World: The Disabled in the Law of Torts." *California Law Review* 54 (2): 841.

Theben, Bettina. 1999. "Bürgerrechte Behinderter Menschen: Das Urteil des OLG Köln und Seine Implikation für Die Gleichstellung" [Civil rights of people with disabilities: The judgment of the superior court in Cologne]. In *Qualitätssicherung und Deinstitutionalisierung: Niemand Darf Wegen Seiner Behinderung Benachteiligt Werden* [Quality control and de-institutionalization: Nobody shall be discriminated against because of disability], 285–95. Berlin: Marhold.

Thornburgh, Richard. 2008. "Globalizing a Response to Disability Discrimination." *Washington Law Review* 83:439.

Tokoro, Hiroyo. 2013. "Employment Quota System to Promote the Employment of Persons with Disabilities in Japan." Unpublished presentation at the Conference on Disability Law and Policy in Japan and the United States, Loyola Law School, March 13. On file with author.

Totsuka, Etsuro. 1990. "The History of Japanese Psychiatry and the Rights of Mental Patients." *Psychiatric Bulletin* 14:193–200.

Tsutsui, Kiyoteru, and Hwa Ji Shin. 2008. "Global Norms, Local Activism, and Social Movement Outcomes: Global Human Rights and Resident Koreans in Japan." *Social Problems* 55:391.

Tucker, Bonnie. 2001. "The ADA's Revolving Door: Inherent Flaws in the Civil Rights Paradigm." *Ohio State Law Journal* 62: 335.

UPIS [The Union of the Physically Impaired Against Segregation]. 1975 "Fundamental Principles of Disability." http://disability-studies.leeds.ac.uk/files/library/UPIAS-fundamental-principles.pdf.

Waddington, Lisa. 1996. "Reassessing the Employment of People with Disabilities in Europe: From Quotas to Anti-Discrimination Laws." *Comparative Labor Law Journal* 18:62.

Waddington, Lisa, and Matthew Diller. 2000. "Tensions and Coherence in Disability Policy: The Uneasy Relationship between Social Welfare and Civil Rights Models of Disability in American, European and International Employment Law." From Principles to Practice: An International Disability Law and Policy Symposium, October 22–26. http://www.dredf.org/international/waddington.html.

Ward, Robert, and Yoshikazu Sakamoto, ed. 1987. *Democratizing Japan: The Allied Occupation.* Honolulu: University of Hawai'i Press.

Wasserman, David. 1998. "Distributive Justice." In *Disability, Difference, Discrimination: Perspectives on Justice in Bioethics and Public Policy,* edited by Anita Silvers. Lanham, MD: Rowman & Littlefield.

Waterstone, Michael. 2009. "Returning Veterans and Disability Law." *Notre Dame Law Review* 85:1081.

West, Jane. 1991. *The Americans with Disabilities Act: From Policy to Practice.* New York: Milbank Memorial Fund.

Williams, Wendy. 1984. "Equality's Riddle: Pregnancy and the Equal Treatment/Special Treatment Debate." *NYU Review of Law & Social Change* 13:325.

Wilson, Charles. 2005. "The Other Movement that Rosa Parks Inspired." *Washington Post,* October 30, B01.

Young, Jonathan. 1997. *Equality of Opportunity: The Making of the Americans with Disabilities Act.* Washington, DC: National Council on Disabilities.

Young, Jonathan. 2000. "Same Struggle, Different Difference." Unpublished manuscript, on file with author.

Index

Note: Locators in *italic* refer to figures and tables.